KINSTOWN
L No. 558159

799
11

402

61

15.

15

26.

29.

07.

18. JUL

5. AUG

COARSE FISHING
IN IRELAND

HUGH GOUGH

UNWIN

HYMAN

LONDON SYDNEY WELLINGTON

This book is dedicated to all my angling friends and to all the kind landowners in Ireland who have allowed me access to fishing.

First published in Great Britain by Unwin Hyman, an imprint of Unwin Hyman Limited, 1989

Unwin Hyman Limited
15/17 Broadwick Street, London W1V 1FP

Allen & Unwin (Australia) Pty Ltd
8 Napier Street, North Sydney, NSW 2060, Australia

Allen & Unwin New Zealand Ltd with the Port Nicholson Press
Compusales Building, 75 Ghuznee Street, Wellington, New Zealand

---

British Library Cataloguing in Publication Data

Gough, Hugh
   Coarse fishing in Ireland.
   1. Ireland Coarse fish. Angling
   I. Title
   799.1′1

   ISBN 0–04–440287–2

Set in 11 on 12½ point Bembo
by Nene Phototypesetters Ltd, Northampton
Printed in Great Britain at The Bath Press, Avon

Contents

Acknowledgements

Ned O'Farrell, Prosperous
Jimmy McMahon, Carrickmacross
Larry Ward, Drumconrath
Brid Halloran, Bailieborough
Brian Hanly, Ballybay
Eamon Gray, Arva
Ivan Price, Ballinamore
Jack O'Neill, Carrigallen
Francis McGoldrick, Ballyconnell
Martin Mitchell, Vincent Regan, Boyle
Marion Maloney, Mohill
Sean Egan, Athlone
Bill Burton, Ballinasloe
Dermot Killeen, Shannonbridge
Owen O'Carroll, Portumna
Joe Maloney and Joseph Maloney,
    O'Brien's Bridge
Brian Cullo, Tulla
Bill Lawlor, Durrow
John Farmer, Monkstown
Oliver and Ronan Ryan, Moycullen
Barrie Nicholson, Ardlougher
Una Plunket, Bawnboy
John Lefroy, Emerald Star, Portumna
Michael Brehony, Carrick Craft, Carrick-
    on-Shannon

Shauna Swords, Tullycoe, Cavan
Seamus Hartigan, Matt Nolan, Michael
    Cleary, Shannon Regional Fisheries
    Board
Danny Goldrick, Western Regional
    Fisheries Board
Bill Reidy, Jim O'Brien, Paul Burke,
    Eastern Regional Fisheries Board
Ted Sweeney, North-Western Regional
    Fisheries Board
Joe Caffrey, Biologist, Central Fisheries
    Board
Sean Taaffe, Northern Ireland Tourist
    Board, England
Ian Hill, Northern Ireland Tourist Board,
    Belfast
Eamon Hoey, Fermanagh Tourism
Leslie Watson, Department of
    Agriculture, Ballinamalard
Robert Buick, Belfast
Peter Brooker, Belfast

Dr Michael Kennedy's booklet, *Coarse
Fish in Ireland*, has been an invaluable
source of information.

Introduction

It all happened in Cavan.

The excitement of digging for worms, the bicycle journey to the River Annalee near Butlersbridge, and catching those perch – that was my routine during the school holidays. The big waters of Lough Oughter provided the next adventure, when with Brendan Coulter I fished and explored the vast complex, where no more than twenty or thirty regular anglers were to be seen.

I recall the day when I saw a stranger sitting under an umbrella. He had a strange net in the water. He was from Birmingham and he told me that he was fishing for bream. I knew that he was wasting his time at that spot and I advised him to move 300 yards up the bank, to the precise place where I knew the bream to be. Later that day, when that angler lifted his keepnet from the water, I was flabbergasted at my first sight of a big bream catch. The English angler thanked me profusely for putting him on to the catch of his lifetime.

That incident put me on the track of coarse fishing for the rest of my life.

I made up my mind that anglers be told about our great fishing and also be guided to the right places to make such wonderful catches. I was also determined to learn how to catch those bream and, more urgently, to buy some of the specialized tackle in which I was conspicuously lacking.

We set up a tourist association in Cavan to promote and develop the waters for coarse fishing tourism. We produced spe-cialized brochures and maps. We prepared water stretches for anglers, erected stiles and footbridges and put up signs to the water. We also arranged accommodation for anglers in farmhouses.

As the business expanded to other parts of Ireland, I met other voluntary workers and we launched a nationwide body to cater for our needs. I was then Secretary of the National Coarse Fishing Federa-tion. I looked abroad to fellow anglers and the next progression was to affiliate to the Confédération Internationale de la Pêche Sportive (CIPS). I was encouraged by members of that organization to have an Irish team participate in the World Championships in England in 1966. The standard of Irish coarse fishing was abys-mally low then, and when I acted as Irish team manager in the following years we drew up plans to improve and promote coarse angling as a sport at home. I was motivated all the time by that one pledge I had made years previously: that more anglers should know more about the sport and enjoy our fishing.

It was as President of the CIPS Tourism Commission that I learned of the great interest shown by my Continental col-leagues in Ireland's coarse fishing and there followed a great influx of pike anglers to this country.

With that background, I moved on to take up a full-time job as Angling Officer with the Inland Fisheries Trust. In that state organization I found staff who had a rare vitality and an enthusiasm to develop and promote the waters of Ireland. My job took me to all the coarse-fishing waters of Ireland, organizing the sport and assimilating information. The compulsion to share the great Irish fishing with others was my driving force.

When Merlin Unwin approached me to write a book on Irish coarse fishing, it was Des Brennan, of the Central Fisheries Board, who advised and encouraged me to take up the task. At last I would pass along my impressions of Irish waters to others and I would fulfil my dream which started so long ago when I met my first English angler at Killykeen.

This assignment could never have been accomplished but for the assistance of my colleagues in Fisheries and I offer all of them a big word of thanks. To all my angling friends throughout the country, including Robert Buick and Peter Brooker in Belfast, I pay tribute for their generous help. A special word of thanks to Des and to my good colleague Bridie Fleming for all their help in bringing my dream to fruition.

The sketch maps shown in this book are a general guide to the fishing and I advise you to use Ordnance Survey maps (scale ½ inch to 1 mile) for all travel.

All the waters described in this book have been researched by me personally, yet such is the wealth of angling in Ireland that there are undoubtedly other waters worthy of exploration by the visiting coarse fisher.

HUGH GOUGH

The Fish

Historical evidence indicates that the natural fish in Irish waters were salmon, trout, char, pollan and eels. We can assume that all other species were introduced, mostly from England by the Normans and then by the owners of large estates.

I know that in recent years an angler brought carp from England to some ponds in the north-west. There is also evidence to suggest that an angler brought chub from England and introduced them to the Boyne system. Some years ago a group of Continental anglers were observed with an aerated tank beside a lake at Strokestown. That tank held live fish which had been brought in from France. Are we about to encounter some new species in Irish waters?

While pike are widely distributed all over Ireland, there is no evidence that this species was in the island before the twelfth century. *Gailliase* is the Irish word for pike and its meaning, 'strange fish', suggests that this fish was also brought to Ireland from England.

Roach now spreading throughout the island were introduced to Ireland in 1889. The first roach were brought here in cans to be used as bait for pike in the River Blackwater in Cork. Those cans, left overnight in the river, were swept away in a sudden flood and the fish escaped.

Soon the Munster Blackwater had a stock of roach.

After the turn of the century roach from the River Blackwater were introduced to the waters in the Baronscourt demesne at Newtownstewart. From there the roach spread into the River Mourne system. It was in the late 1950s that roach were noticed in the Erne waters and by the mid-1960s anglers were catching a few roach in a day's session in the river at Belturbet and Killykeen.

The spread of roach through Irish waters is something I have lived with and I can testify that anglers have played a big role in transferring this species to other systems. Roach from Belturbet were taken as livebait by Continental pike anglers fishing at Lough Kinnale on the River Inny in the Shannon System, whence they moved down river and entered Lough Ree at Inny Bay. And roach brought from the Erne system to Drumgorman Lake near Drumshanbo by a local angler led to the spread of the species in the upper Shannon waters. Roach from Co. Cavan were introduced by English and Irish anglers to the River Shannon at Roosky and Richmond Harbour at Clondra, and others from the River Annalee at Butlersbridge were introduced to the Corrib system by pike anglers visiting the Moycullen district in Co. Galway.

Dublin anglers transferred roach from Cavan to the canals at Dublin and Irish anglers also brought roach from the River Blackwater at Mallow to the River Shannon at Annacotty and the East Clare Lakes.

At the time of writing only one small section of the River Shannon, from Shannonbridge to Killaloe, does not have roach in numbers.

COARSE FISH SPECIES

The following coarse fish are found in Irish waters:

Cyprinids

Bream *(Abramis brama)*
Roach *(Rutilus rutilus)*
Rudd *(Scardinius erythrophthalmus)*
Dace *(Leuciscus leuciscus)*
Tench *(Tinca tinca)*
Carp *(Cyprinus carpio)*
Gudgeon *(Gobio gobio)*
Minnow *(Phoxinus phoxinus)*

Others

Pike *(Esox lucius)*
Perch *(Perca fluviatilis)*
Three-spined stickleback *(Gasterosteus aculeatus)*
Ten-spined stickleback *(Pungitius pungitius)*
Stone loach *(Noemacheilus barbatulus)*
Eel *(Anguilla anguilla)*

Anglers will encounter great numbers of hybrids where cyprinids are present. In the Erne waters, the common hybrid is between roach and bream. These also occur in the upper Shannon, whilst lower in that system and in other Irish waters rudd × bream hybrids are common. In some waters anglers find difficulty in recognizing hybrids, and this is understandable when roach × rudd also occur.

PERCH *(Perca fluviatilis)*

Irish Record   5 lb 8 oz (S. Drum, Lough Erne, 1946)
Specimen Weight   3 lb (1.361 kilos)

The perch is widely distributed throughout the country. It spawns on bulrushes, reeds and sunken roots and trees from mid-April to mid-May, when the water temperature is about 10°C.

Young perch at first feed on Cladocera (water fleas) and then, after their first or second year, shrimps, water lice and insects make up their diet. Perch will feed on small fish and during the summer months large shoals of fry can be seen scattering in the shallows as the hungry predators are on the move.

The perch is colourful and has a double dorsal fin, which has sharp, thorny projections. The body has dark stripes and is covered in rough scales. The opercular bones have sharp edges and care must be taken when holding the fish.

Perch Angling

It was with a bent pin and worm as bait that many young boys and girls are introduced to the sport of angling. In most cases perch respond easily to that simple presentation. In Ireland they have always been popular as a tasty bite to eat.

Perch move in shoals and are found in both still and running water. They can be found in weed and, during the summer, under bridges and jetties.

Being predators, perch will take a great variety of baits. In Irish waters the most successful baits are dead minnows and worms. On one occasion a perch took my legered herring in 20 feet of water! Small artificial spinning baits will always get results in the summer months.

Big perch are rare in Irish waters and the specimen weight of 3 lb is reached only occasionally.

ROACH *(Rutilus rutilus)*

Irish Record   2 lb 13½ oz (Lawrie Robinson, River Blackwater, Cappoquin, 11 August 1970)
Specimen Weight   2 lb (0.907 kilos)

Roach, now widely distributed, are spreading throughout Irish waters. They spawn in slow-moving or still water in May–June, when the water temperature is about 15°C. Roach feed on young stages of aquatic insects, shrimps, water lice, snails and surface insects. They will also eat filamentous algae and shoots of vascular plants such as moss and Canadian pondweed.

Canals, river and lakes all hold roach, but it is important to remember that this species migrates during the spawning period. Where a river flows into a lake, roach will move from the lake into the river to spawn. In a river, they will move considerable distances to find suitable spawning ground.

The fecundity of roach is high and in some waters they become stunted, with fish of 4–5 oz being common. Good-quality roach over 1 lb are to be found in some isolated waters and particularly in

the River Shannon and its tributaries. As roach become established in some of the rich limestone waters, we can expect the Irish Record to fall in a short time.

The roach has a blue and silvery colour, with dirty red fins. The dorsal fin is situated nearly in line with the ventral fins. The lateral line scale count is 40–46. The roach is often confused with the rudd.

Roach Angling

The roach will sometimes feed close to the surface but most fish are taken mid-water to the bottom. The popular roach are located in all types of water and the methods used to catch them range from legering and float fishing to pole fishing. They will also respond to fly fishing.

There is considerable skill in catching roach and care must be taken in presenting the bait on carefully chosen terminal tackle. The common bait for roach in Irish waters are red maggots. The big and often shy roach will respond to bread or worms, particularly in the productive winter and spring months.

RUDD *(Scardinius erythrophthalmus)*

Irish Record   3 lb 1 oz (A. E. Biddlecombe, Kilglass Lake, Strokestown, 27 June 1959)
Specimen Weight   2¼ lb (1.021 kilos)

This lovely red-finned fish is common throughout the country. A prolific fish, the rudd produces about 30,000 eggs per pound of body weight. It spawns when the minimum water temperature is 15°C in May–June. The rudd feeds on filamentous algae, corixids, vascular plants and surface insects.

Rudd are located in big lakes, small ponds, canals and rivers which have a moderate to fast flow and they prefer a weedy habitat. Rudd have declined in numbers in waters where roach stocks have increased.

The bright-red-finned fish with golden scales is sometimes confused with the roach. Distinguishing marks are that the rudd has a protruding lower lip; the dorsal fin is set further back than the ventral fin, and the lateral line scale count is 39–44.

Rudd Angling

Rudd are primarily surface feeders and are most active when water temperatures are high. They will feed on those hot summer days, but it is in the evenings that rudd fishing is at its best.

They are shy fish and move in large shoals at a fast pace over considerable distances in lakes. A sharp eye will reveal the pattern of their cruising and you can then set out to catch them with bread or maggots as bait. A heavy concentration of loosely mashed bread will help to hold the fish and, in a river, a constant but small trickle of carefully thrown loose feed is essential to pinning the rudd down.

In the Irish waters which hold big rudd, long-distance casting is my method. I use a Drennan crystal waggler at 20–30 yards. I always bring my fish quickly to the side of the shoal, so as not to frighten away the others, especially when fishing in the shallow margins.

Big rudd respond to big pieces of fresh bread flake. A bunch of maggots on a size 10 hook will also get results. Rudd feed freely during the warm summer from May and go off from mid-September in most waters except canals.

TENCH *(Tinca tinca)*

Irish Record   7 lb 13¼ oz (Ray Webb, River Shannon, Lanesborough, 25 May 1971)
Specimen Weight   6 lb (2.721 kilos)

Until about the mid-1950s, tench were limited to waters mostly in the centre and lower parts of the country. The then Inland Fisheries Trust carried out an extensive stocking of this species and now they are to be found in many parts of the country. There are isolated lakes in Cavan, Leitrim and Monaghan which provide good sport for tench, which were formerly known only in the middle Shannon Region.

Tench spawn in shallow, weedy water when the minimum water temperature is 20°C, in late June and July. They are to be found in rivers, canals and lakes, but their natural homes are ponds with an abundance of aquatic vegetation and muddy bottoms.

The tench is cylindrical in shape and is covered with small scales. It is brownish-green in colour, with a bright-red eye. The large fleshy mouth carries a pair of minute barbels. The male fish has thick fin rays and enlarged ventral fins.

Tench Angling

Fishing for tench conjures up a scene of a small weedy pond on a warm summer's morning or evening.

Tench mostly like weedy, muddy water and pick up their food by rooting along the bottom. Their presence is often betrayed by patches of bubbles rising to the surface. Tench often respond to ordinary groundbaiting but careful preparation of a swim will get better results. Raking the bottom and then baiting with chopped worms or maggots is a good preparation. Morning and evening fishing is the normal pattern for taking these great fighting fish.

I was fortunate to be instructed by the master, Fred J. Taylor, on how to use the lift bite. In shallow water this method is still the most successful. Tench can also be legered for in our deeper, weedy waters. Those who have worked at surveys in fisheries and have seen many tench with small hooks and fine line sticking from their mouths are only too conscious of the dangers of fishing with light tackle. It is better to step up on your tackle and miss a fish than have a damaged fish escape with hook and line attached.

Tench fishing is best in May and June. After spawning, the fish are more difficult to catch but in some waters they return to give good sport up to mid-September, and in the canals tench are caught even on very cold winter days.

BREAM *(Abramis brama)*

Irish Record 11 lb 12 oz (A. Pike, River Blackwater, Monaghan, 1882)
Specimen Weight 7½ lb (3.402 kilos)

Perhaps the only places where bream are not to be found are some of the coastal regions. They spawn in May–June in shallow, weedy water when the critical water temperature is 15°C. Like most cyprinids, young bream first eat Cladocera and then feed on shrimps, water lice, caddis larvae, chironomid larvae, snails and nymphs. Bream frequent big and small lakes, rivers and canals. They can be found in clear or muddied water and they feed freely from April to October. In my opinion, the best fishing months for bream are from late June to mid-September.

In the River Erne system young bream are known as *shade* when their colour is silver. They are not to be confused with the silver bream (*Blicca bjoerkna*), a species which does not occur in Ireland.

The bream is characterized by a humped back and a dark bronze colour. The head is relatively small and the fish has a big mouth, which is used for sucking its food off the bottom. Outstanding is its heavy coating of slime, which the angler is also well aware of.

Bream Angling

Bream move sometimes in very big shoals. While they can be found in moving water, they seek out the sluggish places to rest. Using my echo sounder, I have studied bream shoals and have discovered that they remain very tightly packed. This point should be noted when baiting and casting for bream.

Bream feed primarily on the bottom by grubbing in the mud and gravel. They will also take food off the bottom, and this occurs in a lot of rivers as particles move down with the current. Shoals of bream move considerable distances, and in seldom fished waters locating and holding those fish presents the angler with problems. The use of substantial quantities of groundbait is essential to attract and hold bream in some big Irish waters. On many of Shannon waters I have stayed in one swim for three or four days without a bite, but when those bream finally found my bait my patience was richly rewarded. A constant baiting is vital to successful bream fishing.

Bream come on the feed in April and fishing improves as water temperatures rise. When the first good warm days come in May bream shoals begin to move to their spawning area. From mid-June fishing really picks up and the summer months through to October provide great sport. In canals bream remain fairly active during the winter.

The habits of bream, like those of all fish, are dictated by changes in water temperatures. During the hot summer days bream may not feed, but then the angler should try fishing in the mornings and evenings. This applies particularly to some waters holding big bream, where the fish may come on the feed only in the late and early hours and stop feeding when the sunlight hits the water.

The most successful hook baits for bream in Irish waters are worms, bread and maggots. Among the best baits is the small red worm, or brandling, with casters. Methods of bream fishing are all well known and in Ireland the fish can be taken on leger or float. Bream are a delicate fish and should always be handled with care. Bream should never be kept for a long period in a keepnet. They should never be tossed out on hard ground. Always return bream to the water quickly, gently and with care.

RUDD × BREAM HYBRID

Irish Record   5 lb 13½ oz (Peter Dighton, River Shannon, Lanesborough, 12 April 1975)
Specimen Weight   3 lb (1.361 kilos)

It takes more than the eye of an angler to identify a hybrid. In many cases scientific knowledge is necessary to tell just what the species is. However, the experienced angler can in many cases identify a hybrid without studying the vital clues such as the shape of the mouth, the position of the dorsal fin, the branched ray count of the anal fin or the scale count of the lateral line. It is the colour of the fish that anglers quickly note before they rightly or wrongly put a name to it.

The rudd × bream hybrid has pinkish red fins and often has a light golden tinge on the scales. These hybrids are found where rudd and bream are present. In some waters they are in great numbers whilst elsewhere there may only be a limited stock.

In some waters they grow to 5 or 6 lb and are much sought after by anglers because of their great fighting power. Having fished extensively for rudd × bream hybrids, I have noted that they usually behave in a similar way to big rudd. They move in shoals, often close to the surface, and cover a great expanse of territory at a fast pace. They are shy fish and must be approached with care.

They can be fished for like rudd, by casting at long distance with a waggler and with maggots on a size 10 or 12 hook, set at about 2–3 feet. They can be held on their cruising path by baiting with mashed bread and, when they are present, only casters or floaters are necessary to keep them in the swim.

ROACH × BREAM HYBRID

Irish Record   4 lb 4⅝ oz (Garnett Coulter, Lough Shark, 8 April 1989)
Specimen Weight   3 lb (1.361 kilos)

The roach × bream hybrid has brownish fins. The scales have a silver-blue and slight bronze colour. These fish are common in waters that hold roach and bream. Since roach have become established in many bream waters quite a few specimen hybrids have been recorded.

CARP *(Cyprinus carpio)*

Irish Record   25 lb (Andrew Ferris, The Lough, Cork, 28 March 1989)
Specimen Weight   10 lb (4.536 kilos)

An introduced species, carp are to be found in only a few waters in Ireland, they are common throughout Europe and many parts of the world. However, on this island the sustained temperature of 22°C required for spawning rarely occurs. Carp will spawn in some shallow, weedy waters in June–August. They inhabit slow-moving or still waters and can be found in waters where there are tench.

Carp are found in The Lough, Cork City, and Galmoylestown Lake near Mullingar and some fish have been transferred by anglers from the latter to the nearby Ballinafid Lake, the canals near Dublin and other waters.

Carp Angling

Carp in Irish waters are mostly loners and can be located in the shallow lakes on calm days as they create bow-waves or cause bubbles to rise to the surface as they root in the bottom. In the two public carp fisheries in Cork and near Mullingar, the fish are becoming wary, and sometimes specialized baits are required to catch them.

The private carp fisheries in Ireland which are rarely fished hold big fish which still respond to sweetcorn and bread. Carp are powerful fish and when they take up the bait your tackle will be truly tested.

DACE *(Leuciscus leuciscus)*

Irish Record   1 lb 2 oz (John T. Henry, River Blackwater, Cappogquin, 8 August 1966)
Specimen Weight   1 lb (0.4536 kilos)

Dace were introduced to the Munster River Blackwater in 1889 and have not spread to other Irish waters. They are a shoal fish encountered mostly in fast water. The dace moves into shallow water over gravel in the winter and spring when great numbers of these small fish can be caught.

Dace Angling

The normal method of fishing for dace is by long-trotting with light tackle. The careful use of loose feeding with maggots is critical for holding the dace in the fast water. Dace have a soft mouth and their bite is fast. It is important to use light tackle and to strike sharply.

EEL *(Anguilla anguilla)*

Irish Record   6 lb 15 oz (John Murnane, Lough Droumenisa, Bantry, 12 June 1979)
Specimen Weight   3 lb (1.361 kilos)

The eel, a migratory fish, is found in virtually all Irish waters. Eels breed in the Sargasso Sea and the larval forms drift for three years in the North Atlantic current before reaching European coasts. In the coastal waters they metamorphose into 2½-inch-long elvers and then run up the rivers to lakes and ponds. The eel then remains in fresh water for several years before returning to the sea during the dark, rainy nights of autumn.

Eel Angling

Small eels are common but the bigger eels of over 3–4 lb are scarce and harder to find. The best fishing for eels is at night. They like to hunt from a secure vantage point and should be sought where there is underwater cover. Eels will take worms, small dead baits and baits that are particularly smelly.

Eels are caught by legering in water that has been well prepared with bait, including chopped-up worms or pieces of fish. Remember that eels may be taken only on rod and line. A licence is required to take eels by any other method.

PIKE *(Esox lucius)*

Irish Record River Pike 42 lb (M. Watkins, Bagnelstown, River Barrow, 22 March 1964)

Irish Record Lake Pike 38 lb 2 oz (Brendan Hardiman, Lough Corrib, 25 February 1973)

Specimen Weight River, 20 lb (9.072 kilos); Lake, 30 lb (13.608 kilos)

Pike are widely distributed throughout Ireland. They are to be found in lakes, rivers, canals and small ponds. When the water temperature is about 10°C, from February to April, pike spawn in shallow flood margins. In their early life pike eat aquatic insects and then move on to feed on young fry. They feed increasingly on fish as they grow and adults are entirely predatory.

The pike is a lone hunter and lies in ambush with little movement. When fodder fish come within range, the camouflaged pike moves with remarkable speed to attack. Pike thrive in waters which hold a good stock of roach, rudd, perch and bream. In waters where roach have become established, pike too have flourished. They are also partial to brown trout. To maintain itself in a year, some authorities estimate that a pike will eat roughly five times its own weight. This means that about 25 lb of fish would be consumed by a 5–16 lb pike in a year just to maintain its weight alone.

The pike is a long fish with a long pointed head and a big mouth. Perfectly camouflaged, with green colouring, it can attack its prey with speed and is known to eat all kinds of water animals and fish. The stories told about pike in Irish pubs are legion. I have certainly seen pike rise to the surface and strike at small moorhens and rats which shows that they are rapacious gluttons.

The population of *large* pike in any water will be reduced by their removal or killing. The message that I want to go out from this book is that the much maligned pike must be conserved.

Pike Angling

I shall make no attempt to go into the details of how to tackle up and fish for pike. There are many books on the market to describe the intricacies involved in tempting and landing pike. My words are aimed at tourist anglers who visit Ireland and also at the young generation at home who are starting out to fish.

Pike are found in all kinds of waters and the most important thing to remember is that they are never far away from their natural food – small fish. The pike's feeding habits vary as its source of food moves with the changing seasons. Pike are caught at all times of the year. During the summer months they live happily in waters where the fodder fish are plentiful and they do not need to travel for a meal. It is in the colder months from September when the water temperature drops that the pike becomes more active and angling is at its best. Pike are known to hunt by sight, sound and smell. The common techniques for pike fishing are spinning, trolling and dead-baiting.

Spinning

This is the method of casting and retrieving an artificial bait. The variety of lures, spinners, spoons, divers, buzzers, floaters and plugs is confusing to the beginner. Some work, others just look good, but at one time or another most of us will simply buy one to have a go.

Local knowledge is important when using artificials. A small dead bait can also be set up, cast out and retrieved. This 'sink and draw' method is successful on many Irish waters.

Trolling

Trolling can be a skilled method for piking on big Irish waters. The art of trolling a bait behind a boat is something that comes after years of experience of the boat and how to use it in conjunction with a bait which may spin, wobble or dive.

I recall using a big 18-foot boat on Lough Allen, powered by an electric motor, and deep trolling at 40 feet along a smooth-bottomed section of that big lake with the master pike angler, Fred J. Taylor. I have since used that technique with great success elsewhere.

Dead-Baiting

During the cold months of the year this method is highly successful. Some knowledge of the pike's haunts is essential to success. Once a hot-spot has been located, a dead fish (roach, rudd, mackerel, herring, smelt or other fish) is cast into the area and legered.

Pike Conservation

All pike should be returned alive to the water.

The newcomer to pike angling must learn to respect the fish and never to be afraid of it. You must have the proper tackle and know how to use it so as not to harm the fish. First, the pike angler must have a large, strong landing net, then a mat or some soft material to lay the fish on. A garden glove to open the mouth, a good long-handled wire cutter and a disgorger must be in your tackle box. The fish is weighed in a big pike or carp sling, and then returned promptly to the water.

To ensure the safe handling of pike, the following simple procedures should be adopted by all anglers:

1   Do not use big hooks in your bait. Size 8 is about right, but you may need to use bigger or smaller hooks when using different methods.

2   It is important that you learn to strike the fish quickly and not allow it to swallow the bait. Remain alert and always keep in touch with legered dead baits.

3   Land the fish carefully with a big net. Never use a gaff.

4   Place the pike on a mat or soft material but never on a hard stony bank.

    You must now handle the fish with care and with firmness.

    Lay the pike on its back and with the fish between your legs insert your gloved hand into the lower jaw and the mouth will open. With the other hand, you can then remove the hooks with a disgorger.

5   Weigh the pike in a sling. Never insert the hook of a balance into the fish.

6   Return the pike quickly to the water. If the fish turns on its side, hold it by the tail until it recovers and swims away. This is a wonderful sight, as the pike shakes its tail and quickly slips into the deeps. The best pike is the one swimming freely in its natural environment.

Anglers should be aware that many clubs in Ireland prohibit the killing of pike in their local waters. Fishery bylaws are given in the Appendix but at this point I would like to highlight the following:

1   Live fish as bait is prohibited.

2   Only two rods are permitted.

3   Live roach must not be transferred from one water to another.

RECORD AND SPECIMEN FISH

It is every angler's wish to catch a big fish and for this purpose the Irish Specimen Fish Committee has set up a schedule of specimen weights for all species. Many waters in Ireland hold specimen fish, though for various reasons many go unrecorded with the Specimen Fish Committee.

The Specimen Fish Committee issues claim forms and if you catch a notable fish of specimen weight you are invited to make a claim by completing the form and sending it to the Irish Specimen Fish Committee, Balnagowan, Mobhi Boreen, Glasnevin, Dublin 9.

In the case of rudd, roach and hybrids, the body of the fish must be examined by a biologist of the Central Fisheries Board.

You should note one or two points when making a claim for a specimen or record fish. The scales on which the fish is weighed must be certified by a Weights and Measures Authority *before* the fish is weighed. If you want to record a claim for a rudd, roach or hybrid, you could arrange to have the live fish examined by a biologist.

An angler who has a specimen fish claim accepted receives a certificate and badge. The Specimen Fish Committee issues an annual report listing all specimens and records taken in Irish waters.

CO. DONEGAL

· DERRY

MAGHERAFELT·   · TOOME

· ANTRIM

COOKSTOWN   Lough
                Neagh   BELFAST

OMAGH   · LISBURN

DUNGANNON

                   · PORTADOWN

Lower
Lough   DOWNPATRICK
Erne   ENNISKILLEN

                   ARMAGH   BANBRIDGE

Upper
Lough   LISNASKEA
Erne
                                · NEWRY

        CO. MONAGHAN

CO. CAVAN

                CO. LOUGH

Northern Ireland

Northern Ireland

Northern Ireland has within its boundaries a great variety of good coarse fishing in lakes, rivers and canals. It was in Northern Ircland that the second colony of roach exploded and the quality of fish remains high. Anglers concentrating on roach in heavily fished stretches soon discovered that good bream were also present, particularly in the big, deep waters, and roach and bream are common throughout the province. On the other hand, waters holding carp and tench are rarer in the six counties than in the Republic.

The angler fishing in Northern Ireland will find access to the waters easy and well signposted. In most areas there are car parks at the waterside and good access to the water on foot. Fishing facilities along the banks are all of a high standard and where the margins are soft and reeded, fishing stands are provided.

The main difference between fishing for coarse fish in the Republic and Northern Ireland is that in the north a permit is required as well as a rod licence. Details are given in the Appendix.

THE NEWRY CANAL (J10 25)

The Newry Canal was built in the early eighteenth century to carry coal from the Tyrone coalfield to the sea at Newry.

Linking the Upper Bann with Newry, and incorporating fourteen locks, it operated for only a short time before the upper

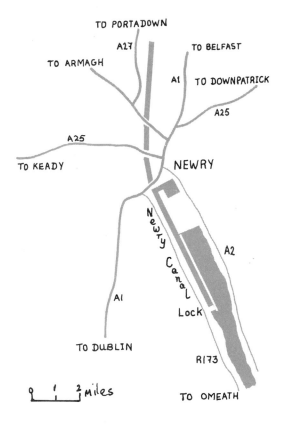

Northern Ireland, Newry

section went into disuse when the coal trade died and the port of Newry began to lose trade to Belfast. Fish, however, had time to colonize this waterway and now the stretch from Newry to the sea holds good stocks of bream, roach, some rudd, hybrids, perch, pike and eels.

To reach the canal take the A1 south of Newry and then take the Omeath road (R173) on the southern side of Carlingford Lough. This road runs alongside the canal. The grass margin between the canal and the road is narrow, so care must be taken with your tackle. The opposite bank is also narrow, forming a barrier with Carlingford Lough. This long, featureless stretch, nearly 3 miles, has depths varying from 10 to 20 feet, and there is some weed.

Fishing on the canal varies from season to season, but during the summer the clouded water will yield bream and roach, while in the colder months the clear and deeper water at the Albert Basin will give the best sport. During the winter months the canal yields some good pike to the sink-and-draw method.

The canal is a match stretch and produces its best results at pegs 25–85 and 100–150.

RIVER QUOILE, DOWNPATRICK

This shallow river, controlled by the Department of Agriculture, is a first-class rudd water. North of Downpatrick fishing from the right bank can be reached from the main A7 road bridge. Here there is a wide bay in the river where you will find an abundance of rudd in 4–5 feet of water with some weed.

Below the Old Barrier, along the A25

Downpatrick–Strangford road, the river is narrow and runs moderate to fast. This is a lovely water to fish a stick float in shallow water. A waterside path and some stands have been provided and a disabled anglers' car park is now in use at the Old Barrier.

Rudd to 1 lb are common and some fish to 2 lb come to the net. Catches of 40–80 lb of rudd are taken in this cracking river.

CAMLOUGH LAKE   (J25 4)

This big water lies near the A25 Newry–Newtownhamilton road west of Newry and near Camlough village. Originally a trout water, it now holds a big stock of roach, bream, hybrids, perch and pike. It is a big and rich water, serious attention is needed to bring those big bream and big hybrids on the feed. Fishing is into 10–15 feet, but in some areas the bank shelves to a depth of 25 feet close in.

During the winter months Camlough Lake offers some great pike fishing.

LOUGH SHARK (Acton Lake)   (J6 41)

This rich and shallow water lies just off the A27 Scarva–Newry road. It holds a good stock of quality bream over 6 lb, but it is essential to treat the water with serious intent. Heavy groundbaiting and long casting are the order of the day – and then keep to it. The water also has a good head of roach, perch, hybrids and pike.

UPPER RIVER BANN   (J54 2)

The River Bann flows through Counties Down and Armagh, through Portadown, enters Lough Neagh, and leaves the big lake at Toome. In the past, massive shoals of quality roach moved from Lough Neagh into the river in the colder months of the year. Catches of more than 100 lb of roach were common and, indeed, records fell here time and again. After spawning higher up in the shallow waters of the river, the fish moved back into Lough Neagh in June. Thus it was that observant anglers were able to track the up-river progress of the roach after they left the immense reservoir of Lough Neagh in the autumn.

However, there has been a dramatic change, as roach stocks have decreased greatly in Lough Neagh and the Upper Bann. No longer can you take those great catches which raised so many eyebrows in the angling world. Some roach do remain, but don't expect those big catches – they are now history.

With the decline of roach in the Upper Bann, however, we can now expect an increase in the stocks and in the quality of bream in this area. Access and fishing facilities in Portadown are first-class. From Point of Whitecoat to the Boat House there is a path along the left bank. Access is also easy between the Boat House and the Shillington stretch. The river has a steady pull and depths fluctuate, but average 6–12 feet.

Bream are present in limited sections of the river and the stretch from the Dumps to the Boulevard is sure to yield catches of fish of about 3 lb in the summer months. The river is accessible at several points in Portadown. Hoy's Meadow has access from the A3 Craigavon–Portadown road by Bridge Street. After the Bann Bridge, take the second left into Watson Street, which brings you to the amenity area via the tunnel under the flyover. The Hoy's Meadow stretch is closed on Sundays. The Boulevard is approached from the A3 Craigavon road to Bridge Street. First left after the bridge to Bridge Street south, and then to the car park, which is to the left.

LOUGH NEAGH   (H00 80)

The largest lake in these islands, Lough Neagh is a remarkably shallow water, with an average depth of 7–10 feet. There is a great growth of weed during the summer.

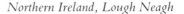

Northern Ireland, Lough Neagh

Approached from the M1 motorway, Kinnegoe Marina offers a chance to fish the big lake. The long breakwater here is a good place for bream and roach fishing in the early summer months. Catches to 50–80 lb can be taken here, but do remember that at weekends the marina becomes alive with boats, canoes and surfers.

LOWER RIVER BANN

The River Bann is now controlled by Bann Systems Ltd; do not forget that in Northern Ireland fishing permits are required as well as rod licences. Leaving Lough Neagh at Toome, the river passes through Lough Beg and moves at a moderate to fast pace through Portglenone and on through Coleraine to the sea.

Toome   (H99 91)

The river at Toome Bridge is fishable along the right bank. Here there are 30 pegs, where the depth is 15–25 feet and there is a considerable pull on the river. The water level is controlled and levels can rise quickly to flood level. This stretch yields good catches of small bream and roach × bream hybrids, with some roach and perch.

Portglenone   (C97 4)

At Portglenone, there is a good stretch up-river on the left bank. Here there are good swims which produce catches of roach well over the magic figure of 100 lb. During the summer months, this rich river yields some great bream over 9 lb

and great catches of quality fish have been recorded.

The river is deep here and flows fast. Fishing may be by leger, pole or waggler. You can step up on hooks to size 12 or 10 and use 6-lb BS line here, with red maggots or casters as bait. It is essential to make your groundbait heavy in this water, with a depth of 15–20 feet and with a hard pull.

The Portglenone stretch is a first-class fishery and must be put on your list of waters to fish in Northern Ireland.

Below Portglenone there are many game-fishing stretches, but down-river from Agivey bridge near Ballymoney you will again find some good bream and roach fishing.

Canal Stretches

The Lower Bann has some quiet canal stretches which also provide good sport.

The Toomebridge canal stretch can be reached by turning left in Toome village off the A6 Belfast–Randalstown road towards Derry. The stretch yields good roach and perch catches. The canal can also be reached to the north by turning left and left again off the A54 Portglenone–Kilrea road ¼ mile north of Kilrea. Here you will find perch fishing below the lock and during the winter good pike are taken along this stretch.

The Monanagher canal stretch produces small bream, roach and some good pike. It can be reached by taking the Ballymoney road from Kilrea over the Bann Bridge to McLoughlin's Corner. Here turn left and left again and follow the B64 road for over 2 miles to the road to Monanagher Fish Farm.

Lough Beg   (H98 95)

Lough Beg means 'small lake' in Irish but is, in fact, quite a big water north of Toome. The River Bann flows through the lake and it holds good stocks of roach, bream, hybrids and perch. It is for big pike that this rich water has gained a reputation, particularly during the winter months.

LURGAN LAKE   (J8 58)

This is a shallow water in the Town Park in Lurgan. Access is easy and there are facilities for all. With a depth of about 4 feet, the water near the golf course yields good catches of good bream over 5 lb. You can also have good sport over most of the year for roach and perch.

CLAY LAKE   (H83 32)

A public reservoir, this 120-acre lake lies beside the B3 Castleblaney–Keady road 3 miles from Keady. Permits to fish are available from the Department of Agriculture. Access is easy along the stony shore. This water holds a big stock of perch and some good quality roach. With good fodder fish, pike are also of good quality here.

RIVER BLACKWATER

It was in the Upper River Blackwater that the Irish Record bream of 11 lb 8 oz was taken in 1882. But since then this water has changed a lot, as roach are now present. A great fishery, this river can be fished at many places along its course, but mostly from Blackwatertown to Lough Neagh.

Blackwatertown   (H84 53)

This water is a mixed fishery so make sure that you have the proper permit to fish. In the early season down river from the bridge you will find some swims for good roach in 6–8 feet of water.

Moy   (H85 56)

Up river in the village the river is slow-moving with a depth of 9 feet, and it is here that quality bream of over 6 lb are taken. At the bridge some great roach are taken in April and May.

Down from the bridge, where the depth is 7–10 feet, you will have good sport with bream, roach and perch.

Up river from Bond's Bridge, the river widens and the depth is 8–12 feet. In this deeper part of the river good catches of bream are taken. Below the bridge, where the depth is about 13–15 feet, there is a big head of small bream. The stretch at Bond's Bridge also holds roach, perch and pike.

Verner's Bridge   (H88 61)

Verner's Bridge can be reached from the M1 motorway between Dungannon and Craigavon. Here the Blackwater is much deeper. In 15–20 feet of water you can fish for quality bream of over 5 lb, though in such a big water heavy baiting is essential.

Roach can also be found, but since they migrate between the river and Lough Neagh their presence is at times unpredictable. As roach stocks have decreased in Lough Neagh, we can expect also a decline in the roach which move up the river.

STRULE RIVER, OMAGH
(H45 73)

The Strule River, joined by the Fairy Water, flows north-west from Omagh to Newtownstewart, and then as the River Mourne joins the River Foyle to flow north to the sea at Lough Foyle. Roach introduced early this century to the waters of the Baronscourt estate near Newtownstewart from the Munster Blackwater spread through the system and in days gone by the Strule at Omagh shared with the Munster Blackwater a reputation as Ireland's premier roach fishery.

From the beginning, the stretch extending over a mile downstream from the Nestlé factory, to the east of the A5 Derry road 1 mile north of Omagh, set the scene for roach fishing in Northern Ireland. In the summer the water is shallow (3–5 feet), and the top-class roach must be sought in the deep pools. During the winter months, with the water much higher, sport continues in what is a cracking roach water. This rich river holds quality roach of over 1 lb and catches of over 150 lb have been taken here.

The Fairy Water and Strule River are mixed fisheries and you must be sure to get the correct fishing permit.

CREEVE LAKE   (H74 51)

This 45-acre lake lies south of the B128 Benburb–Aughnacloy road. Access is easy and the lake has a path round it. The water is reeded, with forested margins, and fishing stands are provided.

This is a rich water which holds some quality roach, perch to 1 lb, and also some good pike.

ENAGH LAKE   (H76 46)

This 13-acre lake lies alongside the Dungannon–Caledon road 11 miles from Dungannon and 1 mile from Caledon. It offers all the facilities commonly found in Northern Ireland – car park, a path along the water, and fishing stands.

This small but rich water holds some good bream, roach, perch and pike. The depth is 10–16 feet, with some weed, and the water can be fished easily by float or leger.

THE ERNE SYSTEM

The River Erne flows north from Co. Cavan in the Republic and enters Northern Ireland and Co. Fermanagh, where it forms two majestic lakes, linked at Enniskillen by a stretch of river. In the south of Co. Fermanagh the Erne is fed from the west by the Woodford River and from the east by the Finn River. The narrow and slow-moving Finn forms the border between Northern Ireland and the Republic in this part of the island.

The waters of the Erne offer a vast variety of places to fish. There are many river stretches, small tributaries, and countless bays, inlets and islands in the big loughs to entrance the angler. A glance at the map will show the potential of the fishing in Fermanagh.

Visitors to this part of Ireland will be impressed with the first-class facilities provided for those fishing for coarse fish. The signposting of all waters makes them easy to find and car parking in most cases helps to keep the haulage of tackle to a minimum.

River and Upper Lough Erne

On the Cavan–Newtownbutler road take the first right from Newtownbutler by the church, and continue through Landbrock crossroads to Galloon Bridge. This point can also be approached from the Cavan–Belturbet road over the border via Wattle Bridge, turning left before the filling station. Galloon is an island and over the bridge to the left at the end of the road you will find access to deep water, 10–14 feet close in and 30 feet at a long cast. This area produces great bream catches in the early season and reaches its best again in September. Here there are roach, hybrids, perch and pike at other points around this island.

This area offers great scope for exploration. I have fished many of the bays and behind islands along this border area, using my boat as transport, and I believe that it will be many years yet before the true fishing potential of this complex system is fully known. While the match stretches are well known and published, you can also stop off for easy fishing at countless quays and jetties.

Lady Brooke and Lady Craigavon Bridge connect Trasna Island with the mainland and at each place bream and roach provide good sport. The area near Craigavon Bridge, approached from Lisnaskea by the B127 road, offers facilities for all. I have often had great bream fishing directly above the bridge on the upper Lisnaskea side, where there is a steady flow.

Enniskillen   (H24 44)

The island town of Enniskillen has some marvellous stretches for roach and bream fishing right on its doorstep. Beside the Lakeland Forum lies the much-used and productive Broadmeadow stretch, and directly across there are some swims which will produce bream, though they are a bit uncertain. Drop into the Lakeland Visitor Centre here and you will get a wealth of information.

Along the Queen Elizabeth Road there are some swims below the bridge which yield bream and roach, especially when there is a good depth of water.

Leaving Enniskillen by the A4 in the direction of Belfast, a short distance on by the Killyhevlin Hotel take the right turn signposted Lake Acrussel. By this reeded lake the narrow road leads to a car park at the River Erne. The bending river here has some good bank to the left and also has fishing stands. This is The Ring, where bream fishing in the summer months is good, with catches to 80 lb. Roach fishing here is up and down, but winter gets the best results.

Directly opposite here to the right of the Bellanaleck Jetty there are some swims which yield good bream, but during the summer this area has much boating activity. This area is approached by taking the A4 Belcoo road west out of Enniskillen and then turning left on the A509 to Derrylin and Bellanaleck. In the village of Bellanaleck turn left to the river and jetty.

If you continue through Bellanaleck towards Derrylin, a left turn at 200 yards leads by Mill Lough to Schools, another good stretch. This water is also fished from the opposite bank, Corrigans, which can be reached by continuing on from Bellanaleck to the crossroads and signpost to the left for Carrybridge and Lisnaskea. Before Carrybridge, the fishing sign to the left leads to a car park at

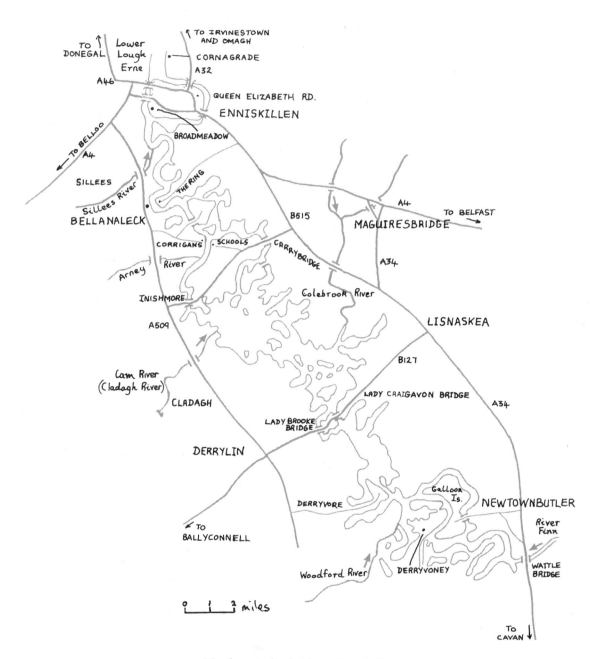

Northern Ireland, Upper Lough Erne

This river stretch of the Erne below Enniskillen at Cornagrade produces great catches of bream and roach

The wide and open stretch of the River Erne up from Enniskillen at The Ring

Tully. The best swims here are to the left and over two fields. Fishing is from stands, but farther on near the bend the bank is good and clean. In the summer, the first fishing stands are popular and there you will find good bream to 3 lb in 6–10 feet of water. Roach and perch are also found here. The best roach fishing is in the colder months.

River and Lower Lough Erne
(H22 50)

At Queen Elizabeth Road in Enniskillen and over the bridge, the first turning on the left – opposite the hospital – leads to the down-river stretch at Cornagrade. Here there is a waterside path and fishing stands in a wide section of the river. This is a follow-through from the upper Broadmeadow stretch and fishing is dictated by the movement of the shoals of roach and bream. With conditions right it can be roach galore, but in recent times bream seem to dominate the stretch. The roach which appear here – and, indeed in most of this middle section of the Erne – are of good quality.

The very big Lower Lough Erne is a designated game fishery and anglers should note that, particularly in the lower section of the lake, all regulations must be adhered to.

Three miles north of Enniskillen on the A52, and just before the Kesh–Ballinamallard road junction, the left turn leads to the Trory Stretch. This great stretch is located in the narrow tail of the

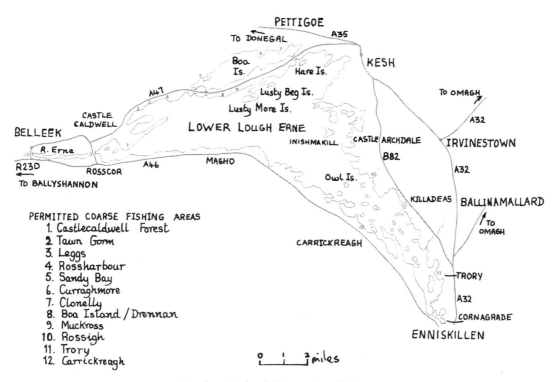

Northern Ireland, Lower Lough Erne

lake and near the historic Devenish Island. Here there is waterside parking and fishing is from stands. Fishing is into 5–11 feet over a bottom of gravel and float fishing in normal conditions is easy. Great catches of bream to 3½ lb will come from these swims and you can expect to catch 50–60 lb here. Roach × bream hybrids are also common here and at the time of writing hybrids and bream dominate, as roach stocks have declined.

Lower Lough Erne is a rich water with rocky shallow margins in places. The quality of the coarse fish present is very good and if you concentrate on the one swim you can expect some fantastic catches.

Erne Tributaries

Record catches of roach have been taken in the many tributaries of the two loughs in the early season, but do not forget that roach migrate to spawn. You cannot assume that tributaries such as the Sillees and Ballinamallard rivers will hold many roach after the month of June.

The Colebrook River is approached by taking the first left on the B514 200 yards north of Lisnaskea. The next left leads to car parks and a very good stretch of this river. The McVitties Mile here yields good bream fishing during the summer. The stretch holds roach and a good head of bream to 4 lb, and your target would be 50 lb of bream and roach.

The Cam, or Cladagh, River, which flows from Swanlinbar in Co. Cavan, is approached from Enniskillen via Bella-naleck (A509), turning left after 8 miles before Carrs bridge. Fishing is in the river to the right. A small river with good clean banks, it is accessible on both banks.

During the summer, small bream are taken here on the waggler or pole. Good hybrids, roach, some rudd and perch are found here.

The River Finn forms the border between part of Co. Fermanagh and Co. Monaghan. The slow-moving and quiet river, which has low banks, holds good stocks of small roach and bream, with perch galore and a good stock of small pike. It can be fished at Annie's Bridge, where access is easy.

DONEGAL

BALLYSHANNON

COOTEHILL

SHERLOCK

CAVAN

BALLINAMORE

GOWNA

DUBLIN

Northern Region

Northern Fisheries Region

The waters of this region are mostly those of the River Erne system in Counties Donegal, Cavan, Longford, Leitrim and Monaghan, and other waters in Sligo. The Northern Regional Fisheries Board is responsible for the protection, development and promotion of fisheries in this region. Addresses and telephone numbers are given in the Appendix.

The countryside in Cavan, Leitrim and Monaghan is mostly of small hills (drumlins) with a great number of lakes and rivers. The attraction to anglers in this part of the country is the vast variety of different places where one can fish for bream, roach, hybrids, perch, pike, tench and eels. The waters of the Erne have good fishing depths of 5–20 feet and the rivers mostly have slow to moderate flow. Up to about 1960, the waters of these parts of the Erne were free of roach, and rudd to 2 lb were then common. Following the invasion of roach in the early 1960s, rudd became scarce and now they have virtually disappeared in many of the Erne waters.

RIVER ERNE

In south Co. Cavan the village of Lough Gowna is surrounded by a maze of lakes and it is from these waters that the River Erne flows. The main inflow to the lakes is the Legwee River, flowing from the high ground in Bruskey, the source of the great river, which we will look at in detail as it flows from Co. Cavan, through Co. Fermanagh, to enter the Atlantic at Ballyshannon in Co. Donegal.

In my early days of fishing for coarse fish I took many good brown trout to 4 lb by spinning the then deadly Voblex bait. Stocks of perch and pike were good then, with some rudd and bream appearing in some of the lakes. It was to these lakes that the first organized groups of English coarse-angling tourists came in great numbers, setting off a tourism industry which was to spread all over the coarse-angling districts of Ireland.

From the Gowna Lakes, the River Erne flows fast to enter the vast complex of lakes named Lough Oughter, between Cavan and Killeshandra. This is a most scenic area, with forests and the Killykeen Forest Park Holiday Village, where anglers have always enjoyed great fishing. Two rivers add volume to the Erne here: the Killegar, or Castle, River entering from the West; and the River Annalee from Shercock and Cootehill joining the main watercourse at Derryheen below Butlersbridge.

The wide river now flows through Belturbet and as it enters Upper Lough Erne in Co. Fermanagh it is joined by the River Woodford from Ballinamore and Ballyconnell. Lough Erne is studded with lovely islands and the whole water area is now navigable by cruisers, which adds to the facilities which abound here.

The River Erne now winds its way round Enniskillen before flowing into Lower Lough Erne whence, as a river once more, it enters Co. Donegal. Here the waters of the river form a reservoir of 1,000 acres for the hydroelectric power station. The River Erne then enters the Atlantic a short distance away at Finner Strand, where as a young lad I built many a castle with spade and bucket.

The slow-moving Erne with its lakes in the drumlin counties offers the angler a variety of fishing. Lakes, big and small, and the parent river with its tributaries present opportunities to use all methods for bream, roach, roach × bream hybrids, perch, tench, pike and eels. Rudd are no longer the common species here since roach invaded the system, but they can be found in some isolated lakes. You should note that whilst I single out only those special waters which hold quality fish, pike and eels are common throughout the system.

LOUGH GOWNA

The little village is situated in south Co. Cavan and near the Longford border. It is surrounded by a maze of lovely lakes collectively called Lough Gowna, which form the headwaters of the River Erne system.

Population 204
OS ½-inch Map No. 12
Cavan 12 miles, Arva 4 miles, Longford 16 miles, Dublin 72 miles
Club: Lough Gowna Anglers' Association

LOUGH GOWNA

Dring   (N30 86)

The lake here is shallow along the margins. There is good parking and access to the waterside car park. Fishing is best here in the early months, when distance casting for roach is the preferred method. The area is frequented by bathers in the summer months.

Aghakine   (N28 88)

The approach to this water is over a narrow lane with several gates. The access over this private ground is open only on special occasions. The bank is clean and firm, with fishing for bream and roach into 8–12 feet of water. The stretch requires extensive baiting to bring the fish on the feed.

Stretton's Shore   (N28 91)

The access to this lovely lake is along a narrow road and through a farmyard. Anglers must get permission to cross this land and you are requested to respect the property of the owner, Mr Hall. The lake shore is of gravel and is firm. I have had great catches of good bream to 4 lb here by fishing close in, where there is a sharp shelf dropping to 21 feet. This is a great bream water where catches of well over 120 lb are taken.

Dernaferst   (N29 89)

There is an amenity area at the waterside here, where access and parking are easy. This is a perfect fishing area for the handicapped angler. There are two lakes connected by a small river. Dernaferst West has good bream beginning 200 yards along the bank, where fishing is into 6–10 feet of water over a stony bottom. There is also an abundance of roach and perch.

The lake to the east is shallower but there are a few great swims at the stile and just to the right for 30 yards near the alders. Bream catches of over 100 lb are common here. Only two or three of the pegs over the bridge and in the wood from the small car park produce bream.

Church Lake – Andy's Point   (N30 90)

A short distance from Gowna, access is through a gate and there is parking beside the lake. The bank is clean and firm, with fishing into 12–17 feet of water. Often the sliding float is the best method here for roach and bream. The best pegs are over the first stile and near the second one further on.

Cloone Lake   (N30 91)

There is a waterside car park here, with easy access to good bream fishing. The

Bobby Smithers from Dublin was the first Irishman to win the CIPS World Championship. Here he is fishing in style on the placid stretch of Lough Gowna at Dernaferst

approach to the best swims is to the left along the bank by the island and then to the point. The walk round the corner is worth it, because I have found that the prevailing wind, coming face on, brings the bream on the feed. The bottom is stony and the depth is 8–16 feet. Bream shoals with fish to 5 lb appear in the late summer. Roach and perch abound here.

As in all the Gowna lakes, eels and pike are common. Big brown trout are also taken on a Devon bait. The Gowna Club controls trout fishing in this area.

Swan Lake   (N31 92)

Anglers are often attracted to fish this lake, which lies near the road at Lough-gowna. While the water holds good-quality roach and some bream, the height of patience is needed to catch them. On some occasions the lucky angler will land on a shoal of big roach and catches of over 100 lb have been taken here. To the east of this lake, approached over a small road, there is a small reeded pond, Black Lake, where the adventurous angler will find some good tench to 6 lb.

AGHANORAN LAKE (N32 90)

Lying one mile to the east of Gowna, this is a big water which is connected to the main system. There is a small lakeside car park here and access is easy over a stile. A river leaves the lake to the right and this has always been one of my favourite places for easy float fishing into 4–6 feet of water over a gravel bottom. The bank is low and liable to flood but from midsummer to October the bream and roach fishing here is wonderful, especially when the wind is blowing from left to right.

There is another access further along the road near the road junction and house. Access is through the gate and to the left to the point beyond the island and stile. The depth varies here but good shoals of bream will respond to heavy baiting and you will find quality fish in windy conditions. Anglers should note that there is no access to this lake along the southern shore.

The river stretch leaving this lake, at Gowna Bridge, has deep pools worth trying for bream and roach.

BAWNDOORA LAKE
                          (N32 91)

Tench were stocked in this lake from 1960 and later some carp were introduced. I have taken tench to 4 lb here, while fishing from stands. But where have all those small carp gone? Access is easy, with waterside parking. The lake also holds roach, perch and some small bream.

WHITE AND BLACK LAKES
                          (N91 34)

These are heavily reeded waters and stands are provided. There is a small stock of small bream, with roach, rudd and perch. My advice is to forget these waters and move on to the next productive lake.

DERRIES LAKE   (N34 90)

Sometimes called Lisanny Lake, which is, in fact, farther down the river system.

There are three approaches to this first-class water. The first car park along the lake is at the exit of the river, and here the water is very shallow. However, roach fishing in the early season, with a float set at about 3 feet, is very productive. Some shoals of good bream appear here in the late season. There is a second car park along the road to the right. Anglers are requested not to park in the field here; please use the car park. Bream fishing in the early season is particularly good when there is a fresh south-westerly wind blowing onshore. Fishing is into 5–9 feet of water, with a gravel bottom. The third access is from the same car park to the left and over the wooden bridge to Deignan's Point, where the bream feed freely in windy conditions. The depth here is 12–14 feet and to the left it shallows to 3–4 feet, with some perch and roach fishing only. It is to the left here that the main source of the Erne system, the Legwee River, enters the lake. All these waters hold good stocks of pike and eels.

RIVER ERNE

Sallaghan Bridge   (N32 94)

Here along the Gowna–Cavan road the narrow River Erne appears for the first time. Parking is along a busy road at the bridge and access is by foot over one field and a footbridge to the short up-river stretch. Here there are about five swims and fishing is into 10–12 feet of water with a slow flow. There are, however, some submerged hazards here. There are good roach in this short stretch in the early season. Down river, roach move into a deep pool and fishing can be great in the early months. This fast water was once noted for its brown-trout fishing. Please respect the landowner's property here and do not park in the field.

Dingin Bridge   (N33 95)

Parking is along a narrow and busy road. Fish just 50 yards down from the bridge along the right bank, where there are interesting pools, with roach. Using a stick float, I have enjoyed many a session for roach in this short and quiet stretch. Note that bank space is limited along this water.

Wateraughey Bridge   (N34 96)

The river continues to look like good trout water and, in fact, produces some fish to 3 lb. Above the bridge there is a very shallow short stretch where good sport can be had by floating at 3 feet for roach. It is important to bait lightly and to keep a low profile along this exposed bank. Overbait or make noise here and you can go home!

KILL LAKE   (N42 91)

High in the hilly country of Co. Cavan and near the village of Kilnaleck are the topmost waters of the River Erne system. Parking for this lake is on private property and every consideration must be given to the kind landowner. The bank is low and the lake floods easily. For directions see the entry below.

This has been one of my favourite lakes, and produces good-quality roach. Using a Peter Drennan 3- or 4-swan waggler, a long cast into 6–8 feet of water, facing the sun and in breezy conditions will always get a catch of 40–80 lb of good roach to 1 lb. Bream also come into this area in the late summer.

Benny Ashurst with a good netfull of roach and roach x bream hybrids on Kill Lake,
one of the waters at the top of the River Erne system in Cavan

CORGLASS LAKE   (N42 92)

Corglass Lake lies close to Kill Lake and has a bigger stock of bream. Fishing is from stands or, for the adventurous, further along the bank under the steep hill. Good-quality roach abound here. Pike removed from Lough Sheelin were tagged and stocked into this lake.

This lake is reached by turning left at the Granard sign ¾ mile from Kilnaleck on the Kilnaleck-Cavan road and to the left at the Granard sign. After a further ½ mile a right turn leads to Kill Lake, but for Corglass continue a little farther and turn right at the crossroads. Then at 1 mile turn right and along a small road by a house, through a gate, and at the end you are one field from the water. This is a private access road. The low bank has a fringe of rushes, where I have cut some swims. Float or leger here for quality roach – catches to 80 lb or more can be taken. From here the small river flows on to become the Bruskey River, then the Legwee river, which enters the Gowna Lakes.

ARVA

Arva a small village in the farming area of south Co. Cavan and close to Counties Leitrim and Longford. It lies within the upper waters of the River Erne system.

Population 407
OS ½-inch Map No. 12
Gowna 5 miles, Cavan 14 miles, Carrigallen 5 miles, Dublin 85 miles
Club: Arva Tourism Association

GARTY LAKE   (N28 98)

This big lake in Arva village has only a fair stock of good-quality roach, which are best fished for from a boat in the far bay to the right. There are also some perch and pike here and, as bank space is limited, I would advise you to try the more productive lakes in this area.

HOLLYBANK LAKE (N26 98)

Tucked under a hill at the village, this is a rich water which gives great sport. Fishing is from one side where the bank is good and the depth 10–12 feet. The bank faces the sun and the prevailing wind, which when fresh brings on the bream, and there is also an abundance of roach which will keep you occupied. A good water. Access is off the Carrigallen Road and ½ mile from Arva.

GUINIKIN LAKE   (N27 96)

Just a short distance from Arva, this small lake was stocked with tench in 1960 and remains a fair water for fish to 4 lb. It has easy access from the Ballinalee–Longford road. The lake also holds roach and perch. Fishing is into 6–8 feet of water, with a good bottom.

LOUGH NABACK   (N25 95)

Lough Naback must be mentioned even though here I am dealing with coarse fishing. With an area of 29 acres and a depth of 36 feet, it is unique in being the only natural salmonid water in this region which holds char. The water is listed under the National Heritage Inventory. If you find roach in this water, the Fisheries Board would like to hear about it.

TULLY LAKE   (N22 97)

Follow the Carrigallen sign from the Drumlish Road at Moyne. After ½ mile continue ahead along Aghavas road and 1 mile farther on turn right at Carrigallen sign. At ½ mile turn right at the lake sign and then through the gate to waterside parking. Fishing along this clean bank is very good for bream to 4 lb, with good roach too. This water also produces good pike fishing.

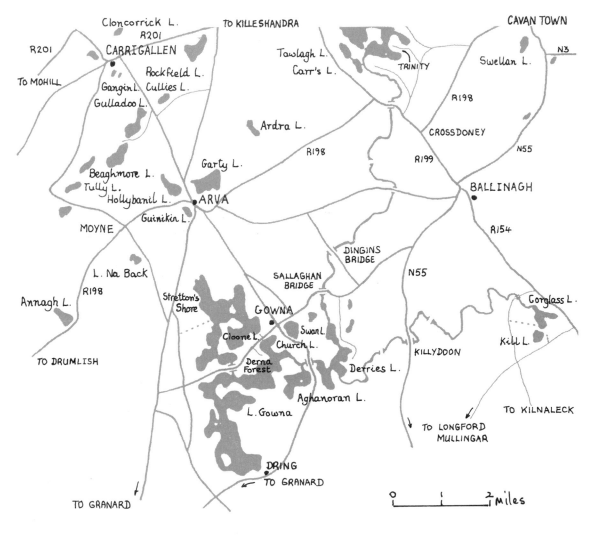

Northern Region, Arva

CARRIGALLEN

This small town, situated in Co. Leitrim, is surrounded by lakes which form part of the Erne system and drain into Co. Cavan and Lough Oughter.

Population 261
OS ½-inch Map No. 8
Arva 4 miles, Killeshandra 5 miles, Cavan 18 miles, Ballinamore 10 miles, Dublin 90 miles
Club: Carrigallen Angling Club

TOWN LAKE   (H23 3)

This is a 40-acre lake with shallow margins and has a maximum depth of 25 feet. Access is easy and fishing is from stands. This water holds a good stock of tench to 5 lb, which come on the feed in May and June. Fishing here calls for some skill and is best in the early morning at first light, with bread as bait. The lake also has a good stock of roach, perch, small bream, eels and pike.

GANGIN LAKE   (H24 3)

This water close to Carrigallen has easy access. The entry is off the Carrigallen–Killeshandra road and there is parking beside the water. The surrounds are soft and weedy here, but there are some good swims for bream and roach. There are also some tench to 4 lb in this water. The nearby Mosies Lake can be fished in comfort only during dry conditions but it does hold tench to 5 lb.

CLOONCORICK LAKE
    (H24 4)

The access to this lake is from a farm and you should respect the landowner's prop-

erty. Foot access is over one long field. The rich water is reeded and has soft margins. Fishing space is limited mostly to stands. The area is weedy and fishing is into 4–10 feet of water. A perfect water for tench, but stocks are limited so patience is required. There is a big stock of roach, with some bream and perch.

GULLADOO LAKE   (H25 1)

Two miles from Carrigallen off the Arva road there are two big lakes known as Gulladoo Upper and Lower, though sometimes the lower lake is called Errew. The first lake has an abundance of roach and bream to 3 lb. The best swims are midway up the lake, where it narrows, and still further along. The depth is 4–8 feet here with a firm bottom with some submerged hazards. Access is from the narrow road and down a steep hill.

The second lake, further along the road and bridge, has some swims near the cottage. The margins are shallow and fishing here is best at the swims to the right, casting out with a 1- or 1½-oz lead.

CULLIES LAKE   (H26 2)

Cullies Lake lies to the east of the Carrigallen–Arva road. There is easy access with waterside parking at this good lake. Fishing in this 15-acre lake is into 10–15 feet of water and there are good stocks of bream, roach, hybrids and small perch.

BEAGHMORE LAKE (N22 99)

Four miles from Carrigallen, this is one of a series of good lakes. The waters are reeded and have some good swims for bream to 4 lb, roach and perch. Pike stocks are good here and anglers are reminded to return all pike alive to the water.

TULLY LAKE (N22 97)

Above Beaghmore Lake in the chain of lakes, this 40-acre lake has parking at the waterside. Fishing is from a clean bank and it is a productive water for bream to 4 lb. Catches to 100 lb are taken on this good fishery, where there are also roach, perch and pike. (See also under Arva, above.)

GLASSHOUSE LAKE (H24 1)

This is a big water with private access. The banks are firm and fishing is into 7–12 feet of water over a good gravel bottom. The lake holds an abundance of roach, bream and perch. This water needs heavy baiting to bring the bream on the feed. There are good bream to 5 lb and your target would be a catch of 100 lb. Fishing is good throughout from May, but this lake is at its best from midsummer on to October.

KILLYGAR RIVER (H26 5)

This is a slow moving and small river which flows through many lakes, – Rockfield, Glasshouse, Derreskitt, Disert – to the Town Lake in Killeshandra. Above Glasshouse Lake, there are a few deep pools, with much weed. I have often enjoyed good sessions here in the calm summer evenings, when some good bream to 3 lb come on the feed. Remember not to bait heavily here. The waters all along this system hold good stocks of eels and pike.

KILLESHANDRA

A small and industrious town set in the heart of the active farming area of Co. Cavan, Killeshandra is surrounded by lakes and the Killygar, or Castle, River, which flows into Lough Oughter.

Population 508
OS ½-inch Map No. 8
Cavan 11 miles, Carrigallen 6 miles, Belturbet 10 miles, Dublin 82 miles
Club: Killeshandra Holidays

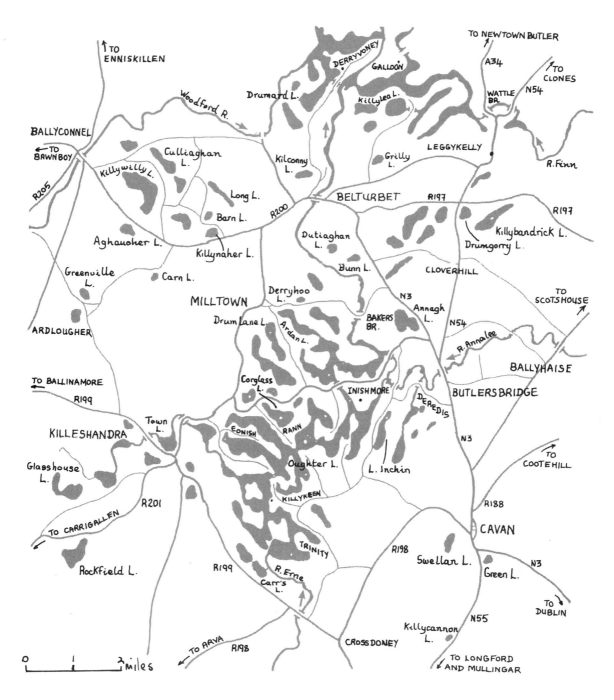

Northern Region, Killeshandra

TOWN LAKE (H28 8)

Access to this water is easy from the waterside car park off the Belturbet road. A big water with a river flowing through, it produces good catches of bream and roach. The best fishing is to the right into 6–10 feet of water. The lake also holds an abundance of perch and has produced pike to over 30 lb. The best swims are 30–40 yards to the right of the entry gate. Below this lake, the New Bridge River is very good for roach in the winter months to early summer. The depth is then about 3 feet, but during the summer the flow is reduced to a mere 6 inches.

GREEN LAKE (H32 7)

This is a small lake tucked below the Cavan road and surrounded by hills. Fishing is from stands and access is down a steep slope. It is only a fair fishery, producing some small tench, roach, perch and small bream.

TULLYGUIDE LAKE (H32 8)

The lake lies beside the road to Killykeen Forest Park. Access is easy and the banks good. This is a suitable water for handicapped anglers. Fishing is into 8–12 feet of water with a good bottom. There is an abundance of roach, perch and bream to 3 lb. This is a good water for small matches, with even pegs along the stretch.

CASTLE RIVER (H30 7)

The Castle River leaving Tullyguide Lake is small, with overhanging trees from the forest. Below the bridge the left bank is open with good but limited swims for roach in the early season. The flow is slow

and the depth 3–6 feet, with a muddy bottom, but there are some submerged hazards. Good roach can be taken here by using a stick float from February to May. Small bream, perch and small pike are common along this stretch.

EONISH LAKE, LOUGH OUGHTER (H35 8)

Once an island, it is now connected to the mainland and the road runs along the waterside. The approach is off the Killeshandra–Killykeen road. There is now a match stretch here for 50 anglers and the good solid bank faces south. Access is easy and suitable for handicapped anglers.

Eonish is a big open water and fishes best when there is a fresh breeze blowing from the south-west. The margins are stony and fishing is into 8–12 feet of water with some variations in the low-numbered pegs, where it shallows. However, a depth of 20–25 feet can be reached by long casting. Heavy baiting is essential here to bring the good shoals of bream (to 4 lb) on the feed.

Just before the start of the match stretch, and in front of Eonish Lodge, there is easy access to good fishing. The swims directly below this house and also those 100 yards to the right yield great catches of good bream. The bank is clean and fishing is into the most scenic of lakes. Please respect Mr O'Reilly's property and leave no litter on the bank.

The lake is also fishable from the southern shore in Gartnanoul, which is along the approach road to Killykeen. To the left at the Sandy Point, the lake narrows and fishes well for bream. The depth is 20–23 feet with a stony bottom. To the left and around the corner in the bay the bottom is stony and the maximum depth is 37 feet. Fishing along this stretch is good for bream in windy conditions. There is also the usual good stock of roach, with perch and pike. This lake will also turn up the occasional big brown trout in the early months of the year.

Catches along the near and middle sections exceed 100 lb in the late summer.

DERALK LAKE (H34 10)

Access to this good water is uncertain at the time of writing. It holds just a few shoals of quality bream to 6 lb, with roach, perch and rudd. Hit those shoals of bream after prebaiting and you will not be disappointed.

CORGLASS LAKE (H34 9)

This roadside water is approached off the Lough Oughter west road from Killeshandra. There are good swims along the lake towards the island. This area is approached by the entry at the stile on the hill. Here the bank is good and firm and fishing is into 6–12 feet of water over a gravel bottom. Many a good day's fishing I have had here for bream to 3 lb. There are some rudd in this lake, and with roach also there is an abundance of hybrids. This good water deserves more attention from anglers and fishes best after June.

TAWLAGH LAKE (H33 3)

The entry is off the Cavan–Killeshandra road and foot access is easy. The bank is clean and fishing is into 5–8 feet of water over a soft bottom. Waggler fishing here with red maggots in the early season has produced 100-lb catches of bream and roach. The lake is normally shallow and is connected to Carr's Lake, which in turn drains into the River Erne. This area has a vast stock of roach and bream, with perch and pike.

CAVAN

The county town of Cavan, known in Irish as 'The Hollow Place', is surrounded by hills. In medieval times this was the territory of Breifne and the home of the powerful O'Reilly clan, whose castle on Tullymongan Hill dominated the town. Anglers will also look over at another O'Reilly castle in Lough Oughter, where bream and roach abound. Cavan is my home town, where I sharpened my first hook.

Population 4,973
OS ½-inch Map No. 8
Dublin 71 miles, Virginia 19 miles, Cootehill 16 miles, Belturbet 10 miles, Killeshandra 11 miles
Club: Cavan Tourist Association

KILLYCANNON LAKE (N39 0)

This small lake lies beside the N55 road 3 miles south of Cavan. Access is easy from roadside parking, and there is a fishing stand and another swim at the rock to the right into 8–12 feet of water. This water has an abundance of small roach together with perch and some rudd. There are also small bream and a fair stock of hybrids. The lake was stocked with tench, which are now established and producing good sport in May and June.

You are requested to respect the land-owner's property and leave no litter.

SWELLAN LAKE (H39 4)

This lake lies below a hill in Cavan town. It is fed by springs and has limited access only to the east shore. The bank is firm and the bottom of gravel. Fishing is into 5–20 feet of water and in the early season good-quality roach respond to heavy feeding. There is also a fair stock of good tench to 6 lb, which are best fished for in May and June with bread as bait. I have always found this slow water to come alive at first light during the short tench season. With housing development in the area, permission for access around the shore is necessary.

LOUGH INCHIN (H39 8)

This is a long, reed-fringed lake, approached off the Killykeen road west of Cavan. At the time of writing, parking is along a narrow road where extreme care must be taken. Access to the fishing stands is easy. A favourite water of mine, years ago I took rudd to 2 lb here. Now the abundant roach respond easily to the maggot-baited hook and a few rudd appear. There is a good stock of bream to 3 lb and they are taken by float fishing at 8–10 feet, particularly from the stand to the left of the entry. The lake also holds perch, and pike of 5–8 lb. In recent years, tench have become established and it is

now yielding good fish to 5 lb in May and June and later in September.

KILLYGOWAN LAKE (H38 8)

A big lake, which forms part of the Lough Oughter complex of waters, Killygowan is connected to the River Erne. Access is through the kind permission of the land-owners, as with so many other waters.

The first access is from the short lane at Mr McGovern's house, over the stile at the gate and then over two long fields to the right. The bank is clean and firm. Fishing is into 7–15 feet of water with a good clean bottom, but there is weed further along where the lake narrows. This is a first-class fishery which produces great catches of bream, well over 100 lb. Bream run to 3 lb and there is a heavy stock of roach, perch, and some rudd and pike.

While the walk to this lake is long, it is well worth it. The bank I have mentioned is also accessible by boat from the river and other lakes, but in the summer the lake is very weedy.

LOUGH OUGHTER

The River Erne from Lough Gowna enters Trinity Lake, the first of a vast complex of waters through which the river flows. The name Lough Oughter (in Irish, Loch Uachtair – the Upper Lake) is the general name for this labyrinth of lakes, which are joined together by short, narrow stretches of the river called 'fords'.

I will first describe the River Erne as it enters the lakes and then move down river, going north towards Belturbet. The waters are accessible to the 'fords' on the eastern (Cavan) and western (Killeshandra) sides, but while anglers might face each other at these narrow stretches access to the other side might mean a road trip 8–10 miles, as there is only one connecting road bridge.

RIVER ERNE, SLANORE
(H35 2)

The approach to this stretch of river south of Lough Oughter is over a narrow road and parking is on private ground. Foot access is over one field. The river winds its way worm-like over low ground and is shallow except in some deep (6–8 feet) pools. There is an abundance of small roach and small bream here, together with perch and pike. Once a popular fishing area, anglers now find the obnoxious fumes from the nearby factory hard to tolerate. The low-lying valley floods easily in the winter months.

LOUGH OUGHTER, TRINITY
(H34 4)

Access to the water is easy and the approach off the Killykeen road is over private ground along which there are gates which must be closed. There is fishing near the end of the lane and the area is suitable for handicapped anglers.

The narrow river stretch is shallow and to the left very stony. There are roach, perch and some small pike here. Down river and in the lake the bream appear. The lake in general is shallow (3–6 feet) in the summer, with considerable silting at the river exit. Bream along the bank to the right respond to heavy feeding. The causeway to Trinity Island served the inhabitants of the Abbey, which dates back to 1237, when no doubt the waterlevel was much higher.

The approach to this water is off the R198 Cavan–Killeshandra road at the Killykeen signpost. After ¾ mile continue on by the Killykeen sign and after 200 yards turn right at the bungalow into the narrow road. After a further mile, turn sharply towards the lake, now in view, and through the gate.

LOUGH OUGHTER, KILLYKEEN FOREST PARK
(H36 7)

Killykeen, in Irish, Coill chaoin, means 'the beautiful wood'. This forested and lovely area is approached east from Killeshandra and west from Cavan. The attraction to the angler is the variety of locations available and the consistently good fishing over the year. This area is also suitable for the family. There are forest walks and, at the Killykeen Park Chalets, tennis courts and a children's playground.

River Stretch

The Castle River from Killeshandra enters the lake to the left and joins the Erne in this area. The short river stretch, flowing along the left side, is about 2–3 feet deep during the summer months. The main quarry is the roach, but during the summer shoals of good (1 lb) perch move in. In high water, conditions change dramatically. If the water extends across the full channel from wall to wall, then there is a flood and you should take care not to fish into what is in normal times a grassy bank.

Dennis White on his way to winning the 1988 King of Clubs match at Killykeen Forest Park Stretch, Lough Oughter

The outflow at the left side below the bridge is shallow with many submerged snags, while along the right bank it is rocky.

Chalet Stretch

Many are attracted to the first swim directly down from the car park at the majestic copper beech. Fishing at this place at the beginning of the river stretch is into water where there are rocks and the depth is only about 2–3 feet. Forget this area and move up by the Hanging Tree, to near Peg 1, where there is a good depth and the first sign of bream. This long match stretch can accommodate 50 or 60 anglers, and for such high numbers foot access is better over the forest road from the barrier.

The bank is good and can be fished when the waters are high in other parts of Lough Oughter. The depth of water along this stretch up to and by the boat-house is of importance to the angler. At Peg 1, there is a narrow shelf close in and then a drop-off to 22 feet. At Peg 2, beside the bushes, the drop-off is sudden, to 26 feet, and at Peg 3 there is a sharp drop to 30 feet.

Let's look closely at this section of the Killykeen area. The waters at this point hold an abundance of coarse fish – bream, roach, hybrids, perch and pike. In the early months some big brown trout also appear in this section of the lake. When a fresh westerly wind is blowing onto the shore, the bream feed very close in near the sharp shelf. I leave it to you to work out where to cast and how to land those big bream over the shelf. The message is plain and simple: face that strong wind, prepare your bite indication method properly and the bream will oblige.

Along the match stretch, the sharp drop-off continues but the depth declines gradually to 23 feet at Peg 15 and 18 feet at Peg 28. Those heavily fished pegs from 23 to 35 are always productive in the colder months of the year.

At the boathouse there is a distinct change in the underwater contours. Here the sharp shelf has gone and there is a gentle decline to 12 feet. As the lake narrows approaching Peg 50 the depth drops to only 5 feet across the lake. Quite a change from Peg 1!

Trinity Island is further along to the left and after ½ mile the lake remains very shallow in the summer months. In the early and late months the boathouse pegs in the high numbers produce roach, and catches to 20–30 lb are taken. However, having fished this stretch extensively, I know that those bream move up and down, remaining in the shallow waters, particularly in midsummer. But during one September I took some great catches of good bream (3 lb) at Peg 43. The whole stretch holds a very big stock of bream of about ¾–1 lb, which augurs well for future fishing in this consistent stretch.

Sometimes bream bites here can be very delicate, so do not expect your tip to swing sharply as at other waters. Precise and careful attention to tackle and bait is often necessary to catch bream in this stretch.

This area fishes well for pike from September to January, when the best method is legered dead bait. I will reiterate my earlier comments on pike and request anglers to return all pike to the water alive.

Restaurant Stretch

On the Cavan side, park at the restaurant car park and walk down the steep hill. Fishing here is into Eonish Lake below the footbridge and river exit. The Eonish match stretch is opposite, to the right. This is another great fishing stretch but it does call for careful and controlled fishing. The exit of the river is silted and has submerged snags. The water flows strongly across the lake towards the next channel at Buck Island. Bream shoals frequent the edge of the flow and often remain there even if the flow is slack. Long casting with a feeder is essential here to contact the bream. Remember when groundbaiting that the strong flow will carry your mix to the right. Close in, the bottom is rocky and you are liable to lose tackle; if that is the case, you should cast farther, where there is a gravel bottom at 20–25 feet.

Bream and roach are in abundance here, with good perch in late summer.

It was in the river to the left here that I once set out to provide an advertising agency with a fish for the camera. My first cast with a spinning bait from my pike tackle box was rewarded with a whopper of a fish. I was into a 10-lb brown trout and my photographer was more than happy that I had obliged so readily. That was absolute luck but I did not tell that to the photographer.

Bathing Stretch

I record this because this sandy bay on the Gartnanoul side opposite the cottage is reserved for bathing during the summer. Anglers are often attracted to this shaded and calm area in windy conditions. My advice is to face the strong wind and catch bream along the cottage side. The area farther up and facing the chalets has shallow margins but produces good bream only at the limited few swims where there is an opening to allow trees to be brought over from the island opposite (Inch Island).

EONISH LAKE   (H33 8)

See under Killeshandra, page 00.

LOUGH OUGHTER,
SALLY LAKE   (H35 6)

This is the shaded lake to the right within the Forest at Killykeen. There are two stands in this water which attract anglers in stormy conditions. It is weedy here with a depth of 4–6 feet. This lake has a fair stock of small roach, some small bream only, and perch. My advice is not to consider this lake for serious fishing.

LOUGH OUGHTER,
RANN AND INISHCONNELL
(H36 8)

This part of the lake is near Killykeen and the narrow approach is along the road once named 'Cromwell's Road'. To the left, the lake at the slipway is in general shallow (3–4 feet) and only holds some bream in the early season. At the end of this road there is a car park near the ford, or short river stretch. To the left it is shallow and rocky. The river is about 2–3 feet deep in the summer and there is some silting at the outflow. The best bream swims are to the right and near the birch tree. The flow from the river moves out towards the castle and, as in the outflow from the Killykeen river stretch, the bream frequent the edge of the flow in normal conditions.

This is a great fishing stretch for 6 or 7 pegs only, because further along this bank the lake shallows and there is weed in the bay. The bream can be reached by long casting with a feeder.

I am so familiar with this water that I know exactly where to aim my balls of groundbait, which must land within my target area. The depth is 15–18 feet, over a gravel bottom. I prefer to fish the spots I know the bream shoals haunt naturally, near the river flow through the lake, rather than bait close in and wait for them to appear. Trotting out from the river exit will yield an abundance of roach.

This scenic lake is dominated by Cloughoughter Castle, once the residence of the O'Reilly family.

LOUGH OUGHTER,
DERRYNA   (H37 8)

This part of the River Erne system is approached off the Butlersbridge–Killeshandra road beyond Caratraw Bridge. The road leads to the water at another river channel, which is only a fair fishery with varying depths. Bream move in here only at certain times and fishing is not consistent. This water does hold an abundance of small roach and perch.

TIRLIFFIN LAKE (H36 9)

This good lake lies to the right of the narrow road to Derryna, and you must park carefully. Access is through the gate and over private ground. Many a good day's fishing for bream I have had here, in 10–12 feet of water at the rocky bank to the right of entry. This stretch faces the south-west and produces good bream catches when the prevailing wind is blowing onshore. Heavy baiting is critical since the shoals seem to travel to other inaccessible parts of the lake. Roach, hybrids, pike and perch are also present.

LOUGH OUGHTER, FLYNN'S PASS–DERRYNIGGAN (H37 8)

Access to this section of the River Erne is off the Cavan–Killykeen road via Farnham. The rambling river here flows at the foot of a steep hill down from the car park.

Directly in front of the car park the river is shallow with low banks and so floods easily. This spot holds roach, perch and small pike. The bream swims are to the right along the green bank close to the reeds. Bream shoals move along the shallow reeded channel and come into the clear swims after heavy baiting. Depths vary here but most fishing is in 12–15 feet of water, with some weed to the right.

The limited swims produce great catches of bream and roach. My record here is 150 lb of bream.

The River Erne splits here, going to the left by Carratraw Bridge and to the right by Derryheen and Urney Bridge. There is boat access through weedy waters to the right into Killygowan Lake.

RIVER ERNE

Carratraw (H37 10)

The 200-yard stretch of river has one pool which holds some small bream, and in the faster water there are roach and perch. During the summer months this stretch is shallow and is not worth fishing.

INISHMUCK LAKE (H37 10)

The River Erne from Carratraw Bridge rushed into this lake and flows to the right and then around the island of Inishmore.

There are many snags where the river leaves the lake but good shoals of bream frequent this area in midsummer, often feeding off the bottom and to the sides of the flow. I like fishing along the right side here by long-distance floating for good-size bream to 4 lb. Roach move in here to the left in the early summer. There is a big stock of hybrids in this lake, together with perch and small pike. If you are adventurous and fit, walk along the bank to the right. At the green bank and opposite the pumphouse bream fishing can be out of this world. Every year I go there by boat and have fabulous catches, close to 200 lb of bream. Fishing is into 4–8 feet of water with a clean soft bottom. The river then moves to the right and into another channel known as the Weir.

Inishmuck Lake can also be approached by an access road directly across from the car park at Drumlane Lake. This small road here, after a right turn, leads to the old causeway to the island. Fishing at both sides here can be very productive for bream and roach.

Inishmuck Lake also holds good stocks of roach × bream hybrids, perch, pike and some tench.

RIVER ERNE

The Weir and Carafin Lake
(H37 11)

The access to this area is over the road to Mr Mee's house and then by foot down a long steep hill. The fast water flows into a deep pool. The banks are open and clean but there are many submerged trees which cause problems when legering. This pool holds some good bream to 7 lb, but the average weight is about 3 lb.

Carafin Lake has a big stock of bream, roach and perch. It has good banks in many places but access entails a long walk. The clean and firm bank behind Inishmore House in Mr Lynch's land produces great catches from a well-baited swim.

RIVER ANNALEE

Curraghanoe to Knockfad
(H43 12)

Downstream of Cootehill the Annalee has many fast and shallow stretches which hold some brown trout, and in the few deep pools there are bream. Roach and perch are common throughout.

There is good slow water down river from Ballyhaise. The stretch is approached by a road at Ballyhaise village to the car park at Curraghanoe Bridge (1 mile). The fast water at the bridge enters a pool 18 feet deep and then takes a turn, where the depth is 6 feet. There is another pool which is 28–35 feet deep, about 650 yards from the bridge. This stretch and the deep pools hold an abundance of roach and some good bream to 6 lb. The stretch from here to Knockfad can cater for 60 anglers. The lower part of the river stretch is approached from the narrow and hilly road between Ballyhaise and Butlersbridge and then to the waterside car park beside Rabbit Island. The river to the left of this car park is shallow and fast, while the stretch up river is slow with a depth of 6–10 feet. There is a big stock of roach and small perch here with some good bream to 4 lb. Heavy baiting will reward you with catches to 80–100 lb of fighting bream. It should be noted that roach migrate to the bridge area in late May–June.

Butlersbridge
(H41 11)

In summer conditions the river just below the bridge, which is easily accessible along the left bank, has a depth of 2–4 feet with weed. The Annalee at this point fishes best when there is about 4–5 feet of water in the early months. Small perch and roach are common here.

Further down there is a pool where there are bream to 2–3 lb. There are some submerged hazards here and fishing is only fair by local standards.

Deredis
(H40 10)

Here the Annalee is joined by the Cavan River. There is rapid water flowing into a wide pool, where the occasional big brown trout lurks. The pool has a few swims for roach, rudd, hybrids, some small bream and small perch. In general, the pool is shallow and produces eddies, making float fishing interesting. The narrow Cavan River holds small roach in the winter months.

Derryheen   (H39 10)

There is parking at the bridge and fishing up river along the two banks or down river for 300 yards along the right bank to the deep pool. Anglers must respect landowner's property, keep to the water's edge and never park cars in fields. Do not cross meadows.

The up-river stretch above the bend has a depth of 12–16 feet and holds bream and roach. Do not bother to fish at the bend above the bridge. Bream fishing is good 650 yards further up at Montgomery's Ford Pool. This area is approached by Ford House, through Mr Mundy's land. Catches up to 100 lb of bream are taken in this pool.

The pool below Derryheen bridge is 16–18 feet deep, with some good shoals of bream to 4 lb. The banks are good and the bottom clean. The pool can be fished from both sides. Access to this water via the church is over private grounds and only with the permission of the landowner, Mr West.

This pool is at the confluence of the River Annalee and the River Erne. The area is liable to flood in the winter months.

RIVER ERNE

Urney Bridge   (H39 11)

Access is from the car park and over the stile near the cemetery. The river here now gains additional strength, having left Lough Oughter and many other lakes behind.

Seldom fished, the few swims here have given me great sport for good bream, roach and rudd over the years. There are varying depths, with water coming around the point of Inishmore Island. Interesting waters for trying out your floats!

The river now continues north towards Bakersbridge and the town of Belturbet.

BELTURBET

The River Erne dominates the whole area round this busy and industrious town. Now its middle regions here, the river has gained strength and flows through the town in a more stately manner than upstream.

Population 1,208
OS ½-inch Map No. 8
Cavan 10 miles, Ballyconnell 8 miles, Killeshandra 10 miles, Dublin 81 miles
Club: Belturbet Coarse Angling Club

DRUMLANE LAKE   (H34 12)

Near Milltown village, this is one of a group of rich waters which hold good stocks of fish but which are also slow to produce catches.

Parking here is at the waterside and access to the left is easy. The bank is good with fishing into 12–15 feet of water. To the left there is an island and to the right on the opposite bank is Drumlane Abbey. The bottom is stony and there is some

*Hugh Gough clearing a swim on Drumlane Lake near Killeshandra with a little help
from some friends*

growth of lilies. This water presents problems and extreme patience is required to get results. My best fishing for bream to 7 lb here has been at first light, with bread as bait. There are also good-quality roach, which are best sought in the early months, when fish near to 1 lb can be taken.

There is a second access along a narrow private road to the lower section of this lake, which has a narrow waist of reeds at the top. Good-quality bream and roach are here too but you must not expect the fish to come to the usual tactics. Try the early morning, with bread as bait.

TULLY LAKE   (H34 10)

A small water along the Butlersbridge–Killeshandra road, Tully Lake is con-nected by a narrow river to the rich Garfiny Lake, which is inaccessible. Fishing is from stands on this reeded water. Good roach fishing in the early months produces catches to 50 lb. Bream to 6 lb are here but catching them is a slow business and requires experimentation.

ARDAN LAKE   (H36 12)

Ardan lies beside the Butlersbridge–Milltown road and parking is dangerous in this narrow and busy road. Foot access is over the stile and across one field to the limited swims. There is a depth of 8–12 feet and fishing is perhaps only fair for bream to 2½ lb, with an abundance of roach and perch. There is another access to the lower section of the lake by the narrow by-road to the east of the water.

DERRYHOO LAKE   (H36 14)

This is a 2-acre lake near Ardan and parking is dangerous on the narrow twisting road. Do not park in fields or block entries. Swims are limited in this sheltered water, but it does produce good catches of small bream, roach and perch. The bank is good and fishing is into 4–10 feet of water over a muddy bottom.

RIVER ERNE

Bakersbridge   (H38 12)

Here the river was once rated highly for good bream, but the abundance of small roach has changed the fishing pattern. The first access is up river along the right bank from the bridge. The deep (12 foot) pool holds bream from the swims close to the fence, with the island to the right. Above here the river is shallow and rocky, but 500 yards farther up river at the sharp left bend there is a lovely section for fishing. The wide and slow-moving river here produces great catches of bream and roach. This area is well worth the long walk from the bridge. The pool above the bridge can be approached off the narrow lane beside the bridge. Fishing from the attractive green left bank is only fair, as the flow of the river is to the right and long casting into the flow is essential for bream fishing. The river all along has a big stock of small roach and perch.

On the left bank 300 yards down river there is a pool and farther along by the island there is a good bank facing down river. From this point there is great bream fishing and many a good day I have had float fishing in 4–8 feet of water where the bank faces north with the island on the right.

The river then flows through shallows and deeps for many miles. There are isolated shoals of bream and some of these may be located near Putiaghan, a few miles above Belturbet.

TULLYROANE LAKE   (H39 15)

This lake is 7 miles from Ceavon and 3 miles from Belturbet. It is near Parisee Lake and Round Lake. This weedy water lies under Hill Top Farm and can be fished from stands or a boat. A rich lake, it offers good fishing for bream and roach. The water also yields some good rudd of over 1 lb and hybrids to 3 lb. Heavy prebaiting is vital to success here as the shoals move around in the weedy water.

BUN LOUGH   (H38 15)

Access to this 21-acre lake is from a car park on the N3 Belturbet–Cavan road and then over two fields. The lake is heavily reeded and fishing is from stands. It is a weedy lake with a soft bottom; the depth is 10–13 feet. This is another lake I often visit during May–June for good tench to 4 lb. There are good bream here, too, together with roach and perch. Some years ago small carp were stocked in this lake. If you catch one, report it to the Fisheries Board. This is a good all-round fishery.

PUTIAGHAN LAKE   (H37 15)

Parking here is at the top of a hill with foot access over one field and down a very steep hill. Heavily reeded and with a thick growth of lilies, this 40-acre water is fishable from stands or boats. There are varying depths and the bottom is soft with weed.

The water yields good tench to 4 lb and also some good bream to 4 lb. There is a big head of roach and small perch with pike and eels here too. Boats may be hired from Mr Sean Fitzpatrick, Putiaghan. Remember, when using a boat, not to interfere with anglers fishing from the stands.

DRUMLANEY LAKE (H43 18)

This water is approached by a small road near the pub on the N54 Cavan–Clones road at Leggykelly. Fringed with reeds, it is fished from stands. Depth is 10–13 feet with a gravel bottom and some weed. This water yields some good catches of bream to 4 lb, with roach, perch, pike and eels.

Anglers fishing in Co. Cavan will often ramble on to the very small lakes and the River Finn in this area. You should note that the waters may in fact be in Co. Fermanagh, where there are different fishing regulations (see the appendix).

KILLYLEA LAKE (H39 21)

Killylea Lake lies to the left of a bridge down a narrow lane off the Belturbet–Clones road. The narrow road leads to a bridge and to the left is Killylea Lake, which is connected to the nearby River Erne. Swims in a reeded part of the lake which has a good bank can be reached by crossing a field to the left of the bridge. The lake yields good catches of bream to 3 lb and has a heavy stock of roach, perch and pike. The other side of this good fishery can be reached by crossing the bridge and turning left. The ruined buildings and church were once the property of the Saunderson family, who owned an extensive estate here.

RIVER ERNE

Creamery Stretch, Belturbet
(H36 17)

The river is navigable for cruisers from Belturbet down into Lough Erne.

The water to the left of the jetty is 2–4 feet deep and during the winter months produces great catches of roach, but in the summer the water drops and the roach shoals disperse.

There are some good swims down river along the left bank. To reach them you must cross private ground and you should seek permission from the landowner.

Tully's Stretch (H36 18)

Access here is from the car park and down a long hill. To the right and up river towards the moorings opposite at the bend there are several good swims for bream. The exact swims are downstream of the sharp bend in the river.

Further down there is slightly faster flow, which holds mostly roach and perch.

McHugh's Stretch and Lough Dooley (H36 19)

Continuing down river there is an attractive pool at a bend, but my advice is to ignore it as it seldom yields good catches.

At the end of the road to the McHugh's Stretch, which is signposted, and across a field to the right the slow river contains good stocks of bream and roach.

Further down river, a rocky section

where roach and small perch abound, the river widens considerably in the district called Lough Dooley. The bank is reeded and during the early summer superb catches of good bream from some of the swims can be taken.

Down river the river continues slow and deep with good bream fishing.

Clooniny and Foley's Bridge (H37 20)

Access is off the narrow road signposted Clooniny and down a private road through a farmyard to the left to a car park, and then by foot over one field to a clean bank and slow-moving water. The gradual bend in the river is a first-class bream water and also contains a big head of small roach, hybrids, perch, pike and eels.

The next access is over the bridge from the car park and across two fields. Fishing here is from a good bank into 8–12 feet of water. At the marker 300 yards downstream the river narrows and is shallower. Here is wonderful bream fishing and catches to 70 lb have been taken – a lovely stretch, with limited swims for trotting. Anglers should always respect landowners' property and leave no litter. Ask for permission to cross lands.

LOUGH ERNE, DERRYVONEY (H38 23)

Further along the narrow road you will find parking in a car park at a right-hand

Tony Dench fishes Lough Erne at Derryvoney near Belturbet. This lake produces catches of bream and roach

bend. Access is to the left of here and then over a stile to the right. The best swims in this lovely lake are near the stone ditch. At this point you will find great shoals of bream to 4 lb, and when the fish are on the feed the magic figure of 100 lb can be easily broken. The lake holds roach, hybrids, perch, eels and pike – in all, a very good fishery. The bank opposite is in Northern Ireland.

WOODFORD RIVER, AGHALANE BRIDGE AND McCABES   (H36 20)

The traveller using a road map will be surprised to find that there is now no access here at Aghalane to Enniskillen. There is access to the river to the right, where the water is slow-moving with varying depths. Fishing for roach and perch is good in the spring months. The river is best fished when approached off the Derryvoney Road and to the left. Parking is near the house and foot access over one field. There are good bream and roach here, in 3–8 feet of water with a slow flow. Remember that access is over private ground and that you should respect landowners' property.

BALLYCONNELL

This well-kept village has been a National Award winner in Ireland's Tidy Town Competition. It lies in the midst of beautiful scenery beside Slieve Rushden (the local name is Russell), which offers extensive views. The Woodford River, once canalized, flows through the town to Lough Erne.

Population 605
OS ½-inch Map No. 8
Belturbet 8 miles, Ballinamore 12 miles, Cavan 18 miles, Dublin 90 miles
Club: Ballyconnell Tourist Association

KILLYWILLY LAKE (Cranaghan)   (H30 17)

The lake can be reached by a narrow road north off the R200 Ballyconnell–Belturbet road. Park carefully and walk to the water over a long field. The lake is reeded and fishing is from a stand into 8–13 feet of water over a clean bottom. The lake has a good head of bream to 3½ lb and provides good catches to 80 lb. Roach, hybrids and perch abound in this lake, with pike and eels. Sometimes bream fishing on this water is slow in the summer months, but it may be that early-morning or late-evening fishing would crack this.

TOMKIN ROAD LAKE   (H31 18)

Access to this lake is easy but parking space is limited. The bank along one side faces north-west and offers good fishing into 8–12 feet of water. A good fishery, but one that needs extensive groundbaiting to bring the limited bream on the feed here. The water has good roach and sometimes good perch, with pike and eels. Not an easy water for those bream, so have patience and experiment.

CUILLAGHAN LAKE (H31 19)

The small, narrow Rag River flows from Killywilly Lake into Cuillaghan Lake. Access is down a long lane to near the water. This is a big reeded water which produces quality fish. There are only some clear swims here and fishing is into 8–12 feet of water over a clean bottom.

This good water yields great catches of bream to 4–5 lb and also has an abundance of rudd, that species so rare in Erne waters today. At the time of writing Cuillaghan Lake has limited fishable swims.

BARN LAKE (H32 16)

Approached off the R200 Ballyconnell–Belturbet road at Killynaher, the entry to the lake is over a stile on the right. Fishing here is only fair for some good roach, small bream, and also some rudd.

LONG LAKE (H33 27)

The next right turn after Barn Lake leads to Long Lake. The road here is narrow and parking is dangerous. The narrow – and indeed, long – lake lies two fields away. It has good swims and yields some good roach, some rudd, bream and hybrids. Fishing is into 8–12 feet of water and your target here is 30 lb.

GREENVILLE LAKE (H28 13)

This lake lies beside the road near Ardlougher. Fishing is from stands, with the margins reeded. It holds a good head of bream to 3 lb and roach, producing catches to 30 lb. The water provides some good tench fishing in May–June with fish to 4 lb, which respond to most baits.

CARN LAKE (H30 14)

This small lake is approached off the Ballyconnell–Ardlougher road, with parking at the roadside and foot access over a long field. Fishing is into 6–8 feet of water over a muddy bottom. The lake yields some tench to 4 lb, perch and small roach.

WOODFORD RIVER, BALLYCONNELL (H27 17)

The Woodford River flows from Garadice Lake through Ballinamore. It was once canalized and it flows through several lakes. Above the village at Skallan and Ballyheady Bridge, the small river has deeps and shallows. Accessible again just above Ballyconnell, the river yields an abundance of small roach and perch. Small bream appear in the slower water and deep pools. The river also produces a lot of small pike. The Woodford River flows on to Lough Erne but en route is sometimes heavily coloured.

BAWNBOY

Four miles north of Ballyconnell, this tidy village is situated in a most scenic area, with lovely views of the Cuilcagh Mountains to the north-west.

Population 190
OS ½-inch Map Nos 7 and 8
Swanlinbar 7 miles, Ballinamore 10 miles, Cavan 22 miles, Dublin 93 miles

DERRYCASSAN LAKE
(H32 12)

The Woodford River flows into Derry-cassan Lake from the shallow Ballymac-govern Lake. Access is limited and from the side of the forest near Burren Bridge. The bank, however, is clean and some good catches of bream are taken. In my opinion the long trek here is only for fit anglers. There is another access from a small road ½ mile from Kilnavart church, and the limited swims there produce some good catches.

COOLOGUE LAKE   (H24 13)

In general, this is a shallow lake, with many areas of weed. Access is near Burren Bridge, where the river leaves the lake. Sometimes there is weed in this particular area and fish stocks are affected. This water holds a good stock of roach and some really good bream to 6 lb. Float fishing in this area may be difficult at times but the limited shoals of rudd moving in here during the summer evenings give great sport, with a bread-baited hook set at 1 foot. A good water, but the growth of weed will test your skills.

WOODFORD RIVER   (H25 15)

Below Coologue the river flows fast, with good roach fishing in the early months of the year. The river slows down at Skallan, where there is an old canal lock. Below this there are some bream and a lot of roach around 5 oz. From here the river flows on to Ballyconnell by Ballyheady Bridge.

TEMPLEPORT LAKE (H22 17)

This is a rich and productive water 3 miles south of Bawnboy. Branch off to the left at one mile on the Ballinamore road and then take the small road to Templeport church. Access is along to the left. Fishing on this good reeded water is from stands. I have taken good-quality bream to 5 lb in this water and had catches up to 180 lb, with roach and rudd, from the stand on the left.

BELLABOY LAKE   (H20 17)

A good lake just 1 mile from Bawnboy, it has easy access from the nearby Bawnboy–Ballinamore road. The bank is low in this area and so liable to flood. Fishing is into 8–12 feet of water over a clean bottom.

A good catch here would be 60 lb of bream to 3 lb with roach, perch and pike. Waggler fishing gets good results with red maggot and small worm as bait.

LAKEFIELD LAKE   (H20 18)

To reach this water take the first sharp right after the church along the Ballinamore road from Bawnboy and up a steep, narrow road. Park carefully. The lake is over one field beside Frank Dolan's house.

Fishing is mostly for quality roach in 8–10 feet of water along a clean bank, and the sport can be wonderful.

BUNERKY LAKE
(Gortnacorriga Lake)   (H11 7)

The next lake along this road has parking at the waterside. Fishing is good for roach to ¾–1 lb, but the shoals respond only to heavy baiting. Along the forest and reeded side there are some good rudd. On the left there are some submerged trees, while on the right, from the green field, there is a good depth to 10 feet. Bunerky is a good roach water and also has nice pike, which respond to dead-baiting at the point to the right during the winter months. This water holds a big stock of crayfish.

BRACKLEY LAKE   (H20 21)

One mile north-west of Bawnboy, this scenic water lies beside the R200 Bawnboy–Swanlinbar road. There is a waterside amenity area, with easy access, and water activities are common here in summer. The margin to the left is shallow (2–4 feet) but it does produce good roach and perch catches by waggler fishing.

A point projecting out into the lake along its northern (Prospect) side offers superb fishing. Access is 500 yards north of the lake, on the Swanlinger road. Turn left at the crossroads. Then the next road to the left leads to the gate entry. It is important that you note that access to this section of the lake is over private ground. Entry is to the right (western) side of the point and through one gate. Parking is on private ground at the first gate only – do not drive further into this field. Then walk down the hill to the right to a good bank. Fishing is from 6–15 feet of water, with a stony bottom. This lake holds limited stocks of bream to 6–7 lb and quality roach. Catches of well over 100 lb are regularly taken on this highly rated fishery.

Brackley Lake lies amidst lovely scenery not far from the Cuilcagh Mountains where the River Shannon rises.

BALLINAMORE

A small town in Co. Leitrim, Ballinamore occupies a pleasant site in an area of small hills and lakes, with the Woodford River flowing by. Here the waters of the Erne are close to the watershed of the Shannon system, just south of Garadice Lake and at Lough Scur.

Population 1,209
OS ½-inch Map No. 7
Carrick on Shannon 18 miles, Ballyconnell 12 miles, Cavan 25 miles, Dublin 100 miles
Club: Ballinamore Angling and Tourist Association

KILTYBARDAN LAKE
    (H8 11)

The lake lies beside the R208 Ballinamore–Carrick road. There is waterside parking and access is easy. The bank is clean with some shallow margins. Long casting into 8–12 feet of water over a gravel bottom yields good catches of

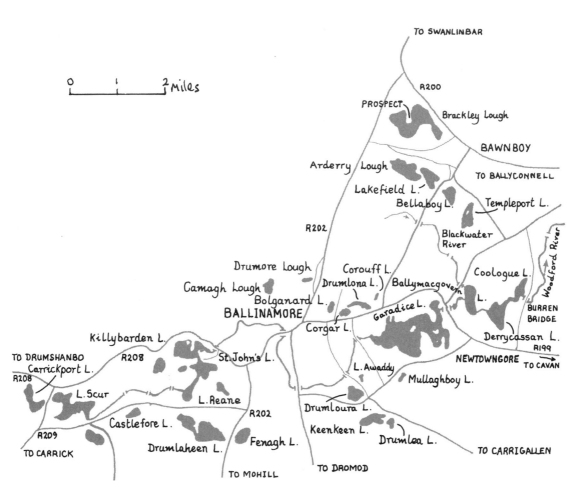

Northern Region, Ballinamore

small 1–2-lb bream and small roach, with lots of small perch and pike.

ST JOHN'S LAKE (H8 11)

Also beside the Carrick road, the approach here is to the left at Ballyduff Bridge and over a lane, by a farmhouse, to a car park. There are some swims opposite the car park but the good swims are over a field along the bank of the small river. This short green bank at the point stretch, facing north, is opposite the main road. Here the fishing is into 6–9 feet of water with a good clean bottom. This good fishery has a big stock of bream around 1½ lb and you could catch 50–80 lb on a good day. Roach and perch are common throughout the waters of this area.

WOODFORD RIVER

Ballyduff Stretch (H9 12)

A road runs along the bank of this small slow-moving river where it leaves St John's Lake. The depth is 3–4 feet here and it is a nice water with easy fishing for small roach, perch and small bream. There are a few deeper holes, which give entertaining fishing.

The narrow road here was once the base for the rails of the Cavan–Leitrim narrow-gauge railway. A local farmer told me that as the train slowly made its way from Belturbet to Drumshanbo the driver often stopped here to bait a swim and then fished on the return journey – but I don't believe that!

DROMORE LAKE (H13 13)

This water is just off the R202 Ballinamore–Swanlinbar road and has access by a narrow road. Access by foot is then over a field to the reed-fringed lake. Stands on one side of the lake provide fishing into 4–7 feet of water with a muddy bottom and some weed. A second access on the opposite side leads to stands where the depth is about 12–14 feet. A good water, which will give sport for bream to 4 lb with roach, hybrids and perch.

DRUMLAHEEN LAKE (H8 8)

This big lake lies south-west of Ballinamore along the R209 Keshcarrigan road

via Fenagh. There is easy access with a car park. The lake is heavily reeded and holds a big stock of roach and perch, with some good shoals of bream, which can be fished for from some clean bank. This water must be baited heavily to get results. It also has a good stock of pike, as do most waters in this area.

CASTLEFORE LAKE (H6 8)

Access to this roadside lake, not far from Fenagh, is easy. It is reeded, with some soft margins, but there are a few clear swims on the roadside and also along the shore directly across. Fishing is into 8–20 feet of water with some weed on the bottom. The lake has a good stock of small roach and perch, with some shoals of bream to 4 lb.

CARRICKPORT LAKE (H1 9)

This big water lies beside the Carrick road at Drumcong. There is parking along a narrow, busy road and access to the water is easy. This is a good water which calls for heavy baiting and serious attention. Do just that and you will get the bream going. The stock of 2–3-lb bream is good, with roach and good hybrids, perch and pike. The bottom is sometimes weedy and the depth goes to 22 feet. Fishing is from a good bank which is sometimes soft, but there are stands to make things easier.

LOUGH SCUR (H3 10)

This lake can be reached from the R280 Drumshanbo-Ballinamore road and also from the road at Keshcarrigan. The first access is over a field in front of a house and to parking near the water. The big lake has many areas of shallow and weedy water but at this point there is a rocky shore with fishing into 6–10 feet. Pegs are limited here, but when there is a south-westerly blowing onto the shore bream fishing can be very good. The lake holds a big stock of bream around 1½–2½ lb, with roach, perch and pike.

The opposite shore is not quite as good, which perhaps illustrates that the onshore wind helps to put the bream on the feed.

There is boat access and parking along the main R208 road and winter piking in the shallow section has produced fish to 30 lb.

KESHCARRIGAN LAKE

(H4 7)

Beside the village of Keshcarrigan and along the Mohill road, this lake has easy access and parking. Fishing is from stands into 8–10 feet of water, with a soft and sometimes weedy bottom. While there are limited shoals here, bream to 3 lb do respond to heavy baiting and catches to 80 lb have been taken.

WILLOWFIELD LAKE

(H14 11)

Near Ballinamore town, this is a small, shallow and weedy pond. Fishing is from stands into 3–5 feet of water over a soft weeded bottom. This lake holds a big stock of small roach and small rudd with some small bream. The water is a reservoir of all kinds of hybrids. There are also small tench to 3 lb.

LOUGH AWADDY   (H16 10)

Lough Awaddy lies not far from Drum-coura Lake and there is parking beside the water, with access to the waterside over a few stiles. The margins are soft and peaty with some reeds. Fishing is easy here with a waggler, as the depth is 6–8 feet. This interesting lake holds some dark-golden-coloured rudd to ½ lb and also roach. There are also some bream to 3 lb.

I am always fascinated with this water, which produces good fighting hybrids.

DRUMCOURA LAKE   (H16 8)

This good water can be approached from Ballinamore via the R199 Killeshandra–Cavan road or the Carrigallen road. Parking is along a narrow road and access is easy over a short field. The west-facing low bank is open and clean with fishing into 3–6 feet of water close in. There is a slow graduation to 10 feet and, at a 1-oz bomb cast, into 15 feet. There is a little weed and the bottom is of gravel. Fishing in the early season, I have taken great bream catches, with fish to 4 lb, in the left corner near the crossroads. This good fishery also has a big stock of roach, perch and pike.

KEENKEEN LAKE   (H16 7)

Just off the Ballinamore–Carrigallen road, this is a rich water. There is a limited stock of bream to 6 lb here but they only respond to patient fishing after heavy groundbaiting. The roach stock here is of better quality than other waters in the area. The water also has hybrids, perch and pike.

Access to a rocky shore near a bay is past two farmhouses and over private ground. The depth here is 10–12 feet, with a weedy bottom. There is also easy access via a lane with parking at the waterside. However, the fishing along this good shore is not much to shout about.

DRUMLEA LAKE (Black Lake) (H17 7)

This water lies beside Keenkeen Lake and is approached from a road opposite the church. Access is over private lands and the landowners' property must be respected. Swims on the lake are limited. Fishing is from stands into 6–10 feet of water. There is good fishing for roach, rudd, some bream and a variety of hybrids.

BOLGANARD LAKE (H15 13)

The lake lies off the Ballinamore–Cavan road and you must park with care, so as not to obstruct entries. Access is easy to the reed-fringed lake, which has fishing stands. There is some weed and fishing is into 5–9 feet of water. I have always found this lake hard to get results from. There is a fair stock of bream to 5 lb, with some rudd, roach and hybrids. Perhaps you will have better luck!

CORGAR LAKE (H15 12)

Near Bolganard lake, this 35-acre lake is a different water and provides good fishing. It is reedy, with soft margins, and fishing is from stands. Here I have used a float and enjoyed watching my lift bites in about 6 feet of water. When raked in May–June the weedy margins will produce good tench of over 6 lb. The lake also holds the usual roach, some rudd and bream. Try this water in the morning or evening and you will have great sport.

DRUMLONAN LAKE (H16 12)

The approach to this long, narrow and weedy 40-acre lake is from a road off Ballinamore–Cavan road. The access road is to the right and through a gate. All gates must be closed along this access road.

Access is then easy to the fishing stands on the right. The reedy but rich water with one or two deep holes (10–12 feet) has a good stock of roach, rudd, some bream and hybrids. The lake also holds a small stock of tench to 6 lb, with perch and pike. Drumlonan Lake can also be fished from a stand approached off the main road at a dangerous bend. I advise that you approach the lake from the road along the northern side of the water.

WOODFORD RIVER, CARRICKMAKEEGAN BRIDGE (H16 11)

The river here is canal-like, being slow-moving and narrow. The bank down from the bridge is clean, with a depth of 3–5 feet. There is a fair stock of small roach and small perch here. In the early season, great shoals of Garadice Lake bream move into the lower stretch of the river. Approach along the left bank and over the footbridge. The long walk is worth it.

My advice is to explore the lower stretch in late May–June. If the bream are there you can crack all records.

Always remember that access is only through the good will of landowners. Seek permission to cross fields.

CORDUFF LAKE   (H13 17)

Just off the Ballinamore–Bawnboy road, access is easy. Fishing in this small lake is easy from stands. There is some weed here and in May–June you will find tench to 5 lb in the early mornings. The lake also has a stock of small roach, perch, rudd and small pike. I found fresh bread a good tench bait here.

MULLAGHBOY LAKE

(H18 9)

This is a reeded water which has some fishing from stands. The margins are soft and there is a growth of lilies. The water holds a small stock of roach, some rudd, small bream and hybrids. However, evening sessions on this small water have given great catches of bream and roach.

GARADICE LAKE

This is the jewel in this part of Co. Leitrim. A very big water (1,200 acres), it is a rich fishery with a big stock of bream (2½–3 lb), roach, some rudd, hybrids, perch, pike, and eels. The Woodford River flows through the lake, which has many islands and bays. The lake can be fished at many accessible places. The facilities for fishing and parking around this lovely water are perfect.

Haughton's Shore

Access is off the R199 Ballinamore–Cavan road near the junction road to Ballyconnell. There is a waterside road, making access for handicapped anglers just perfect. The shore, facing west, is clean and has a capacity for 40 anglers. The depth from 8–12 feet graduates to 4–5 feet at the lower swims, where there is some weed. The bay at the extreme end, shallow and weedy, holds some shoals of rudd. There is a big stock of roach here, with a lesser stock of bream.

Church–Cully's Shore Garadice Park

This part of the shore is well developed with all facilities. There is parking for coaches and foot access to the water is also easy. The extreme end pegs can be approached via the narrow road through the trees. Here there is top-class bream fishing from a clean shore just a rod-length from your parked car. Fishing is into 8–10 feet of water, which drops to 15–22 feet farther along. While many float-fish this stretch I prefer to leger at a distance, and with worm and caster as bait great catches of bream can be taken. There is a graduation in depth back towards the bay and the main car park. Here it is sandy and on summer weekends, when the sun is shining brightly, this area is used a lot by swimmers.

Over the stile to the right of here is a short but very good stretch which produced the winning catch of bream in the national Coarse Fishing Championships. The depth is 6–10 feet and the bottom good.

Creamer's Shore

This stretch is reached down a long narrow road between the Boeshill and Garadice Park areas from the Ballinamore–Cavan road. The bank is clean but the margin is varied, with submerged rocks and shallows. However, after the usual heavy baiting and with a fresh southerly blowing into your face, the limited swims here will produce champion catches of over 100 lb of bream and roach. Please seek permission to cross lands.

Boeshill Shore

The fishing here is not up to the high standard of the other stretches and has fishing into shallow water only. In my opinion it is not worth the long access.

Maxwell's Shore

This stretch at the south-western side of the lake has limited bank space for fair fishing but it is an excellent spot to launch a boat to fish the bays for bream in May and June.

Connolly's Shore

Approached from the road south of the lake, access is along a narrow road to the car park at Mr Connolly's house. Please respect the landowner's property here. Park your car in the car park, walk through a field and close the gate. The bank is clean and faces north. Fishing is into 6–10 feet of water, with a gradual drop to 16–18 feet at long leger distance.

I have topped the 100 lb of bream here by float fishing at 8 feet with a fresh wind blowing from right to left. This great stretch with about 10 swims will respond to heavy baiting. Bream, roach and perch abound in this area. I repeat, please respect the kind landowner's property and do not park in the field.

Garadice Lake is a great coarse fishery and even as I write I feel reluctant to leave it. This big water holds good stocks of pike, which the local Tourist Association urges anglers to return alive to the water.

WOODFORD RIVER LITTLE GARADICE LAKE
(H20 12)

Flowing from Garadice Lake under Ballinacor Bridge, the Woodford River bulges into Little Garadice Lake. Parking here is at the access to Haughton's Shore and then by foot across the main road at a dangerous bend. Left of the bridge, able anglers can reach a clean bank with about 4 swims. With the river flowing fast from right to left, fishing here is a good test for the stick-float expert. Along the right side the backwater or small lake is easier to fish and will produce an abundance of small roach and small bream. Fishing is into 6–8 feet of water but sometimes high water brings hazards down the river.

Farther down the Woodford River is a mixture of pools and fast shallows with overhanging trees. However, you can find interesting small nooks to fish the pools in absolute solitude for roach and small bream. The Castle Stretch is such a place and is approached over private ground off the Ballymacgovern–Ballyconnel road. Then there is the Monk or Brickyard Pool, where there is lovely quiet fishing for roach and small perch.

BLACKWATER RIVER BALLYMACGOVERN

(H21 13)

This river, which at one time rewarded me with many a good brown trout, now has a stock of roach. Roach shoals migrate from the shallow Ballymacgovern Lake up this river and in the early season fabulous catches of over 100 lb are taken by using a waggler at 2–3 feet just above the bridge.

The small stretch of river between Ballymacgovern Lake and Derrycassan Lake has some areas which produce bream catches, but only in the early season.

COOTEHILL

This town in east Cavan, with a wide main street, takes its name from Sir Charles Coote, who founded it in the seventeenth century. The Annalee River flowing from Shercock south of the town is joined by the smaller Dromore River and then wanders on to Butlersbridge and the River Erne.

Population 1,510
OS ½-inch Map No. 8
Ballybay 10 miles, Bailieborough 12 miles, Cavan 15 miles, Shercock 10 miles, Dublin 64 miles
Club: Cootehill Tourist Association

ANNAMAKERRIG LAKE

(H59 21)

From Cootehill, this lake is approached via the R189 Cootehill–Newbliss road. It is a lovely lake, situated in a forest, with access over private land.

During the weekends, the lake is sometimes used by water skiers but on other days your fishing will be in quiet and scenic surroundings.

Parking is along the road to Annamakerrig House and access is easy. Near the boathouse, there are two easy swims for handicapped anglers.

Along the boathouse (northern) shore in normal summer conditions the water is up to the bank at the trees. But then the water may only be one or two feet deep up to 20 feet out and then 3 feet for another 10 feet out. There is then a sharp shelf, which drops to 11–13 feet.

Roach and good-quality roach × bream hybrids to 3 lb feed close to this shelf and sometimes bringing up bigger fish presents a problem. This is a good water which also holds good bream, good perch up to 1 lb, and pike. Catches of 100 lb of roach, hybrids and bream are taken here in the early season. Fishing in the late summer is also first-class.

The open swims below the forest gates and green field are attractive, but forget it – the depth is 3–4 feet only, with a few roach!

Do not be surprised if you catch a crayfish here, as there is a good stock of them in this lake. There are other swims 500 yards along the left side, but the forest gate is open only on special occasions.

DRUMGOLE LAKE (H59 19)

The best swims in this lake, on the bank opposite the road, are reached by a long walk over private land from the road junction to Annamakerrig Lake. There are some good bream here in 10–12 feet of water. The lake also holds roach, perch and pike.

DRUM LAKE (H56 18)

This 20-acre lake, like others in the vicinity, is fringed with reeds, with a shallow area near the small reeded island. There is waterside car parking with access for a boat. However, at this parking area there are a few swims where you can cast a float into 8–10 feet. There is a good stock of quality roach and rudd, with some perch and pike.

DRUMSHEIL LAKE (H55 13)

Leave Cootehill on the Belturbet road and after 3 miles turn left at the crossroads then left again after ½ mile down a small lane to a car park. Then walk down the long field to the 12-acre lake. This good fishery tucked away in the drumlin country produces good bream to 4 lb. I fish this water close in for bream, in a depth of 6–10 feet with some weed. It has a good stock of roach, with some rudd, hybrids, perch and pike. A lovely water and well worth a try.

WHITE LAKE (H57 14)

This small lake lies alongside a narrow road which connects with the Cootehill–Belturbet road and the R188 Cootehill–Cavan road in the district of Ashfield. It is reeded in most places but there are some clear swims at the waterside parking, which makes it accessible for handicapped anglers. The lake has a depth of 15 feet and is a lovely water to fish in the summer evenings for small roach, some rudd, hybrids and the occasional tench to 4 lb. The lake fishes slowly during the day and best results are in the early and late hours.

RIVER ANNALEE, CORICK (H58 13)

The river flowing from Shercock is often shallow and weedy in the summer. During the spring months, the clear and deeper stretches produce some good roach, perch and small bream. Up river from Corick Bridge and along the Cootehill–Cavan road there are some deep swims and just below the bridge and car park where roach, small perch and some skimmers can be taken.

DOUNG LAKE (H62 13)

At the junction of the R190 Ballybay and R192 Shercock roads, this small lake is approached over one field from Mr Brady's farm. Like many of the small isolated lakes in this area, it holds rudd and roach with some hybrids and perch.

LISNALONG LAKE (H64 16)

Beside the twisting R190 Cootehill–Ballybay road, this 25-acre lake has a heavy fringe of reeds. It is fishable from stands and has some good swims. With a few hours to spend one evening, and being tempted once again, I stopped here to find bream to 4 lb come quickly to my loose feeding of casters and wormcaster bait combination. I had eight bream in two hours, but the cream came in fading light, as I took four tench around 4 lb. This rich water also has a good stock of roach, hybrids and perch. There is a depth of 6–9 feet at casting distance, with some weed.

KILLYVAGHAN LAKE

(H64 16)

This 80-acre lake is near the Dromore River. From the first car park at the bridge a long walk brings you to the eastern shore, under the green field. The margin here is shallow but by long-distance legering you will find 6–12 feet of water. Facing south-west, this shore fishes best with a strong wind blowing into your face. There are a few shoals of big bream to 6 lb here and heavy baiting is vital to success. Some great catches are taken in this section of the lake. There is another access from the car park beside the lake. Here and to the left at the rocks the fishing is mostly for roach, small perch and hybrids. The big lake holds pike, which are best fished for from a boat along the south-eastern margins. Always put pike back alive.

DROMORE RIVER

Ballynascarva Bridge   (H65 17)

The narrow river here is a mixture of pools and weedy shallows. A hundred yards up river along the left bank and above the bush there is a deep pool which holds bream to 4 lb. There are also some smaller bream in the limited deep water below the bridge. There is an abundance of roach and perch here. The river fishes best in the winter and spring, but then, with low banks, the river is liable to flood. In summer there are many shallow and weedy stretches when fishing conditions are difficult, but in the clear swims you can have great sport.

New Bridge   (H60 23)

This bridge, on the Cootehill–Rockcorry road marks the boundary between Co. Cavan and Co. Monaghan. There is a small pool above the bridge with easy access. Here there are small roach and small perch. Up river along the right bank there is fishing from a stand for small bream. This forested river has soft margins and is reeded, but there are many good swims which produce good catches of bream to 2–3 lb.

There is a big stock of small roach, small bream, hybrids and perch here. The banks of the river are low and so liable to flood. Above this point the river has formed some lakes, where access is private.

DRUMLONA LAKE   (H64 18)

The approach is down a long, narrow lane to a car park, and then by foot over two fields down to the lake, where there is limited bank space. In high water conditions there is difficulty fishing here, but during a normal summer there is a good bank. Fishing near the rock is into 8–12 feet of water with a good bottom. There is a pull from left to right as the river flows through the lake. Some great catches of bream (3½ lb) are taken here by legering at long distance. This water can produce well over 100 lb of bream and roach in a good session.

NOTE   While still close to Cootehill, rivers and lakes higher up the system are listed under Shercock and Ballybay.

SHERCOCK

This small village on the east side of Lough Sillan in Co. Cavan marks the eastern limit of the River Erne system.

Population 692
OS ½-inch Map No. 8
Cootehill 9 miles, Carrickmacross 13 miles, Bailieborough 8 miles, Cavan 25 miles, Dublin 65 miles

LOUGH SILLAN   (H70 7)

This is a lovely lake at the top of the eastern arm of the Erne system and from here the river Annalee flows on by Coote-hill to Butlersbridge. There is easy access to some swims at the roadside amenity area and caravan park. Fishing is from a clean bank into 5–10 feet of water over a bottom of gravel. Roach fishing here is best during the winter and spring.

There is another access from the lake-side car park at Annafarney on the western side, which is approached from the Cootehill–Shercock road.

Please note that access to the water is only by the stiles and along the margins of the lake. To the left of the car park, there is a good long stretch with fishing into 20–32 feet of water with a gravel bottom. Just to the right of the car park, down a private lane, there is a short stretch which is deep in the middle section then shallows at the point and also back towards the car park to the left. In all these stretches there is roach fishing with roach × bream hybrids and perch.

It is remarkable that stocks of bream in this lake are limited and are located most-ly by boat fishing in the reeded bay at Annaghfarney to the right of the car park. Roach-fishing patterns change consider-ably on this big water and some stretches do not have consistent fishing. There are greatly varying depths in Lough Sillan and perhaps some day we will be able to track down those big roach and their pattern of movement.

MUDDY LAKE   (H72 6)

This 13-acre lake off the R178 Shercock–Bailieborough road is reached by a small lane. Fishing swims are limited to one place at the dangerous 'Bilberry Rock'. This lake holds small roach, some bream and perch.

Anglers should note that access to other parts of this water is not permitted. At all times, no matter where you go, seek permission from landowners before crossing land.

STEEPLETON'S LAKE
(H72 5)

This 9-acre lake lies close to the village of Shercock. A muddy bottom with weed growth indicates that this is tench water.

Good fish to 5 lb are indeed taken here in May and June.

CORRANEARY LAKE

(H65 5)

Sometimes called Church Lake, this 150-acre water has an average depth of 12 feet. It is approached from Cootehill via the Bailieborough road or from the Barnagrow Lake and Lough Sillan roads. Parking is along the road and the lake is reached by foot, with the permission of the land-owner, over a long, hilly field. The bank is good, with fishing into 10–12 feet of water, sometimes over a gravel bottom. This is a first-class lake which yields good catches of bream to 6 lb. It also has a good stock of roach, hybrids, rudd, perch and pike. Your target here would be about

50 lb, but catches of more than 100 lb are taken. Some good swims with fishing into 8–10 feet of water can be reached along the road near the church.

BARNAGROW LAKE   (H67 8)

A big lake lying under the lovely hilly country around Cootehill and Shercock, Barnagrow has many bays and short fishing stretches. There are two access points from the R192 Cootehill–Shercock road. The first is along a very narrow lane to a hilltop car park along the northern side of the lake. Fishing from here to the left or right of the pumphouse at the foot of the hill, I have found the laborious walk to the right rewarding on many occasions, and have taken good bream to 3 lb after heavy prebaiting. The bank is

The drumlin (small hills) country produces countless waters in Co. Cavan. Corraneary Lake, between Cootehill and Bailieborough is popular for its great bream catches

clean and fishing is into 12–20 feet of water.

The second access is beside the waterside and then along a path to the right through the trees. Good bream fishing appears from the fifth peg on and over the first stile. Then there are some pegs with perch and small roach. The lake holds a good stock of roach, with hybrids, pike and some brown trout. The bank here fishes exceptionally well in windy conditions but heavy baiting is vital in this good fishery.

LOUGH TACKER   (H69 8)

Access to the car park is down a small road from the crossroads on the R192 Cootehill–Shercock road. The banks are clean and fishing is into 6–10 feet of water with a gravel bottom. There is a good stock of roach but only some bream, with pike and perch. A fair fishery, but I would not waste much time here with richer waters just around the corner.

KNAPPAGH RIVER   (H69 11)

This small, shallow and narrow river holds brown trout and is controlled by the Bawn Rod and Gun Club. The water flows through about eight lakes before entering the River Annalee. The productivity of the string of lakes here is only fair and general stocks of coarse fish, particularly bream, are nothing to shout about. There is, however, a fair stock of perch, roach and pike throughout the waters of this area.

DERRYGOONEY LAKE   (H70 11)

This is one of the Knappagh lakes mentioned above. It can be reached from a point near Cortubber post office, over a stile and then across three fields; or from the Billy Fox Memorial Park and over one field near the river outflow. The bank is good but reeded in many places. The water holds a big stock of roach, perch and small pike.

BALLYBAY

Ballybay along the shores of Lough Major near the headwaters of the Dromore River in Co. Monaghan.

Population 1,270
OS ½-inch Map No. 8
Cootehill 10 miles, Castleblaney 8 miles, Clones 16 miles, Dublin 66 miles
Club: Ballybay Tourist Development Association

TONYSCALLON LAKE   (H76 21)

This lake is at the head of the Dromore River which flows to Lough Major at Ballybay and then to Cootehill, where it joins the Annalee River. Sometimes called Dernaglug Lake, it is near the R182 Ballybay–Castleblaney road and can be reached over private ground beside the house. Ask permission first. Fishing here is for bream, roach, perch and pike.

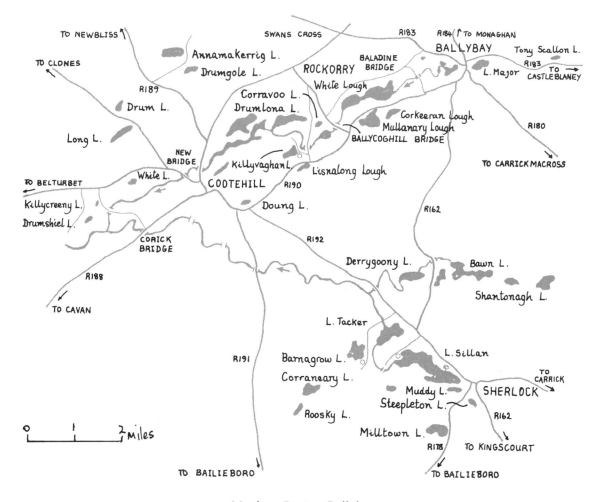

Northern Region, Ballybay

LOUGH MAJOR (H72 20)

The 200-acre lake is in Ballybay and has easy access all round. The best access is near the junction of the Carrickmacross and Cootehill roads and there is parking beside the water. The lake has some reeded margins and some scrub but there are good clear fishing swims where legering or waggler methods are used. Along this eastern shore there is excellent fishing for bream and roach with catches of 50–80 lb taken often. Depths vary in this lake with 6–12 feet in most places. Fishing is also available along the park side, which is approached from the R182 Castleblaney road.

This is a very good fishery for bream, roach, hybrids and perch.

DROMORE RIVER LAKES
(H71 20)

From Lough Major the Dromore river flows through a low lying valley, with reeded marshy margins. Here it forms several lakes which provide first-class coarse fishing at some limited swims. The area is liable to flood in the winter months. Access is easy from the high road overlooking the waters.

In what was called Wilson's Lake, good bream to 7 lb were once common in pre-roach days, but now you will encounter fish of 3–4 lb. Rectory Lake, also beside the Clones road, yields bream to 3 lb with roach, hybrids and perch.

DERRYVALLEY LAKE
(H70 21)

This small lake, easily accessible from R182 the Ballybay–Clones road, is fishable from stands. Fishing is into 6–8 feet of water, with some weed and a soft bottom. The lake holds a small stock of tench to 3 lb with roach and perch.

DROMORE RIVER

Balladine Bridge
(H70 20)

The river here is narrow and shallow. Fishing is mostly for roach and perch, with best results coming during the win-ter months. There is access up river along the right bank and then down on the left bank. Always seek permission to cross land and respect landowners' property.

WHITE LAKE (Bairds Shore)
(H67 19)

The Dromore River flows on to enter this reeded lake, which is also known as Bairds Shore.

Access is easy, with parking beside the water by permission of the landowner, Mr Joe Baird. The bank is clean and fishing is into 8–12 feet of water. This is a good water and bream are present in great numbers. The best swims are about 150 yards from the end, on the river side. Catches to 60–80 lb are taken here, with roach, perch and pike. The bank is low and is liable to flood easily.

DROMORE RIVER

Ballycoghill Bridge
(H66 17)

Below White Lake the banks of the river are low, which allows the area to flood during the winter. The average depth is about 3 feet. The flow is slow and there are clear banks. Below the bridge there are just a few swims for roach, perch and some small bream. Fishing in this section is only fair.

CORRAVOO LAKE
(H65 19)

The lake is approached from the R190 Cootehill–Ballybay road and then along the R193 Rockorry road, over Bally-coghill Bridge and left at the crossroads ½ mile further on. Parking is on private ground overlooking the lake and care should be taken when parking a car. The fishing stands are close by at the foot of a steep slope. Fishing is into 6–12 feet of water with a clean bottom. This lake has given me great enjoyment, with catches of up to 80 lb of bream to 3 lb. The water holds a big stock of small roach, hybrids, perch and pike. Fishing space on this lake is limited to about seven anglers.

CORKEERAN LAKE (H69 18)

This water beside the Ballybay–Cootehill road is heavily reeded. However, there are a few clear swims just off the road which hold small roach, small bream and perch, but do not expect great catches.

MULLANARY LAKE (H67 18)

This 120-acre water beside Corkeeran Lake is similar to it, with fair fishing only for bream. It is heavily reeded but there are a few swims along the road and to the left of the access area. Big stocks of small roach and perch frequent the inaccessible point opposite the main road. The few roadside swims do produce some roach but do not expect great results.

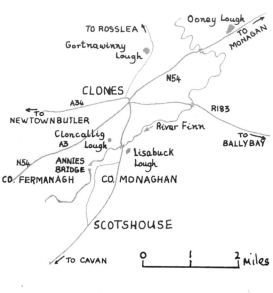

Northern Region, Clones

CLONES

This town is situated in the hilly region of west Co. Monaghan. An ancient Celtic Cross stands in The Diamond and a short distance away are the remains of a round tower. The River Finn, a tributary of the River Erne, flows south of the town.

Population 2,710
OS ½-inch Map No. 8
Cavan 17 miles, Ballybay 16 miles, Monaghan 13 miles, Dublin 75 miles

---

RIVER FINN (H48 23)

The river is slow moving and often canal-like with depths to 8 feet. The most accessible places are in the vicinity of Annies Bridge, which is approached off the Clones–Scotshouse–Cavan road. The banks of the river are low and are liable to

Hidden in the reeds Gilles on the left, in Co. Fermanagh, points to his friend Sophie, in Co. Monaghan, on the right, on the River Finn near Clones

flood. There is a nice growth of lilies along the margins, which offer good cover for the big stock of small roach, some rudd, perch and small bream. This good fishery also has a big head of small pike, which are liable to disrupt your quiet roach or bream fishing.

At the bridge the fast water entering a pool will test your skills with a stick float. There is fishing above and below the bridge for about 1 mile. From the left bank of this narrow river, a miscalculated cast might land your tackle on the far bank, and that is in Co. Fermanagh!

LISABUCK LAKE (H50 23)

A short distance from Clones, just off the Scotshouse road, this 12-acre lake has a good stock of coarse fish and in pre-roach days I enjoyed many an evening taking rudd to 2 lb here. Now the lily-fringed water has a big stock of roach, only some rudd, some bream and many varied hybrids, together with perch and pike. The stands offer easy fishing into 8–12 feet of water with some weed. With serious baiting and fishing, this water will provide catches to 30 lb, mostly of roach and hybrids.

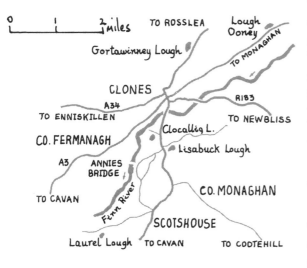

Northern Region, Clones

OONEY LAKE (H56 30)

This 26-acre lake lies beside the N54 Clones–Monaghan road near Smithborough. I have had lovely roach in this rich water, but found difficulty in fishing along the lay-by side of the lake. If the water becomes more fishable, have a go, because the quality roach will provide you with good sport.

CLONCALLIG LAKE (H49 24)

This 7-acre lake to the right of the Clones–Scotshouse road is heavily reeded. Bring your weed cutter and you might improve the two swims here. A nice water for bream to 3 lb with roach and perch galore, but remember that fishing space is limited. Always seek permission to cross land.

BLACKLION, CO. CAVAN

This is a small village on the northern side of the Cuilcagh Mountains, where the River Shannon rises in Co. Cavan. This village, in most scenic countryside, straddles the border with Belcoo village in Co. Fermanagh.

UPPER LOUGH McNEAN (H3 40)

The lovely Upper Lough McNean, a big water along the N16 Blacklion–Manorhamilton road, is the major fishery here, with access in Co. Cavan and Co. Leitrim. The margin at the jetty beside the river is shallow but good-quality roach can be taken by long-distance float fishing. Farther along at Carrickrevagh, approached off the Glenfarne–Killyclogher road, there is a good area where

bream to 4 lb and also good roach can be taken in 6–12 feet of water.

Lough McNean is a rich fishery with excellent stocks of bream, roach, hybrids, perch and pike.

TUAM RIVER
ARNEY RIVER (H8 38)

The villages of Belcoo and Blacklion are divided by the small Tuam River, which holds roach. The river then enters Lower Lough McNean in Co. Fermanagh. From here the Arney River, a designated coarse fishery, flows slowly on to enter Lough Erne near Derrylin. In this lower area there is good roach fishing.

Note that different regulations apply in waters controlled by Republic and Northern Ireland authorities in this area.

BALLYSHANNON, CO. DONEGAL

In south Donegal, the River Erne comes to the end of its long journey to the sea. Above the town, the waters of the river are harnessed to power the hydroelectric station.

Ballyshannon, 140 miles from Dublin, offers lovely sandy beaches in the beautiful county of mountains, glens and rich game-fishing waters.

ASSAROE LAKE   (G90 61)

Assaroe Lake is the 1,100-acre reservoir formed by the dam. It holds good stocks of coarse fish. Quality roach with some bream and perch abound in this unpredictable water. Pike to 25 lb have also been taken here.

This water is controlled by the Electricity Supply Board (ESB) and fishing is by permit only. It is important to comply with all regulations and particularly not to fish near the dam and along the embankments.

North-Western Fisheries Region

North-Western Fisheries Region

This region has rich sea-angling waters along the beautiful coast to the most northern part of Ireland. There are great numbers of top-class game-fishing waters, all close to the sea. Coarse-fishing waters are few in number in this region, but some of them are productive and worth recording.

Near Ballyhaunis and Knock Airport there are some lakes with pike, perch, rudd, and some bream which merit investigation with rod and line. Lakehill Lake nearby is a small water with a big stock of small tench (2 lb) and I recall taking nearly a hundred of those fish in a session.

The natural beauty of Lough Gill near Sligo is unequalled, and to add to its attraction it holds good stocks of bream, rudd, perch and pike. At the time of writing the bream fishing here too is relatively unexploited, but I predict superb sport from this lovely lake.

A mixed fishery, this big lough also holds salmon and trout.

BALLYMOTE

Ballymote is a busy market town in the high ground of south Co. Sligo. An ancient place, it is the site of a strong Norman castle built in 1300, the ivy-covered ruins of which are an interesting feature of the town.

Population 1,657
OS ½-inch Map No. 7
Sligo 15 miles, Boyle 6 miles, Dublin 121 miles
Club: Ballymote Angling Development Association

TEMPLEHOUSE LAKE
(G62 17)

This is a big lake, which in the past gained a reputation as a big pike water – and rightly so. Fish to 35 lb were common. But then followed a number of years when pike-killing Continental anglers attacked the lake and it soon became just another pike lake with small fish. When angling interest dwindled the lake quickly recovered, and now, with a new awareness of the need to conserve pike, it is producing good sport.

Just 2 miles from Ballymote, the lake has wooded surrounds and is best fished from a boat. Approached off the R296 road, the access is at the top of the lake where the Owenmore River enters. With

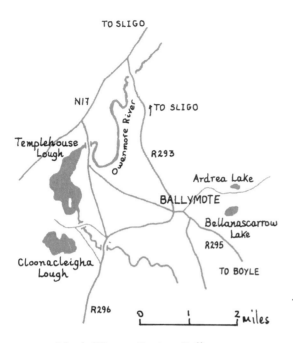

North-Western Region, Ballymote

reeded margins in many places and most of the land in private ownership, this fine lake is just not readily accessible to anglers. But from a boat you can tuck yourself into the reeded margins, bait up and find good bream to 6 lb. Rudd, hybrids and perch are also present but pike are the preferred quarry here. The lake is often weedy, with depths to 30 feet and few sudden drop-offs.

All pike should be handled with care and returned alive to the water.

OWENMORE RIVER (G63 18)

Below Templehouse Lake, the slow-moving river below the road bridge has a lovely deep pool which is attractive to the angler's eye. In the early season this pool attracts the bream too, and if you time it right, as I did once in late May, you could have a cracking time. Float fishing to 8 feet in the quiet pool could produce bream catches of well over 100 lb. But beware! The bream shoals move into the lake later in the year and the pool retains just a small number of fish.

The wormlike and quiet Owenmore River has a fair head of rudd, perch and small pike, but there does not appear to be a good stock of resident bream here.

CLOONACLEIGHA LAKE
(G61 14)

Just south of Templehouse Lake and on the Owenmore system, this is another big lake, which is fishable mostly from a boat. Access is easy from a car park. The margins are of peat in some places and quite rocky in others. There are very extensive shallow areas on the west side, up to 25 acres, which are covered with bulrush, a feature of the lake.

The northern and western margins are peaty and there is a thick belt of rushes. There is a fishable bank on the east where there is little weed. The lake in general has maximum depths of only 12 feet, with vast areas of 4–5 feet where there is abundant plant life – bulrush, stonewort and Canadian pondweed.

This lake has a stock of exceptionally big perch. Spinning my favourite Swiss X bait I have landed fish to 2 lb, and in the summer months the shoals of big perch come easily to maggot-baited hook in the weedy shallows. The water holds some bream and it is no surprise to know that big pike live comfortably on those great perch.

ARDREA LAKE   (G68 16)

This 10-acre lake beside the Ballymote–Riverstown road has easy access to fishing. The shoreline is over blackish marl and fishing is from stands into 8–12 feet of water. The lake holds a fair stock of tench to 3 lb. Bigger fish have been taken but I think that they were exceptional. There is also a small stock of bream and perch.

MOYCULLEN
●
GALWAY
●

○ DUBLIN

Western Fisheries Region

Western Fisheries Region

MOYCULLEN, CO. GALWAY

This small village north of Galway city, along the Oughterard road, is situated on the western side of the big Lough Corrib.

Population 809
OS ½-inch Map No. 14
Galway 8 miles, Ballinasloe 48 miles, Dublin 143 miles

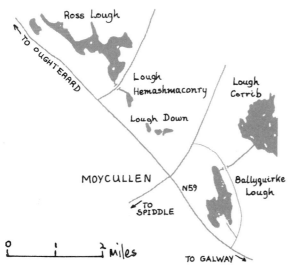

South-Western Region, Moycullen

This region is famous for its great salmon and trout fishing. With the population of roach increasing in the River Corrib system, anglers are experiencing great sport with fish over 1 lb. Take care to have permission to fish in this area where there are many private waters.

The waters in this region are controlled by the Western Regional Fisheries Board whose headquarters overlooks the weir in Galway city.

Ballyquirke Lake   (M23 31)

A narrow ½ mile long canal joins this lake to the big Lough Corrib, well known as a game fishing water. Ballyquirke has two access points, where there are different fishing conditions. The first is 1½ miles from Moycullen along the road to Galway (N59) at the Joinery. The access and parking is on private ground at private house and business premises. You must seek permission to enter here. The lake is only 50 yards away and fishing is from stands.

The second access is further along the Galway road and first left after the small lake. Five hundred yards down this narrow road, turn left again along an even narrower road which leads to a bay of the lake. There is a path along the bank where you can park about 200 yards up into the bay. If a north-westerly is blowing down into the bay that is the sign for good bream fishing.

The depth is 5 to 10 feet and the bottom mostly clean but with some rocks in places. Float or leger can be used, where bream to 6 lb and roach to 10 oz are common. This good fishery also yields hybrids, perch and some good pike.

Lough Down (M21 34)

Along the Oughterard road (N59) from Moycullen and just a short distance from the speed limit signs. The access to this lake is through private property. Permission for access and to fish this lake in State Forest property must be obtained.

Here in fact there are two lakes, joined by a short stream. The second lake is the one which produces good fishing. The margins are soft and stands are provided for those who fish for roach, mostly in the autumn and winter.

Lough Down yields some fine bream to 7 lb and with patience during the summer months, your worm and caster baited hook could attract fish to 8 lb. The water also holds a big head of small perch and small pike.

Hemushmaconry Lake (M20 34)

Further along the Oughterard road (1 mile) turn right at the Cornamuck sign and then after ½ mile there is a small bridge under which flows a stream from Ross Lake to Hemushmaconry Lake on the right.

Parking just after this bridge and bend is extremely dangerous on the narrow road. The path leads to the lake to the right and down the left bank of the stream for 500 yards. Bank space is limited to about 10 swims along this side of the lake. Fishing is into 10 to 15 feet, where the bottom has just some weed. Your catch here will consist primarily of good roach, with some bream, hybrids, perch and pike.

Ross Lake (M19 37)

A big lake with rocky shallows, it is approached as at the previous Hemushmacrony Lake. Access is through State Forest property and swims are limited. This water has a big stock of lovely roach with some bream, hybrids, perch and pike. The nature of the shallow rocky margins makes bank fishing difficult all over this water.

Don't forget to get permission to fish waters in this area.

Clare River (M32 33)

Roach are now established in the Corrib System and there is good sport for the coarse fish angler in the waters already described.

The Clare river along the eastern side of Lough Corrib is a trout fishery with controlled sections. There is, however, at the time of writing very good roach fishing in the lower stretches of the Clare River, where the flow is sluggish. This section is approached from the Galway–Headford (R334) road and fishing is near the road bridge, where banks are good. Being close to Lough Corrib, the roach in the Clare River will migrate and fishing is seasonal.

With local game fishing interests on this river, I advise you to contact the Western Regional Fisheries Board for clarification on where to fish.

Galway City   (M30 25)

The Corrib River rushes fast through the city and, some time ago, a canal was built to allow boats passage from the sea to Lough Corrib. The canal joins with the river a short distance up-river from the weir and is approached on the western (right bank) side of the river near the cathedral.

The narrow canal here has clear water and holds a good stock of nice roach and perch.

DRUMSHANBO
CARRICK ON SHANNON
MOHILL
LANESBORO
ATHLONE
GALWAY
BALLINASLOE
DUBLIN
PORTUMNA
TULLA
LIMERICK

Shannon Region

Shannon Fisheries Region

By far the largest in the country, this region encompasses all the waters of the great River Shannon system – the main river, countless small tributaries, big deep lakes and small shallow ponds, all of which abound with coarse fish.

RIVER SHANNON

It was in the shadow of the Cuilcagh Mountains in west Co. Cavan that my father introduced me to fishing. I recall when he brought me as a small boy up those mountains to see the source of the River Shannon and I came away with no impression at all. Later, when I came to understand my fishing and the waters of Ireland, my next visit through those mountains in the land of the families McGovern, Dolan and Maguire was one of deliberate exploration.

The Shannon Pot, as it is called, is a small pool about 40 feet wide in a field below Tiltinbane (1,949 feet). Legend has it that one could not drown in the so-called bottomless pool, which is almost hidden by overhanging alder and birch trees. My echo sounder recorded a depth of 18 feet in this pool, which is fed by underground streams. The rushing stream, about 4 feet wide, emerging from the Shannon Pot in Derrylahan, enters a lake and then some miles away joins the Owenmore River.

Many a small brown trout I took from this mountain river where the water tumbles over the rocks in the treeless and yet beautiful country. At Dowra village the Shannon is still a small, shallow water, which fills up quickly after rain and flushes itself into Lough Allen a few miles away.

Over 7 miles long and 3 miles wide at the top, this first big lake of the Shannon lies betwen the bleak Slieve Anierin Mountains to the east and the Arigna Mountains to the west. Fishing for pike one cold winter's day in the big bay at Derrynahona, my colleague Seamus Hartigan and I just sat back to admire the barren landscape. Before us were the ruins of countless stone cottages, with nearby the faded patterns of potato ridges in the sparse soil. As we reminisced and wondered how those hard-pressed inhabitants eked out an existence, we had visions of crafty fishermen setting lines baited with frogs to catch the 50- or 60-lb pike which must have been in this big lake in the past. Today, fish to 38 lb are taken and that dream fish, I am certain, is still there.

Lough Allen's waters act as a reservoir for the hydroelectric station at Ardnacrusha near Limerick, 130 miles away. The waters are controlled by sluice gates at the

Una Plunkett stands at the source of the River Shannon – The Shannon Pot in the Cuilcagh Mountains

river outflow at Ballintra, giving Lough Allen a fluctuation of water of nearly 15 feet at times. The margins are remarkably free from the usual emergent vegetation and it is only in the upper bays and the big lower section that you will notice the familiar reeds and rushes which we associate with the Shannon further down.

After Leitrim village the pace of the river slows, and from here the drop on its 200 miles to the sea is a mere 160 feet. Soon the river is joined by the waters of the Boyle River above Carrick-on-Shannon. From Lough Gara, a big rock-fringed water where bream abound, the Boyle River flows through the town of Boyle, where the shallow rapids once produced lovely trout. At Drum Bridge the slow-moving river wanders into the island-studded Lough Key. A beautiful lake, Lough Key is dominated by the forest park and its first-class tourist facilities for cruising, camping and caravanning. Strangely, this big lake has little bank space for angling. Leaving here, the Boyle River drops down by Knockvicar to Cootehall and into Drumharlow Lake and then joins the wide Shannon flowing south.

At Carrick-on-Shannon, the county town of Leitrim, the local population of bream and roach are not at all disturbed by the comings and goings of cruisers at the busy marina. Going south from here we leave the mountains and high ground behind and the river moves at a fast pace by Jamestown and Drumsna, while cruising traffic is diverted by a short canal stretch, of interest to anglers only during the winter months, when roach fishing is good.

Below the tidy Albert Lock and Drumsna, the next group of lakes introduce a change of character to the mighty Shannon, as the now heavily reeded waters to the west near Strokestown boast great colonies of lovely rudd.

Through Roosky to Tarmonbarry, the next interesting area is where the gentle Camlin and Feorish rivers join the big river. The whole section of big river, tributaries and canal will haunt you and keep you coming back, as I do, time and again, to explore. It is here too that tench appear in numbers. As we progress further down river they turn up in the river and particularly in the big lakes of Lough Ree and Lough Derg.

At Lanesborough the hot-water outflow from the electricity power station has created one of Ireland's famous stretches for specimen fish. From 1964 on, great specimen bream, tench, rudd × bream hybrids and rudd came to the nets of the hordes of hardened anglers who made Lanesborough their stamping ground. From late June, most of those big fish move into Lough Ree, a veritable reservoir of quality coarse fish, which extends 16 miles to Athlone. With Rocky and shallow margins, surprisingly few places in this vast expanse of water offer easy access to good swims for coarse fishing. I am certain, however, that with more exploring we will come up with more suitable locations for tackle-laden anglers, who must have fishing within reasonable distance of parking.

The Shannon passes through Athlone and flows through low-lying country which floods easily in the winter months. The monastic settlement at Clonmacnoise looms out in this stretch of winding and thickly reeded water. At Shannonbridge my interest in the Shannon fish is often given a rest, as I am drawn towards another of my passions, local history.

There is more to fishing than catching fish! Preparing your tackle, casting out and waiting for the bite is all very well, but then the ritual of fishing is broken when you stand up, walk around and savour the lovely Irish countryside. But I digress temporarily, as I do so often when I am out fishing, and no doubt I will continue to wander off the angling path throughout this book.

Overlooking the impressive arched bridge at Shannonbridge are the remains of extensive Napoleonic artillery fortifications. There are more of these along the way to Portumna, but the fish stocks in the river were never disturbed back in the early nineteenth century, as those defences were never engaged in any conflict. I wonder how many of the soldiers look down on the big rudd there – or was it the jumping salmon which interested them in those days?

But back to modern days. The hot-water outflow from the big electricity power station attracts great numbers of big tench and other species. This is a great area for all species and is not heavily fished.

The Grand Canal from Dublin connects with the Shannon above Banagher, another base for cruisers. From this point down, there are islands galore, and the still backwaters present ideal situations for quiet and productive fishing.

Portumna is at the top of the largest of

the Shannon lakes, Lough Derg, which extends down to Killaloe, 25 miles away. The high mountains to the south and richly wooded islands make this lake a pleasure for all for cruising, sailing, surfing, or fishing. But where in such a big water does one sit on a good bank to find those bream and rudd? This is another Irish lake that will take years to explore – and another volume to fill on its fishing.

The next coarse-fishing centre downstream of Lough Derg is the village of O'Brien's Bridge. Then there are rapid salmon waters on the way to Limerick, though there is exceptionally good bream and roach fishing in sections of the river above the city and near Annacotty. To the west of here, in Co. Clare, there are scores of small lakes which are seldom fished for bream, rudd, tench and pike. Here, too, you will find a richness not only in fish stocks but in a countryside of scenic beauty and a wealth of Irish character.

DRUMSHANBO

A small town situated at the Southern end of Lough Allen, Drumshanbo is dominated by the great lake and surrounding mountains.

Population 670
O/S ½-inch Map No. 7
Ballinamore 12 miles, Carrick-on-Shannon 8 miles, Boyle 13 miles, Dublin 109 miles
Clubs: Lough Allen Angling Club, Lough Allen Conservation Association, Drumshanbo Tourist Association.

LOUGH ALLEN   (G96 20)

From Dowra village the River Shannon is shallow and mostly fast, with some pools. It enters Lough Allen between Rossmore and Kilgarriff at one of the five big bays at the top of the lake. Seven miles long and near 3 miles wide at the top, the lake narrows into a point near Drumshanbo. The shoreline is remarkable in places, with many shallow areas and sandy beaches. Because of the fluctuating water levels (nearly 15 feet), if ever the boating angler had to study a big lake before going out this is it. The lake is flanked by the Arigna Mountains to the west and Slieve Anierin to the east. A north-westerly wind is common in the winter months, and, so close to the sea, a fresh wind through the gap at the top of the lake can be extremely dangerous. The lake is also exposed to the prevailing south-westerlies and it is vital to your safety to exercise care when going out afloat.

I have taken small roach at the Shannon as it enters the lake, but this is mountain country and access entails long walks from small, narrow lanes. The introduction of roach to this lake has most certainly improved pike stocks, more big pike are to be found in the lower section where rudd, perch and roach abound.

The northern bays near Inishmagrath Island all produce big pike in the early

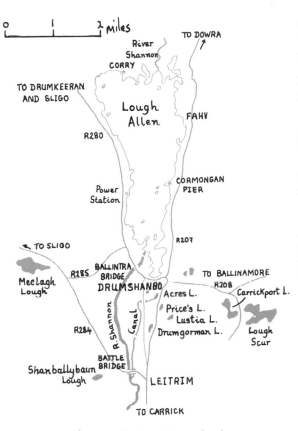

Shannon Region, Drumshanbo

months of the year and there is boat access at Corry, which is approached off the R200 Dowra–Drumkeeran road.

The western side of the lake has great depths and the real interest for anglers begins around the Cormongan area along the eastern side. Here there are a few islands out from the pier and fishing can be good for bream and roach, but only after very heavy groundbaiting. I have had bream averaging 4 lb from the second island to the left and facing north, in 12 feet of water over a sandy bottom.

The Shannon leaves the lake along the western side, not at the southern tip as you might expect, and it is in the lower section that you will find shallow, weedy water with an abundance of good bream, roach, rudd, hybrids, perch and pike. Access to limited bank fishing off the R280 Drumkeeran road is difficult and boat fishing is best. Approached from the main lake by boat, you enter the bottom section through a shallow area which has many submerged posts. Fish halfway down along the western bank at Maha-nagh, where the depth is 4–6 feet, with much weed. A great area, full of fish!

With a supply of fodder fish in the lower weedy and shallow section, it is natural that great predatory pike roam here. There are a few distinct piking areas south of a line drawn from Cormongan to the power station. During the summer months, trolling is the best method and this is done in the area out from the Cormongan Islands to the power station, then down to a point near the marker and up again to the Cormongan area.

During the cold months of the year from October to April, dead-baiting from the points around Cormongan can be rewarding. The roach population remain active in the warmer water near the power station and directly south along the western side.

Around the point at Gubscrabragan, the Arigna River enters the lake and over the years the silt has built up, making a large bay of very shallow (6–4 feet) water. This whole area, where roach are common in the winter months, is the home of those big pike of over 30 lb. Over the years I have learned to use a thermometer when I go fishing and unquestionably it pays to note the changes of water temperature, particularly in the lower section of Lough Allen when fish move from the deeps to the shallows.

Hugh Gough legering with dead bait for pike in Kilgarriff Bay at the top of the big Lough Allen

RIVER SHANNON

Ballintra Sluice Gates   (G96 12)

The river leaves Lough Allen through sluice gates at the south-western corner of the lake. Approached from the R280 Drumshanbo–Drumkeeran road, the water in this area is controlled by the Electricity Supply Board and you should abide by local regulations. This stretch is also controlled by the local trout angling club and information on their club and waters is available locally.

Above the bridge there are just a few swims with fishing into 6–8 feet of water for good bream and roach in the early and late seasons. Downstream there are some swims for about 500 yards along the right bank and the narrow and fast stretch near the overhanging trees can often produce great bream fishing. I have also had many good pike to 20 lb here by carefully casting close to the side and near the trees where fish like to lie in ambush.

Battle Bridge   (G95 8)

A stretch of river at Lurga above the bridge has a fair stock of bream and roach, the best area for roach is below the fast water at the bridge. The roach appear in April, May and June below the point where the Lough Allen Canal enters the river, you must hit the massive shoals when they are on the feed. Fish with a stick float in 4–6 feet of water.

The access here is from Battle Bridge by the lock-house. Parking space is limited, and take care not to obstruct the entry.

LOUGH ALLEN CANAL
(G95 7)

This canal was built in 1820 with the intention of ferrying Arigna coal down the river, but the scheme was a disaster. It was reopened in 1978 for pleasure craft. There is now a stock of fish in this 4-mile reach, which is used as a match stretch. About 4 feet deep and narrow, the water holds small perch, small roach, small bream and some tench to 4 lb. Access is easy from the nearby road.

ACRES LAKE   (G97 10)

The topmost point of navigation on the River Shannon, this is a small lake which has shallow margins and submerged trees. There is a jetty here where you can fish at times, but remember that a cruiser could suddenly come along to berth in your swim. There are roach, perch, some rudd and bream here. Beside the lake there are excellent sport facilities for children.

DERRYNAHOO LAKE
(Price's or Flynn's Lake) (G97 9)

Also beside the R280 Drumshanbo-Carrick road, fishing here is for small bream and roach. The margins are soft and fishing is from stands into 5–8 feet of water with a muddy bottom.

DRUMGORMAN LAKE
(G96 8)

Further out from Drumshanbo along the Carrick road, access to this 15-acre lake is easy. This is a good fishery, which holds a good stock of bream (2 lb) and roach. The banks are sometimes soft and fishing is from stands into 6–8 feet of water with a soft bottom with some weed. Catches to 50–60 lb are taken here and fishing is of a consistently high level.

BLACKROCK POND (G96 11)

Near the Lough Allen Canal at Drumhiver Bridge, this small water has easy access. Shallow, with weed, it has a small stock of tench to 3–4 lb. I have had my fish there in the late evenings only, with sweetcorn as bait.

DERRYHALLAGH LAKE
ROSCUNNISH LAKE (G98 11)

These two lakes near Drumshanbo have only fair stocks of small roach, small bream and perch. Slow fishing here, and I suggest that you move on to better waters in the area.

BOYLE, CO. ROSCOMMON

Boyle is a busy market town near the beautiful Lough Key below the Curlew Mountains. The Boyle River flows through the town and along its banks are the ruins of the Cistercian Abbey which was founded in 1161, in this land of the McDermott clan.

Population 1,850
OS ½-inch Map No. 7
Carrick-on-Shannon 9 miles, Drumshanbo 13 miles, Roscommon 26 miles, Dublin 117 miles
Club: Boyle Angling Club

LOUGH GARA   G71 00)

This big lake was drained in the 1960s and its features were changed, leaving many shallow areas and also rocky shores. The lake is in two sections, connected by a shallow, clean-banked river. The meeting point is Cuil Bridge, and up river from here along the left bank you will find some deep pools which hold good bream to 3 lb. Below the bridge, the river enters the lake in an area where it is shallow with some rocks at a distance.

The fresh water, often coloured, which enters at this point is the home of the great shoals of Lough Gara bream. Particularly from the right side of the outflow, you will find bream to 4 lb in numbers and catches to 200 lb have been taken here in a session. Lough Gara holds a big stock of good-sized bream and all it requires is plenty of fishing to get those great netfuls.

Roach are now in residence there and the river yields good catches in the winter months especially. The big lake yields good pike and, as the margins are mostly shallow, boat fishing is best.

At Cuppanagh Bridge there is some bream fishing with seasonal roach in what is now called the Boyle River. Shallow and weedy in the summer, this river holds some brown trout and then moves fast through Boyle to Drum Bridge, where it becomes sluggish and deep. The few deep pools above this bridge provide interesting fishing for roach and perch, but for bream you must walk down below the bridge.

BOYLE RIVER

Drum Bridge   (G82 4)

The river is navigable to this point, and slow-moving with low banks. Access is along the right and sometimes the clean bank is soft. Fishing is into 4–6 feet of water, for bream, roach and perch. Shoals of bream tend to move here and in the early months they will enter the shallow bay of nearby Lough Key.

LOUGH KEY   (G83 5)

This is one of the Shannon's most scenic lakes. Studded with islands, this lovely water was once dominated by Rockingham House, the ruins of which were

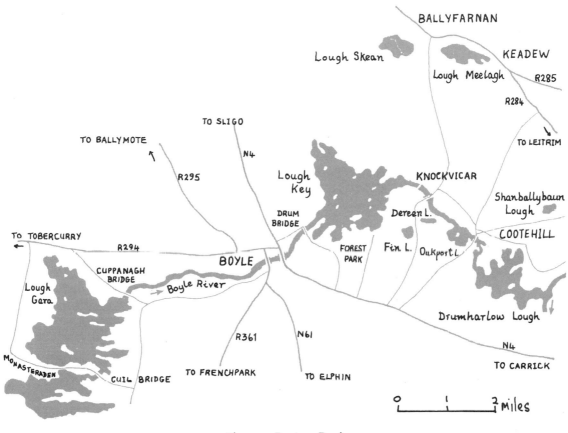

Shannon Region, Boyle

replaced by an ugly concrete tower. In the Forest Park here there are facilities for caravans, camping and boats, and it also has a shop and restaurant. This area is often used by mobile anglers for a few days while touring and fishing.

The shores of this lake do not lend themselves to easy coarse fishing due to rocks, shallows and reeds. There are some swims near Doon, where the Curlew Mountains dip into the lake. Bream to 4 lb are common throughout, with a big head of roach, perch and pike.

FIN LAKE   (G87 4)

This is a 25-acre lake beside the Boyle–Knockvicar road, surrounded by reeds. There are two fishing stands. The first is to the left, through a path in the reeds. The second is approached over a long catwalk.

The lake has clear water, with a heavy growth of stonewort and patches of lilies. Fin Lake has a good stock of tench to 5 lb. Fishing is into 8–10 feet of water over a weedy bottom. This rich tench water calls for serious angling. It fishes best at first light and responds to heavy raking. There is a big stock of small perch with some quality roach, which feed best in the colder months.

DEREEN LAKE   (G87 4)

This lake lies within the property of the Forest Service and access is by a gate off the Boyle–Knockvicar road. The main access gate is mostly closed and permission to enter must be obtained locally. It is a developed fishery and has fishing stands. The first five stands to the right produce the bream. Fishing here is into 13–16 feet of water, shallowing to 6 feet to the left. This quiet wooded water also has roach, some small rudd, small perch and pike.

BOYLE RIVER, KNOCKVICAR   (G87 5)

From Lough Key the river moves quickly over a weir and through a lock. Access to this picturesque stretch is from the bridge, where care must be taken parking. There is a high path above the water, up to the well kept lock area. This stretch has a moderate to fast flow and is 6–8 feet deep, but in one swim at the wooden bridge across the path there is a hole of 15–17 feet. It is here that you will find some cracking bream to 5 lb.

The stretch has a big stock of small roach and small perch, but you should note that the boating traffic is heavy at periods during the summer.

OAKPORT LAKE, COOTEHALL   (G88 4)

The Boyle River flows through the northern side of Oakport Lake. Foot access is from the gate at the bridge and then 200 yards over a field to the first swims, which are to the left of the red marker. At the time of writing, stands are being erected along this fine shore, where there is a belt of rushes. The margin is stony and fishing is into 8–12 feet of water, with some weed in the summer.

This is a great bream water. I have had great sport here float fishing in blustery conditions, when I found that the bream to 5 lb liked to take a moving bait. This rich water also holds rudd, roach, good hybrids, perch and good pike.

The water can also be approached by a nearby slip-road to an amenity area.

BOYLE RIVER, COOTEHALL   (G88 3)

The short river stretch at the bridge moves at a moderate to fast pace and during the summer months has much cruiser traffic. The clean banks are fishable up river along the right bank, reached by the gate, and on the left bank there is fishing from a stand and a good bank.

This tidy and attractive area has some bream and rudd fishing from a stand in Cootehall Lough, which is approached from the bridge along the left side. The jetty area along the road also holds bream, roach and good hybrids. Just to the right of this place, the river turns to the right and the banks are sometimes soft. At this point I have taken good rudd to 2 lb as well as roach and hybrids.

DRUMHARLOW LAKE
(G92 1)

Nearer Carrick-on-Shannon, the river now enters Drumharlow Lake, which has many reeded and shallow margins. The many inaccessible areas retain good stocks of rudd. Along the N4 Carrick–Boyle road there is waterside parking and fishing from a stand. Here you will find some of those rudd but, while I have taken roach here too, I found that small perch ousted all the other species. Along the northern side there are a few accessible places near an old school where the lake is near the road. Here you will find some small skimmers, small perch and roach.

LOUGH MEELAGH   (G12 89)

Between Keadue and Ballyfarnan, beside the R284 road, this lovely part of Ireland along the borders of Roscommon and Leitrim can boast of a very good roach lake. Access is easy to an amenity area where there is a slip.

Fishing is from a stand into 5–10 feet of water with some weed. Good-quality roach to 12–14 oz are here, but it is a big water and you must wait for the shoals to move in.

CAVETOWN LAKE   (M83 98)

Cavetown Lake lies 3 miles from Boyle off the N61 Roscommon road. It is controlled by the Cavetown and Clogher Angling Club as a game fishery, and permission must be obtained to fish.

This is a very deep water, with a depth of 50 feet in the centre. A great part of its margins are reeded and the surroundings are mostly wooded. To the left of the pump-house there is limited space in deep water for fishing.

This rich water, with a growth of stonewort and Marestail, holds a very big stock of rudd. The best rudd fishing is for the adventurous angler who fishes directly across from the pump-house. You could fill a net or two with rudd to 1 lb on a good summer's day on this water.

CARRICK-ON-SHANNON

The county town of Leitrim, Carrick straddles the River Shannon. In the summer months this busy town gains an international flavour as tourists flock to this popular water terminal.

Population 1,973
OS ½-inch Maps Nos 12 and 7
Drumshanbo 8 miles, Boyle 9 miles, Ballinamore 17 miles, Mullingar 56 miles, Dublin 101 miles
Club: Carrick-on-Shannon Tourist Assocation

RIVER SHANNON, HARTLEY BRIDGE   (G94 3)

At Leitrim village the disused canal has some easy fishing for skimmers and roach. The Shannon passes here at a moderate pace, and the margins are low with rushes and reeds.

At Hartley Bridge there is parking along a narrow road with access down a

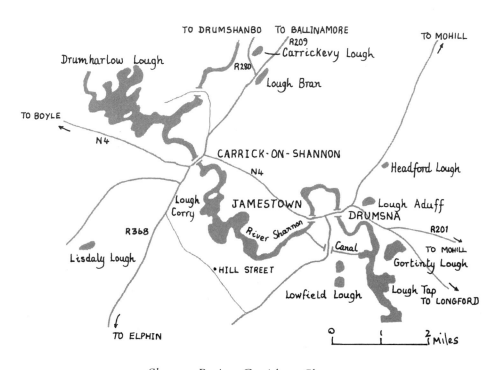

Shannon Region, Carrick-on-Shannon

steep structure to the low-lying right bank of the river. Here you will find great roach fishing as the shoals migrate up river in May. But you must get those fish just at the right time. Bream to 3 lb are taken along this stretch, but it is vital to bait heavily and wait to get them on the feed.

SHANBALLYBAUN LAKE
(G93 5)

Not far from the Shannon, this lake is approached from the Cootehall–Leitrim road and then up a small road to parking at a house. You are reminded that parking and access over private ground is only through permission of the owner. Fishing on this lake is from three stands and you can have good sport here for bream, roach, rudd and hybrids galore.

RIVER SHANNON, CARRICK-ON-SHANNON
(G94 00)

During the summer months the area in the vicinity of the marina can be busy with boat traffic. Note that Saturday is the day when most cruisers change crews. You may think that no sensible fish would hang around here when there is so much quiet water elsewhere. But no, those bream and roach remain and the stretch yields great catches throughout the season.

Access from the N4 Boyle road leads to stands opposite the marina, where there is a depth of 8–12 feet. There are also productive swims – but only in the early season – below the bridge along the left bank at the car park, and then further along the long catwalk to four stands. Below the wide bay here, the river narrows, offering some swims on both banks.

May I remind you always to ask permission to cross land and to park on private property. The swims along the right bank at the Mud Flats are on private ground and you must have permission to enter. The area is approached taking a narrow road just before a bridge 2 miles from Carrick on the Elphin road. After crossing the railway, the private road leads to a farmhouse.

The swims to the left produce great bream catches, with roach, hybrids and perch as well. The swims along the open bank across the river are approached by a small road at a housing estate off the N4 Carrick–Longford road. At Rinacureen there are five or six good swims which yield good catches throughout the season.

LOUGH BRAN   (G3 96)

This is a 60-acre lake at the junction of the R209 Ballinamore and the R280 Drumshanbo roads north of Carrick. Access

from the Ballinamore road to waterside parking makes this a suitable venue for the handicapped angler. This is a good bream water. The bank is clean and fishing is into 12–15 feet, but a long leger cast will reach a depth of 22 feet. There is weed in many swims and particularly near the main road area, where the water is shallow close in.

Fishing stands can be reached just off the main road, and here you will enjoy fishing for tench to 4 lb in May and June. The head of roach and small perch is good here, and don't be surprised to find hungry pike snapping at your small fish!

RIVER SHANNON, JAMESTOWN   (M2 98)

The river passes through the reeded Lough Corry and arrives at Jamestown. Just above the road bridge a stile leads along the right bank to some good swims for rudd, roach and hybrids, and sometimes bream to 4 lb move in. The margin is sometimes flooded and fishing is into weedy water about 8–10 feet deep. Downstream at a wide bend the now fast river forms a pool below the weir where some great catches of bream and roach are taken in the early season. Access is to the left off the N4 Carrick–Longford road just before the village.

JAMESTOWN CANAL, ALBERT LOCK   (N00 96)

There is interesting fishing in the early months for good roach. From the quay the canal enters at the bridge. But from Easter this spot becomes busy with boats coming and going. Below the lock there is a backwater where boats are moored and just at the junction with the river you will find good tench in May and June. My advice is to hit this spot at the crack of dawn before the river traffic starts.

LOWFIELD LAKE   (M95 99)

Just a cast away from the Albert Lock lies the reeded Cartron Lake. Here one or two swims can be fished with some difficulty.

Of greater interest is the nearby Lowfield Lake, which, while heavily reeded, offers fishing from a stand. The approach is off the Carrick-Strokestown road via Jamestown and then left after the canal road. Walk along the stream to the stand, which offers fishing in a weedy area into 6–12 feet of water. This fine tench water is a joy to fish in the morning. I have never seen the likes of the fish activity here, with bubbles flipping lilies up and the occasional dark fin breaking the surface. Specimen tench over 6 lb appear in Lowfield, and don't be surprised if you find some bream to 5 lb here too. A great water!

LOUGH ADUFF   (N00 98)

Access is to the left off the main N4 road about 1 mile from Drumsna and over 2 fields. The lake is surrounded by reeds and fishing is from stands. The margins also have belts of lilies, which help to provide food for the good stock of fish here. Tench to 5 lb respond to bread in the early season. When I tried maggot and worm here I was annoyed with countless small perch.

Bream shoals are few but you will find fish to 4 lb and also some good tench.

HILL STREET LAKES   (M6 91)

These two lakes lie in a state forest and can be reached by turning left off the R368 Carrick–Elphin road to Hill Street and through a forest gate. Reeded and with lilies, these rich waters, connected by a small stream, hold stocks of lovely rudd to 2 lb and some bream.

Many other lakes in this area towards Elphin and Strokestown hold good stocks of big rudd.

GORTINTY LAKE   (N96 2)

This big lake lies beside the River Shannon along the Carrick–Longford road. It is fishable at one place, which is approached off a small side road. Parking is difficult and remember that foot access is over private ground. There is a short stretch with a good stony bank with fishing into 8–10 feet of water with some weed. Heavy baiting is essential in this good water, where catches to 156 lb have been recorded. The lake yields nice bream to 5 lb, tench to 4 lb, and it has a big population of roach and small rudd. It is also worth a try for big pike, which can be taken by legering from this bank.

LISDALY LAKE   (M88 95)

A right turn 4 miles from Carrick on the R368 Elphin road leads to Canbo Lake and farther on to Lisdaly Lake. Cross a stile and a footbridge to the fishing stands. This reeded water holds good bream, rudd and perch. Fishing is into 8–14 feet of water with a weedy bottom. A moody water for bream, it can be sure to provide good sport for rudd in the summer evenings.

MOHILL, CO. LEITRIM

Mohill is a small market town near the attractive Lough Rynn estate, which is now open to the public and offers many facilities.

Population 147
OS ½-inch Map No. 12
Carrick-on-Shannon 11 miles, Ballinamore 10 miles, Roosky 16 miles, Dublin 92 miles
Club: Mohill Angling and Tourist Development Association

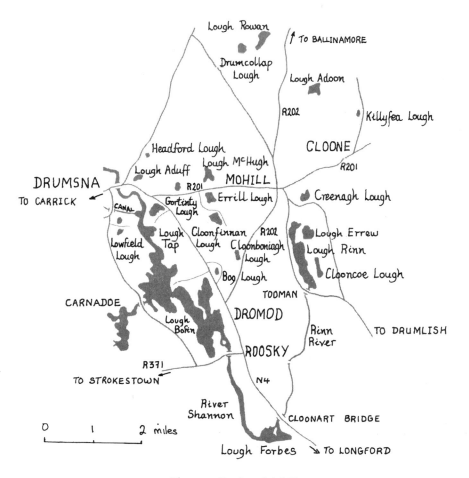

Shannon Region, Mohill

CREENAGH LAKE (N10 93)

This is a rich 45-acre lake 1 mile south-east of Mohill. There is parking at the roadside and access is over one field. Fishing is from stands on this reeded and soft-margined water. The third stand to the right of the entry was always my favourite, and where I have taken great tench to near 6 lb. I could never crack that magic specimen weight but still enjoyed wonderful sport with great catches mostly in the late evening. But this is a moody water.

Big bream to 6 lb are also here, but it does take a lot of baiting up to get them on the feed. Good rudd, once common here, are now replaced by roach in great numbers. Fishing is into 8–15 feet of water, with a maximum depth of 22 feet. For good bream and good tench this is a lake well worth a serious try.

LOUGH RINN (N10 93)

This long and mostly shallow water lies alongside the Mohill–Drumlish road. On the roadside there is access from an amenity area, but fishing here is only fair. Farther along a stile leads to a point where the lake is narrow, and here bream fishing can sometimes be very good.

On the east side of the lake is Lough Rynn House and gardens, which for two centuries was the seat of the Clements Family, Earls of Leitrim. The large estate is open to the public and here the fishing

A lucky peg for those who fish Lough Rinn. The lake can easily be fished by float for bream, roach and tench

stretch offers good bream, roach, hybrids, perch and pike. In May and June there are also tench to 4 lb here, in a depth of 6–10 feet.

There is an admission charge to the grounds and fishing here.

LOUGH McHUGH   (N5 98)

This is a good fishery of 90 acres approached off the R201 Mohill–Carrick road near Eslin Bridge, where a small road leads to lakeside parking. The near side has a good rocky shore, while the rest of the lake has a margin of reeds and sedges. Fishing is to the left of the island, where there is a depth of 10 feet, with 31 feet directly out in the middle. At the margins fishing is into 6–10 feet of water, with some weed.

If you give this rich water the attention it requires, some cracking sport will come your way. Good bream shoals roam this lake and tench to 5 lb are not uncommon. Roach, rudd and perch abound and there are some good-quality pike here too.

ERRILL LAKE   (N5 97)

Access is easy from the R201 Mohill–Carrick road to this heavily reeded 62-acre water. This is a remarkably shallow lake, and in the summer months produces a thick forest of weed. I have tried the lake with little success for the good tench to 6 lb which I know are there in great numbers. If you get them, let me know!

CLOONBONIAGH LAKE   (N6 93)

This is a shallow 26-acre lake along the R202 Mohill–Dromod road, with parking 20 yards from the waterside. The margins are shallow and fishing is from stands. The maximum depth is 8 feet, with float fishing easy at 4–5 feet. The water becomes weedy in the summer months.

There is a good population of bream to 2 lb, with some rudd, roach, hybrids and perch galore. Tench stocks are fair but you could catch fish to 4 lb using sweetcorn as bait.

HEADFORD LAKE   (N1 99)

This small lake lies to the right of the Drumsna–Mohill road, with foot access over a field. I recall fishing this water for pike many years ago, when it held great fish of over 20 lb. But times have changed and now I return for easy bream (2–3 lb) fishing and an assortment of hybrid fishing.

CLOONFINNAN LAKE   (N5 7)

A short distance beyond Errill Lake a narrow road left off the R201 leads to this big water. Park carefully on the road. Access is through one field to the right. A heavily reeded water, Cloonfinnan is weedy and has shallow margins. The lake can produce great fishing, but I have found that patience is paramount, as in so many waters where shoals roam about in the forest of food-laden weeds. One or two blank days are never wasted on this lake if you continue to launch the bait in. You will be rewarded with good tench of 4 lb and bream to 5 lb. During the winter this lake, with good roach, will also yield nice pike to over 20 lb.

ROOSKY, CO. LEITRIM

Rooskey is a small village which straddles the River Shannon between Leitrim and Roscommon. It is a scenic area and attracts a lot of cruiser traffic in the summer months.

Population 274
OS ½-inch Map No. 12
Carrick-on-Shannon 13 miles, Mohill 6 miles, Strokestown 12 miles, Longford 9 miles
Club: Roosky Angling Club

RIVER SHANNON   N5 87)

The River Shannon in this area has some bank space above the bridge along the left bank with easy access from the N4 road. Above this point there are some stands near the inflow of the river, and all along here you will find some bream, roach, hybrids and perch.

Further upriver is Pigeon Island, whose northern end has some swims which yield great catches of bream. The island is approachable only by boat and I suggest that you fish further round to the left, in the slack, where I have had bream to 4 lb with some lovely rudd.

Down from the bridge you will find bream along the right bank below the dry dock, while along the well-manicured left bank there are bream too. However, during the summer months you may find that cruisers cause you problems.

Just below the lock along the left side there are a few swims which hold bream and roach.

RIVER SHANNON, DERRYCARNE   (N2 91)

This area in the big Shannon lake of Lough Boderg is approached off the N4

Carrick–Longford road between Drumsna and Dromod. There is an amenity area here in the Forest Park and to the right, facing west with the black marker to the left, I have enjoyed many a day with great bream of 4 lb and rudd to 2 lb. Fishing is into 8–10 feet of water but there is a rocky bottom with weed here. A good place to loose leger tackle!

RINN RIVER   (N8 84)

This slow-moving river flows from Lough Rinn under the N4 Longford–Carrick road at Cloonart Bridge and then enters the reeded Lough Forbes. There is easy access to the upper side and along the right bank, which is low and liable to flood.

The river has a stock of small roach, perch, some rudd, hybrids, bream and pike. This is a moody water, with roach fishing unpredictable in the summer months. However, like so many roach rivers it can come into its own during the colder months, producing good fishing.

BOG LAKE   (N5 92)

Turn right off the N4 Carrick road 3 miles north of Roosky. The ring road over the railway bridge with Bog Lake to the left leads back to the main road. The small lake has access at a stile, where there is limited parking space. The lake, which is reeded with peaty margins, has limited swims. Fishing for tench with a float is easy, as the depth is 5–6 feet. Fish to 4 lb are taken, with some rudd in the good fishing months of May–June.

STROKESTOWN, CO. ROSCOMMON

Strokestown is a tidy market town with wide and spacious streets. The area here and around Elphin has an abundance of clear waters which are the home of Ireland's best shoals of rudd.

Population 620
OS ½-inch Map No. 12
Roosky 12 miles, Tarmonbarry 8 miles, Roscommon 12 miles, Dublin 89 miles

KILGLASS LAKE   (M98 84)

Just under the high R371 Roosky–Strokestown road, this lake offers a lovely scene which would entice any angler. The view here illustrates the character of so many of the lakes in this area. Shallow margins of open water extend about 10–15 yards to belts of rushes of varying thickness. In the deep water beyond the rushes you will sometimes find lilies and pondweed.

This is the lake that confronted A. E. Biddlecombe from Manchester and his wife in 1959. I recall him telling the story of how he baited up heavily with boiled potatoes in Kilglass and how his wife landed a record-weight rudd. The celebrations were short-lived, however, as he then took a fish of 3 lb 1 oz, a record which stands to this day.

I fish this and the other rudd lakes in the Strokestown area often, so let me tell you of the habits of those lovely golden-scaled fish. The shoals, sometimes of 20–25 fish, are constantly on the move. During the summer days they will cruise in the shallow, clear margins and can be seen easily. Then they can be fished for from the bank by long casting with bread or a bunch of maggots as bait. To be successful here you should bait up in the shallow water and wait for the roving fish.

In the evening, the rudd will enter the reeds and in the fading light they often move out to deeper water on the inside of the belt, and then only boat fishing will get results. The shoals can be stalked by boat in the daytime, but you must be organized to anchor quickly and operate noiselessly.

Here, as in all gin-clear waters, I use Drennan Crystal floats which take 2 or 3 swan shot.

The nearby Grange Lake holds bream and rudd × bream hybrids of over 3 lb with the usual rudd over 2 lb. There are some swims near the quay in this otherwise reeded water.

I have been catching small roach at the mouth of the Mountain River here. I will be saddened when the roach push those lovely rudd out of this area.

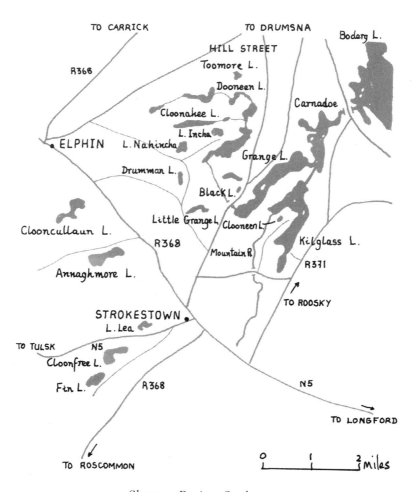

Shannon Region, Strokestown

CLOONEEN LAKE (M97 86)

This reeded lake is approached to the right by Church View Guest House and the Mountain River. At the end of this road, with Kilglass Lake on the right, the access is over private property to the left.

Fishing is from stands into 8–10 feet of weedy water. Clooneen has produced good tench to 5 lb and it holds quality rudd, perch and pike.

BLACK LAKE (M96 87)

This small lake has easy access from the Strokestown–Carrick road. Fishing is from a stand, but submerged tree stumps cause snags. There are small rudd galore here but I have also taken nice tench to 3 lb on maggots during the sunny days.

LOUGH LEA (M92 82)

This is a group of ponds just west of Strokestown which, when in flood, appear as one lake. Some swims in the reedy margins offer fishing for bream, rudd and some tench to 6 lb. There are also some good-quality perch over 2 lb.

ANNAGHMORE LAKE (M90 83)

No year is complete without a rudd session on this great water. A left turn 3 miles from Strokestown on the R368 Elphin road brings you to this rich lake where there is bankside parking.

Here again you will find shallow margins of clear water giving way to belts and islands of rushes all over the water. To the right of the island there is a shallow strip across the middle of the lake which in dry summer conditions makes boat passage difficult.

The lake has an abundance of small shoals of specimen rudd to 3 lb. There are also some tench to be found near the island, as well as perch over 1 lb.

For the keen rudd angler this lake is a must.

DRUMMAN LAKE (M93 87)

Two miles from Strokestown on the Carrick road, take a left and then right at the quarry. This small lake is to the left 1,100 yards on and parking is along the narrow road. The lake is reeded but there are some good swims opposite the roadside.

Near the gate and entry there are just two swims where you can cast for the 2 lb rudd. The lake also has a big stock of small perch and pike.

LOUGH INCHA (Brennan's Lake) (M94 88)

A right turn ½ mile on from Drumman Lake leads to this water, where there is waterside parking. This lake of clear water and reeds is fished from stands, where a short cast will reach 8–10 feet of water. There are few bream present, but good rudd to 2 lb and quality rudd × bream hybrids as well.

I have had great catches of rudd and hybrids here in the evening, and also in the dark, when the latter seemed to come alive.

Nearby is Lough Nablahy and other reeded waters, all of which produce wonderful rudd, though most of them can only be fished successfully from a boat.

CLONFREE LAKE (M91 79)

I tell a story. Many years ago we had organized a big rudd hunt with thirty anglers participating. On one evening I sat in a boat in the near-darkness, peering out in the light of the moon at my peacock quill float, and saw it go under. I struck and the commotion woke up my hidden fishing colleagues around the lake. The fish splashed around as we tried to net it in the dark. I thought that surely the Irish record rudd had taken my big piece of bread on a size 8 hook. Lights were turned on to look at the fish now safely in the bottom on the boat. It was a brown trout, which tipped the scales at 5½ lb!

Clonfree lies 2 miles south-west of Strokestown off the N5 Tulsk road. This reeded water does hold good rudd to 3 lb and tench to 6 lb, and I can also confirm that it holds brown trout.

FIN LOUGH   (M90 78)

Two miles west of Strokestown, this lake to the right of a narrow road has fishing from stands. As in other waters, you can cast beyond the rush belt and get the rudd. Here I advise you to use bread as bait: the abundance of small perch will cause annoyance if you use maggots.

MULLINGAR

Mullingar, the county town of Westmeath, is situated in rich pasture land between Lough Owel and Lough Ennell.

Population 8,120
OS ½-inch Map No. 12
Athlone 31 miles, Castlepollard 12 miles, Longford 27 miles, Dublin 49 miles
Club: Mullingar Coarse Angling Club

SLEVIN'S LAKE   (N45 56)

Turn right 2 miles from Mullingar off the R394 and park at the end of the road. This is a reeded lake with some fishing stands. There is some weed in the summer, and the limited bream shoals come on the feed. The lake also holds perch, pike, some roach, rudd and hybrids.

McEVOY'S LAKE   (N45 57)

This 2-acre lake lies beside Slevin's and has easy access. Fishing is from stands on this reeded water with some weed. This small lake produced rudd to 2 lb in pre-roach days but now that is no longer the case. However, good sport can be had here for roach, rudd, hybrids and perch.

GALMOYLESTOWN LAKE
(N43 61)

This small but very special lake is reached by turning left by the church north of Lee's Cross filling station on the R394 Mullingar–Castlepollard road. The lake is one mile down the road under a hill and has roadside parking at the water's edge. The swims here are ideal for the handicapped angler.

This small and open water has a depth of 4 feet and is mostly shallower where there is weed. The water has good banks and is also fishable from the bank under the hill.

Once stocked with trout, this lake received a stock of carp and now provides excellent sport for fish to 10 lb. Fairly heavily fished, the carp now respond best to the more sophisticated carp baits.

DOOLIN POND   (N46 53)

This, too, was set up by the Central Fisheries Board as an experimental carp

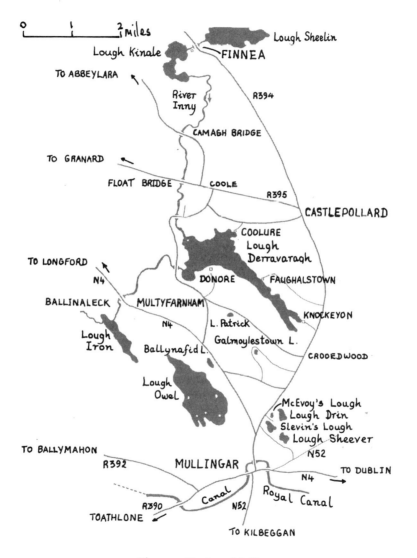

Shannon Region, Mullingar

Brendan Doran with 8 lb carp at Galmoylestown Lake near Mullingar

fishery. The water is approached off the R400 Rochfordbridge road, then left at Gaybrook Cross, over a bridge and left to a bungalow. Access is easy and fishing is from a stand. This is a muddy and sometimes weedy water which yields some carp to 8 lb, but they do not come easily to the hook.

BALLINAFID LAKE (N41 59)

Beside the N4 Mullingar–Longford road north of Lough Owel, the best fishing on this lake is opposite the main road which is approached from the forest road. The banks are soft on this reeded water, which has a stand on the near bank. It once produced good bream to 10 lb but the

fishing for that species has slowed down. Tench to 6 lb respond to late or early sessions here. Carp, which were stocked into this water, are showing good growth and now reach a weight of 13 lb.

LOUGH PATRICK, MULTYFARNHAM (N43 63)

This is a good tench fishery. A short road to the north off the Multyfarnham–Crookedwood road takes you to waterside parking. The reeded water with soft margins is fishable from a boat. Once producing fabulous catches – well over 100 lb of lovely tench to near 7 lb – it declined in fishing some years ago but is now recovering.

This perfect tench water with muddy bottom and a good growth of lilies is a joy to fish. I have had great sport with fish to 5 lb in the early mornings here and I believe that stocks will soon be at their very best.

LOUGH DERRAVARAGH
RIVER INNY (N41 68)

At Coolnagun Bridge above Lough Derravaragh I fished for years for rudd to 2 lb in the moderate to fast flowing water of the Inny. Investigating further in from my boat, I found that the shallow, weedy and silted area of the lake was full of much bigger rudd well over 2½ lb.

I recall, too, catching my first roach there, and that was the signal for dramatic changes in the whole area. Roach introduced by pike fishermen to the Inny at Finnea produced a population explosion downstream at Derravaragh and soon the rudd were nearly all gone.

The big lake which once produced good brown trout became a reservoir to roach to 1 lb and over and then the pike population increased.

This is a lovely lake, shaped like a long leg with two toes. The top wider section has shallow, weedy areas but along the eastern side of the narrow lake there is a great depth of 50 feet close to the bank. The high Knockeyon Hill overhanging the lake offers a great view of the water

Hugh Gough with a big catch of roach at the exit of the River Inny from Lough Derravaragh

and it is a little wonder that there is such a great depth offshore. This is a great area for winter piking with legered dead baits. There is a big stock of roach in the lake, many to 1½ lb and the best results come in the colder months of the year. The most successful area is at the bottom end of the lake at Knockeyon or Clintons, which is approached off the R394 Castlepollard–Mullingar road. Fishing is along the stretch to the right of the parking area and then round under the hill, where you will discover the very sharp drop in depth.

Farther north along the main road to Castlepollard a left turn at the church and left again leads to waterside parking at Faughalstown, where the bank is clean and the depth offshore 30–40 feet. Fishing at this great depth is variable. From Multyfarnham there is access along the western side of Donore, and north of this area winter piking is good.

RIVER INNY, FINNEA
(N40 81)

Here the river flows out of the big trout fishery of Lough Sheelin and drops over a small weir at the village bridge. From the bridge you can reach the left bank downstream, where there are caravans and a jetty. Here the water, about 4–5 feet deep, rushes down with a hard pull.

In this short stretch roach appear in small numbers from late September and the shoals increase to March, when fabulous catches of good rod-bending fish are taken. Some bream appear in early September but it is later that the roach and hybrids come into their own.

No coarse fishing is allowed above the bridge.

LOUGH KINALE   (N39 81)

Half a mile below the village of Finnea the narrow River Inny rushes into Lough Kinale. Surrounded by belts of reeds, this big water is only fishable from a boat. It once produced great pike over 36 lb but sadly it suffered from overkill. After a rest, it has recovered somewhat and is now yielding fish to over 20 lb. This is a lake with varying depths but in general it does not have sudden shelves. It holds a big stock of good-quality roach, some rudd, only a small stock of bream, hybrids and perch galore.

RIVER INNY   (N40 81)

Below Lough Kinale the Inny becomes slow-moving and weedy, with small pike and roach all over. Near Coolnagun Bridge above Lough Derravaragh there is a competition stretch but in summer this water, while producing some roach and perch, is very weedy. The best results here are with roach in the spring, before the growth of weed starts.

At the outflow near Inny Bridge to the west of Lough Derravaragh the short stretch of river again fishes well for roach in the winter months.

ROYAL CANAL, MULLINGAR   (N44 53)

The town stretch of canal is shallow and heavily weeded. In the town centre between the harbour and Green Bridge there are some tench to 4 lb. At Dublin Bridge, opposite Bella Vista, and to the east there are some tench in weedy, shallow water.

Four miles from town, there are some tench and a fair stock of small rudd at

Ballinae Bridge. At Down's Bridge on the Dublin road there are facilities for wheelchair anglers on a narrow stretch along the left bank, where there are some rudd, perch and a few tench.

DYSART LAKES
LOUGH ANALLA   (N57 62)

While they are associated with the Mullingar area, these few lakes are part of the River Deel, which flows into the River Boyne, and come under the control of the Eastern Regional Fisheries Board.

The waters are approached down a narrow road south off the N52 Mullingar–Delvin road. There are two lakes here. The one to the left of the car park has a solid bank with reeds, and fishing is into clean but weedy water. It fishes well for tench to 5 lb and rudd of over 2½ lb.

This is an isolated and lightly fished water. I have visited it many times, armed with my sickle to clear a swim, and have taken great rudd on bread. Then, on lowering my bait to the bottom, I have had tench galore to 5 lb.

The lower lake to the right, through which the river also flows, does not quite offer the same standard of fishing and I suggest that you fish the top lake only.

TERMONBARRY, CO. ROSCOMMON
CLONDRA, CO. LONGFORD

Termonbarry is a small village on the N5 Longford–Strokestown road on the right bank of the River Shannon. Clondra, on the eastern side of the river, is where the Royal Canal connects with the Shannon. Above the village it is dewatered.

Population 345
OS ½-inch Map No. 12
Longford 5 miles, Strokestown 8 miles, Lanesborough 9 miles, Dublin 80 miles

RIVER SHANNON   (N6 76)

Below the bridge over the main N5 road there is a lock and weir. Above the bridge the river from Lough Forbes – a big reeded water into which the Rinn River flows – moves rapidly through reeded margins. About ¾ mile up river on the right, western, bank there are just a few swims which call for exploring. Just ¼ mile up river, there is a small bay with a few swims with fishing for bream and roach in 10–12 feet of water.

Below the lock some good bream can be taken in the summer, but beware – cruiser traffic is heavy here. Farther down the left bank by Clondra there is a road from which you can fish the Cut 1,100 yards from the canal entry. Here the bank is high but you will find some good swims at the bottom of the stretch. In the early months of the year there are some great roach here, real rod-benders of over 1 lb which can be taken on a stick float.

FEORISH RIVER   (N2 78)

This small and sluggish river is approached to the left off the N5 Strokestown road 1 mile west of Termonbarry. In the summer the river is very weedy and the banks are reeded, but this should not deter you from trying this water, which has given me great sport over the years. It holds a good stock of bream of about 2 lb, with roach, hybrids, perch and pike. This weedy water also yields some good tench to 5 lb.

The lower reaches of the Feorish are inaccessible from land but at its confluence with the Shannon there is some great fishing, see Chapter 9.

ROYAL CANAL   (N2 76)

Roach were transferred from the Cavan area to the Richmond Harbour in the early 1970s and the Clondra–Termonbarry area now has a big stock of roach. The larger fish are found in the main river.

The short canal stretch from the Shannon to the lock holds a good head of roach, bream and perch. The banks are good here and I have experienced wonderful fishing at the point along the left bank where the river rushes into the canal. Fishing varies in this stretch as fish – sometimes big bream – move in from the River Shannon.

CAMLIN RIVER   (N8 78)

This river can be reached where it flows under the N5 road between the two villages. The slow-moving and exposed river holds roach, some bream, hybrids and, upriver, good tench to 5 lb. Here again the roach fishing is seasonal, but in the early months there are often great shoals which provide fine sport in 5–10 feet of water.

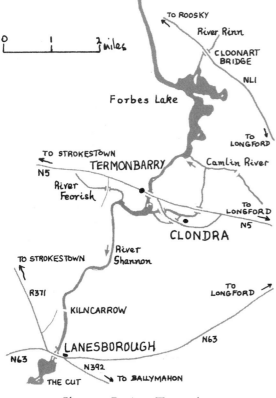

Shannon Region, Termonbarry

LANESBOROUGH, CO. LONGFORD

The River Shannon flowing through bogland from Termonbarry enters Lough Ree here. Dominating the area is the power station, which is fired by peat from the vast areas of bog in this part of the country. On the right bank of the river in Ballyleague there is berthing and a small harbour for the boating traffic.

Population 1,300
OS ½-inch Map No. 12
Longford 9 miles, Ballymahon 13 miles, Roscommon 12 miles, Dublin 82 miles
Club: Lanesborough and Ballyleague Tourist Development Association

RIVER SHANNON

Kilnacarrow (N1 74)

Two miles upriver of Lanesborough, the short stretch at Kilnacarrow, or Bord na Mona Bridge, can be reached down a narrow road through a bog off the R371 Strokestown road. There is parking near the bridge.

The bank below the bridge gives fishing in 6–10 feet of water with a clean bottom. During the winter and spring, if the water is at a low level, you can enjoy good roach fishing on a waggler. In the summer, bream and tench – mostly in the few swims to the right – come to legered bait. The few pegs at the bridge, while having good fishing, can be frustrating with the heavy boat traffic during the summer months.

Lanesborough (N1 69)

It was in the early 1960s that the river stretch caught the eye of anglers. The hot-water outflow from the power station gushed out and dispersed in the waters of the Shannon. Development work on a mid-water island helped to control the outflow of water and diverted it down along the left bank. A dramatic change took place, as the quality fish in the nearby Lough Ree moved up to the warm and weedy water in April and May. The pattern of fishing and the movement of those big fish soon became known and the short stretch became a Mecca for specimen fish anglers. Who would not be attracted in those early days, when the possibilities of landing bream to 9 lb, tench over 6 lb, rudd over 2 lb and rudd × bream hybrids over 4 lb were so great?

Fishing was at night and the bait was bread flake. It was to this stretch that I travelled to fish with Ray Webb, who had his sights set on the Irish record. His persistence and skill rewarded him on the early morning of 25 May 1972, when all in Lanesborough were aroused to weigh a tench which tipped the scales at 7 lb 13¼ oz.

The section below the bridge sometimes produced big fish as they were ambushed on the way to the higher stretch. On receiving a phone call on a Saturday evening in late April 1975, I went to Lanesborough to witness yet another record. This time Peter Dighton and his son were there, with some cracking rudd × bream hybrids. The senior member of the family had one fish which I weighed in at 5 lb 13½ oz – the new Irish record.

The outflow from the power station dictates the fishing, and it is only by observing the stretch over a period of a few days that the movement of the fish will become known. In recent years the few swims down river near the lake get the best results early on. Fish now respond to different baits and, indeed, they no longer only feed at dusk and dawn, as they did in former years.

The depth is 3–4 feet, with much weed

in some swims. Roach have now entered the area and for good sport for quality fish this stretch is a winner in the early months. Some roach × bream hybrids to 2 lb are taken here and I wonder now what change will take place with this wonderful fishery with roach in the stretch!

As lake temperatures rise in June and July, most of the big fish move out into the lake. Do not expect to catch big bream and tench in this stretch after midsummer. The area abounds with small perch which may, in fact, be the only residents here in the midsummer months.

The top of Lough Ree is considered in Chapter 9.

DRUM LAKE, BALLYMAHON   (N12 59)

This small water on the south side of the R392 Lanesborough–Ballymahon road is worth fishing in May–June and September for tench to 5 lb.

There is foot access from the main road to some swims on the forest side. The bank is soft and fishing is into 8–10 feet of water over a muddy bottom. There is a good growth of weed, including lilies along the margins. I found evening fishing good here, using the lift-bite method with maggots as bait.

ATHLONE, CO. WESTMEATH

Athlone is a large and busy town near the centre of the country. It has a long tradition associated with the great River Shannon which flows through the town. After passing over an impressive weir, the river moves slowly through low-lying country to Clonmacnoise.

Population 10,172
OS ½-inch Map Nos 12 and 15
Ballymahon 14 miles, Mullingar 28 miles, Ballinasloe 16 miles, Roscommon 19 miles, Dublin 77 miles
Club: Athlone Anglers' Association

RIVER SHANNON, ATHLONE   (N4 42)

Parking my car near the railway station, I often walk up river along the right bank to the point at the big boulders opposite Charlie's Island. Here the river moves at a moderate to fast pace. There is a forest of ranunculus weed and shoals of good rudd over 2 lb. Float fishing in the shallow, weedy margin is textbook stuff and great sport. Keep a constant trickle of loose feed going in along a precise track and then let your maggot- or bread-baited hook follow. The best time for the rudd is when the river traffic has died down in the late evening.

From a boat the deep hole at the top of Charlie's Island is fishable not only for the rudd but also for good rudd × bream hybrids to over 3 lb. Roach have now appeared in this area and I wonder how long those lovely rudd will remain.

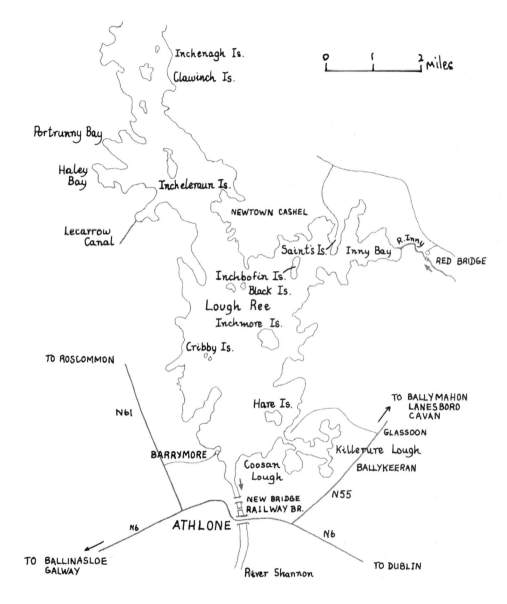

Inchenagh Is.

Clawinch Is.

0   1   2 Miles

Portrunny Bay

Haley Bay

Incheleraun Is.

NEWTOWN CASHEL

Lecarrow Canal

Saint's Is.   Inny Bay   R. Inny

RED BRIDGE

Inchbofin Is.

Black Is.

Lough Ree

Inchmore Is.

Cribby Is.

TO ROSCOMMON

N61

Hare Is.

TO BALLYMAHON
LANESBORO
CAVAN

GLASSOON

Killerure Lough

BARRYMORE

Coosan Lough

BALLYKEERAN

NEW BRIDGE
RAILWAY BR.

N55

N6

ATHLONE

N6

TO BALLINASLOE
GALWAY

River Shannon

TO DUBLIN

Shannon Region, Athlone

Tom Beddar lobs in the groundbait which is necessary on this stretch of the River Shannon at Athlone

Downstream from the weir the river widens between low banks. The Burgess Park stretch to the left and the Meadows Stretch to the right hold big stocks of 4-lb bream from late June on. Catches of well over 100 lb of bream are common along both banks in July, August and September. But at the moment there is a town dump along the bank and several pipes emitting sewage into the river. The scene here at times is not very pleasant and if your preference is for lovely Irish scenery and good fishing you will only get one half of the deal here.

Below the canal, along the left bank, and ½ mile down from the road at the Shamrock Lodge Hotel, there is access over one field to Halligan's Field, where there are some good swims. On this bend of the river fishing is not consistent but after heavy feeding bream catches can be very good. The bank here is high and the depth is 15–18 feet, with the bottom weedy and uneven. There is an abundance of small perch here and in the past year I took some roach which are progressing on their way down river.

LOUGH REE

Barrymore   (N1 47)

This is a short stretch on the west side of the big lough. Access is to the right off the N61 Roscommon road 2 miles from Athlone. The road, by some houses, crosses the railway and leads to the waterside. Fishing is to the left with parking along the bank.

Lough Ree may appear to be daunting, especially when a strong breeze is blowing. It is vital to bait heavily here, so that those shoals can be pinned down in the rich big water. The margins can be float-fished, and this method will reward you in the evening with cracking rudd up to 3 lb. Indeed, the record Irish rudd must surely be swimming around in that part of Lough Ree.

Legering out into the deeper water results in fantastic catches of top-class bream. Specimen bream of over 7½ lb and up to 10 lb move in here and provide great sport in the late summer and autumn. With such bream and rudd, it is natural that hybrids of well over 5 lb are common throughout. Perch, pike and tench also appear in this fabulous water.

East Side (N6 46/N6 57)

Lough Ree has shallow and rocky margins in many places and does not allow for easy bank fishing.

Two miles from Athlone beyond Glasson village, turn left at the sign for Killenure. The long and narrow road leads to the big lake at Killenure, where there are holiday chalets and private houses. Access here is over private ground to the right and permission must be obtained to cross it.

The shore here is very rocky. Directly out is Hare Island. The south-westerlies come from the left and the west wind is somewhat trapped by the opposite island. With those winds blowing and bite detec-

tion difficult, I have taken great bream to 7½ lb as they fed freely in their favourite conditions. Cast far out and you will find a clean bottom in 25–30 feet of water. Farther up the lake there are just a few isolated small sections where you will find the same standard of good bream, but it is open for exploring.

Inny Bay (N10 56)

When my colleagues Jim O'Brien and Michael Byrne carried out technical surveys on this section of the lake many years ago, eyebrows were raised at the results, which showed the presence of vast stocks of rudd × bream hybrids of over 4 lb. This area included the bay from Saint Island across to Muckanagh and in the mouth of the River Inny.

Inny Bay is approached by turning right at the sign 'River Inny – Red Bridge' 2 miles south-west of Ballymahon on the N55. Here there is parking along the riverside, and the water is 3–4 feet deep and pulls moderately to fast. Once a good trout section, it now fills up with good roach in the early season. Half a mile below here the river has a moderate flow with a depth of 10–13 feet and a smooth bottom. The bank is good and open, making fishing just perfect on this fine river, where you can take bream of over 7 lb, roach to 1 lb and hybrids galore.

The River Inny 1½ farther on joins Lough Ree and nearer this point rudd × bream hybrids of over 4 lb appear to add to the sport provided by this great river.

Access to the big lake is farther down the Red Bridge road at Saints Island. Over the old causeway you will find the bank area to the right open and exposed near the church. The lough here is shallow and somewhat stony but I have fished here and found the big bream and hybrids after extensive baiting. Holding these big fish, however, is a problem in such a rich water.

The bream and rudd × bream hybrids move into the inner part of the bay in April, and in early May the whole area can produce record-breaking catches. To reach the inner bay turn off the N55 Ballymahon–Athlone road at Tang and then right after 1 mile over a small road to the low-lying reeded lake. The first sighting is the pumphouse to the left, where there is a river with a high embankment to the left of it. This embankment continues along the margins where dredging operations have opened up a channel to leave a small, shallow, weedy stretch with a high curtain of reeds blocking off the big Lough Ree in front of you. This channel fills up with great bream, hybrids, rudd

and tench to 6 lb in those early months. This area is best approached by boat, as a wide drain along the embankment prevents foot passage.

Parking and access along the open part of the lake is through the kind permission of the landowner, Mr Fox. Please call at the house to ask permission.

A vast spawning area for very big fish is formed by the extensive shallows and often flooded pools where the Inny enters the lake. The fish stop feeding for some time before moving out into the lake for the rest of the year. It is here and in other similar situations that I have found anglers abusing fish terribly by cramming ripe fish into nets and holding them for long periods. Please give our fish a chance and let nature take its course at this time of the year. Always handle fish with care and return them carefully to the water.

CASTLECOOTE, CO. ROSCOMMON

This is a small and tidy village along the west side of the Upper River Suck, 5 miles from Roscommon town.

Population 206
OS ½-inch Map No. 12
Roscommon 5 miles, Lanesborough 7 miles, Dublin 95 miles
Club: Athleague Angling Club

RIVER SUCK (M80 65)

In its upper region, the River Suck has long stretches of fast and shallow water and it is near Castlecoote that good shoals of bream first appear.

Dunamon Bridge

The river is shallow at Dunamon Bridge,

where there is an abundance of small rudd and perch. I have recently been taking small roach from this section of the river and soon this whole river will change dramatically as that species spreads. Below the bridge the river is sluggish and deeper and yields some good bream catches. This section is best approached from Castlecoote over the bridge along

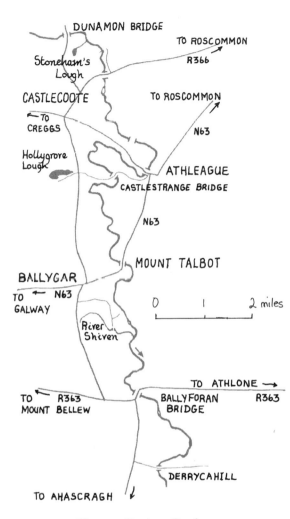

Shannon Region, Castlecoote

great catches here. Seldom fished, this stretch is well worth a try.

Castlecoote

At Castlecoote bridge the river is shallow but the bream shoals appear in the deeper, slower water 2 miles downstream. And so it continues, with long stretches of deep water alternating with short sections of fast shallows, which hold good rudd.

Athleague

Just above the bridge at Athleague there are some good swims along the right bank which can be approached from a point 500 yards down the Glenamaddy road. Here you will find some good bream and rudd. Farther up at Castle-strange Bridge there is access to a short and interesting stretch, with parking before the bridge at the house. The pool to the left has provided me with great sport for rudd to 1½ lb and bream to 4 lb. A lovely place, which is seldom fished. It· has limited space.

Mount Talbot

I seldom cross Mount Talbot bridge without looking over to locate the rudd shoals. In 1 foot of water and with a bunch of maggots on a size 10 hook I have taken rudd of well over 2 lb in the fast water here.

Ballygar

Downstream by the village of Ballygar the river deepens and is slow moving. This is a gem of a stretch, and holds lovely bream to 6 lb, rudd galore and perch. The River Shiven, a good trout water under the control of the Shannon

the Roscommon road and first left after ½ mile. About ¾ mile down the narrow road a stile and a very rough field bring you to the bankside, which is firm and clean.

Fishing here calls for heavy baiting to hold the wild and roving shoals of bream. Legering with caster-and-worm-baited hook in 12 feet of water, I have taken

Regional Fisheries Board, enters the River Suck here. No doubt the variety of fodder fish contributes to the good-quality pike which are to be found in the Suck.

To reach this stretch turn left ½ mile from Ballygar on the Ballyforan road. Access to the river is by another small road to the left about ½ mile on past the cemetery.

STONEHAM'S LAKE (M79 64)

This small lake lies close to the River Suck in the forest to the east of the Castlecoote–Donamon road. It has muddy and shallow margins and is best fished from a boat. This rich water offers great fishing and I often visualize the whole area flooded in the winter with shoals of big Suck bream moving into the still water here. During the summer the rudd and particularly rudd × bream hybrids well over 3 lb abound here to give great sport.

HOLLYGROVE LAKE
(M79 58)

Take the road north off the N63 at Ballygar village and follow it for 6 miles until you reach a crossroads. Here turn left, then left again at the signpost. The heavily reeded 60-acre lake lies to the left of this road. Fishing here is from stands. A quiet water with clusters of lilies, it smells of tench!

Early-morning fishing in mid-June. The mist is hanging over the water, the moorhens break the stillness and my float rises and falls flat. A lovely lift bite and I am into a tench of about 5 lb. That is the way it goes on this lovely water, which yields tench to 6½ lb, rudd to 2 lb, some bream, hybrids, perch and pike.

BALLINASLOE, CO. GALWAY

This busy market town is famous for its horse fair, held in October. The River Suck from Castlecoote, Ballygar and Ballyforan flows through the town on its way to the River Shannon at Shannonbridge.

Population 6,840
OS ½-inch Map No. 15
Galway 40 miles, Athlone 16 miles, Shannonbridge 16 miles, Dublin 94 miles
Club: Ballinasloe Angling Festival Committee

RIVER SUCK

Up River (M82 46)

At Ballyforan bridge, on the R363 road from Athlone and the R357 from Ballinasloe, the River Suck moves up a gear, with bream shoals increasing in numbers and the quality of the fish improving. Fast and slow stretches of river continue to alternate.

Derrycahill Bridge

A good bream section can be reached by turning east off the R358 north of Ahascragh. A signposted road to the right leads over a bog to Derrycahill bridge, which is in flat peat land.

Down river along the left bank there are good bream shoals in the early season at the left bend. Up river a long walk up the left bank will bring you to great shoals of bream to 5 lb. About ¾ mile farther along this bog road a small road to the left leads you close to the water farther up-stream. Here again you will find good bream.

Daly's Grove   (M84 40)

Daly's Grove, where the river has more shallows with weed and good rudd to 2 lb are to be found, can be reached from Ahascragh. However, it is the great bream shoals abounding in the slow-moving stretch which are the attraction. Catches of 3½-lb bream throughout the summer often top the 100-lb mark, making this one of the Suck's most productive stretches.

Please respect the landowners' property here and do not park in fields or block entries.

RIVER SUCK

Down River

Just downstream of Ballinasloe by the Square D Factory at Pollboy, shoals of quality bream to 8 or 9 lb appear, but the

Bill Curton with a lovely 5 lb tench, taken below Coreen Ford, on the River Suck between Ballinasloe and Shannonbridge

water conditions are not pleasant in this area.

Culliagh boathouse lies at the end of a bog road south-west at the signpost off the R357 Ballinasloe–Shannonbridge road. Below here, the wide river holds great bream throughout the summer, but in the early summer the shoals here are mostly located at the high clean bank ½ mile downstream of the boathouse. Along here you will often find rudd, which stay in the lily beds on the far right bank. Farther along the Shannonbridge road, the next stretch is approached at the signpost to the right for Coreen. Half a mile along this road there is a track to the right through the bog known as The 'Plastic Road'. This road joins up with the Culliagh boathouse road and you should beware of travelling here in wet conditions.

The river here also holds bream shoals and some tench. At Coreen Ford car park, access is easy to the pool to the left and here I have taken rudd of over 2 lb just at the edge of the fast flow. Two fields down from here at the bushes there are some productive bream swims, where catches of over 80 lb are taken, with fish to 4 lb. The same water holds good tench to 6 lb, with rudd, perch and pike.

The river now continues slowly to Shannonbridge and the River Shannon, 3 miles away.

SHANNONBRIDGE, CO. OFFALY

This is a small village on the eastern side of the River Shannon. The river is bridged by an impressive sixteen-arched structure, which was completed in 1757. The village is dominated by the large power station.

Population 374
OS ½-inch Map No. 15
Ballinasloe 8 miles, Athlone 15 miles, Banagher 10 miles, Dublin 85 miles
Club: Shannonbridge Anglers Association

RIVER SHANNON   (M97 25)

Up river the banks are heavily reeded at Clonmacnoise and it is just above Shannonbridge along the left (eastern) bank that there are some clear swims.

The western bank has some swims which produce bream in the summer months. Leave the road on the Ballinasloe side, go down the steps at the bridge, and walk ¼ mile up river to the swims, which are behind the island.

Down along the right bank the river is shallow and weedy, producing good rudd. The margin then gets heavily reeded and has scrub but with a struggle you can find some good bream swims 500 yards down. The area also holds great rudd × bream hybrids of over 3 lb.

Excellent fishing can be found below the power station along the left bank off the R357 road. The hot water outflow rushes across the river here and the level of water dictates its direction. Great shoals of bream, rudd × bream hybrids, tench and perch frequent this area and fishing can be superb. The streaks of hot water flowing through the river dictate

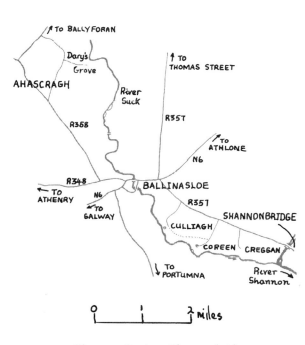

Shannon Region, Shannonbridge

ing into the right stream of water can be critical. Tench of over 6 lb are taken here, while rudd over 2 lb, rudd × bream hybrids over 4 lb and bream averaging 3½ lb are present, making this a first-class fishery.

RIVER SUCK   (M97 24)

From Coreen Ford this river flows slowly between low banks and is liable to flood. The next stretch is approached from the left of the Shannonbridge–Ballinasloe road at the church and signpost. Park with care and do not enter fields or obstruct entries. At the spot where there are some submerged rocks near a bend in the river good catches of bream are taken throughout the summer, though I have always found this area to be patchy and uncertain.

Another stretch is at Rarabeg, closer to Shannonbridge, just a short distance above the confluence with the Shannon. Here I have had good catches of rudd × bream hybrids in 15–25 feet of water, and many of those great fighting fish tipped the scales at 4 lb.

the location of the fish and it is vital that you spend some time in searching for the shoals. When you have found them, cast-

---

BANAGHER, CO. OFFALY

Banagher is a small and pleasant town on the east side of the River Shannon near Shannon Harbour, where the Grand Canal joins the river.

Population 1,500
OS ½-inch Map No. 15
Shannonbridge 10 miles, Portumna 14 miles, Ballinasloe 21 miles, Athlone 24 miles

---

RIVER SHANNON   (N1 16)

The River Brosna and the Grand Canal join with River Shannon at Shannon Harbour, 2 miles up river of Banagher. Below this point, the area known as Bullock

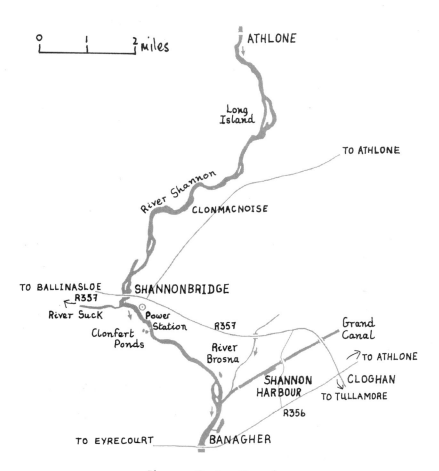

Shannon Region, Banagher

Island has some backwaters which yield fabulous fishing, particularly in the early season. Access is off the Banagher–Shannon Harbour road, just to the west over the bridge at the bend in the road. Permission must be obtained to cross the land here. The small, narrow and shallow backwater holds great stocks of bream, rudd, hybrids, tench, perch and pike. This area can also be reached from the river by a narrow channel, as described in Chapter 9.

Across the bridge at Banagher and down along the right bank there are some good swims which give excellent sport for rudd and hybrids. This area is weedy, but in the evening I have had fantastic sport for those rudd, fishing a waggler at 3 feet.

The vegetable-processing factory (the

'Pea Factory'), a short distance down river off the R356 Eyrecourt road was once a Mecca for bream anglers, but since the factory ceased operating the fish shoals have moved elsewhere. However, not all have gone and there still remains some good fishing for bream and rudd to the left of the entry here.

PORTUMNA, CO. GALWAY

Portumna is a small and tidy town at the head of the last of the River Shannon's big lakes. The Shannon here is also a busy centre for cruisers during the summer months.

Population 1,062
OS ½-inch Map No. 15
Banagher 16 miles, Ballinasloe 20 miles, Dublin 94 miles
Club: Portumna Development Company

FRIAR'S LOUGH, LORRHA, CO. TIPPERARY   (M91 5)

This 12-acre lake is located to the east of Portumna. Turn south to Lorrha 3 miles along the R489 Birr road. Turn right in the village, and right again ½ mile on by the old ruined abbey. This long narrow lane (keeping right) leads to a gate and to a field beside the lake. Access and parking are through the kind permission of the landowner. Please respect the property, close the gate, park carefully and do not leave litter in the field or along the bank.

Friar's Lough is a lovely rich fishery with a good stock of bream, rudd, hybrids, perch and pike. There is a small fringe of reeds, with lilies and other weed. The margins in wet weather will be soft. There is a gradual decline to 8–14 feet in the middle, where the bottom is smooth.

The bream will respond to baiting but excessive noise will put the fish off. The bream run to 4 lb and catches to 100 lb can be expected. While fishing this water I used a leger, but kept my float rod set up for the rudd. Rudd to 1½ lb cruise up and down the middle of the lake, and with a

3-swan Drennan waggler I was able to cast to the middle and pick up some lovely fish.

This isolated lake in Co. Tipperary is easily reached and really must be given an early-morning session for its fantastic sport.

RIVER SHANNON

Portumna Bridge   (M87 5)

At the bridge there is an island whose tip protrudes up river, and here there are swims for about five anglers. The bridge road has heavy traffic and I advise you to drop off your tackle at the gate opposite the bridgekeeper's house and then park along the nearby quay off the road.

The bank cannot be fished in high water. There is much weed in the swims during the summer months and fishing is into a depth of 8–12 feet. In the early season these swims will yield great bream to 7 lb and rudd to 1½ lb. In the summer this area is frequented by boats in all shapes and sizes. If you have problems fishing, pack up and move to the next

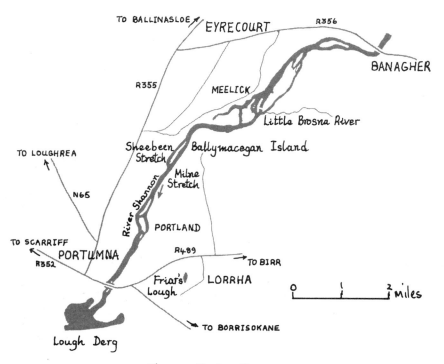

Shannon Region, Portumna

stretch up river at Tirnascragh, which is quiet.

Ballymacegan (Milne stretch)
(M91 11)

Turn north at the sign for Ballymacegan, 4 miles from Portumna on the R489 Birr road. This road, through rich farmland, leads to Milne's Pub and twenty yards farther on an old and narrow lane on the left gives access to the river. This lane was used by those fishing for salmon at White's Ford in bygone days. The story is told that a judge came up from the river in 1884 to partake of some liquid refreshment in the local shebeen. On learning

that the egg-nogg and poteen mixture which made his toes curl up was home-brewed, he forthwith presented the owner with a licence to sell spirits.

Back to the river! The short few swims here in the main channel are never fished and I can report that this is another section of the great Shannon which yields great bream. I took 50 lb of bream to 6 lb just out over the shelf in weedy water, in a virgin swim without any prebaiting. Rudd also to 1 lb made my first expedition to this Milne stretch in Co. Tipperary a pleasure, which I must experience again. This point in the river is opposite Bally-macegan Island and the backwater stretch in Co. Galway at Tirnascragh.

On my first visit to the new Milne Stretch of the River Shannon, north of Portumna,
I took bream and rudd galore on the leger

Tirnascragh–Sheebeen Stretch
(M90 11)

You approach this great stretch off the R355 Portumna–Ballinasloe road at the high pylons, Ferrick's shop and the Eyrecourt sign to the right. After ½ mile turn right at the sign 'Bank Fishing'. The main access to the river is 1 mile on at the sign 'Bank Fishing' and through the gate on the right. Drive through the field and park at the end beside the drainage canal. A short walk of 30 yards and you are at the high and good bank.

The Sheebeen stretch, 80 yards wide, is a backwater of the main river, behind Ballymacegan Island. The flow is moderate and the depth 15–25 feet, with a good bottom. Not open to cruiser traffic, the water is quiet and the bank faces east.

On my first serious approach to this stretch I prebaited with 20 lb of cereal bait with casters. My first cast on the following morning connected with a bream of 6 lb. Throughout the day my tip did not have a moment to settle, as bream after bream came to my size 14 hook baited with red maggots.

This cracking stretch can accommodate nearly 100 anglers and shows the River Shannon at its best, offering bream to 7 lb and rudd to 2 lb. The genial landowner, Mick Madden, will welcome you as he did me, when he watched me take – was it 200 lb?

Meelick (M95 14)

Just a few miles up river from Bally-macegan Island is the complex of water at Meelick. Continue along the approach road to the Sheeban stretch, keep right, and you arrive at the jetty on the River Shannon.

This is at the top of the Meelick water and 30 yards to the left of the jetty you will find bream in a depth of 8–12 feet. There is a considerable pull, as the big weir is just down to the right. The fast but shallow water below the weir is fantastic for great rudd × bream hybrids and rudd, but it is best fished from a boat.

The rapid water then moves quietly around the island, and below the big Victoria Lock there is a quiet back channel along the right bank. This is approached from the Abbey, through the gates and by the pumphouse at the top of the drainage canal. The channel here yields some good bream, rudd and perch. Tench appear in many of the backwater pools and also in this channel in May and June.

The Meelick area is steeped in history and the complexity of the waters makes it an interesting place to look over and explore, with or without a rod.

LOUGH DERG (M82 00)

The last of the Shannon's great lakes, with an abundance of big bream, rudd, rudd × bream hybrids, tench, perch and pike, is seldom seriously fished for those common coarse fish species. The lake has a tradition of trout and pike fishing only, and pinpointing all the accessible bankside swims would take another book and years of research.

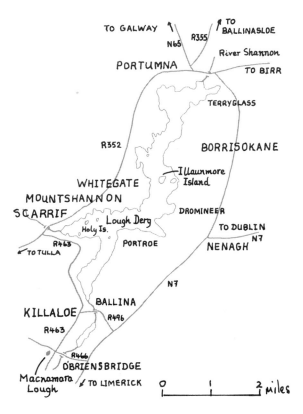

Shannon Region, Lough Derg

In a boat an echo-sounder is a great advantage on this big water, and it has helped me to locate some great shoals. I have seen shoals of tench during the spawning season in late June in the bays near Hare Island and Rinnalough Point churning up the marl in the shallows and colouring great areas of water. The margins of this big water, with rocks and islands of rushes and reeds, are the home of vast stocks of coarse fish. The best method of fishing these areas is from a boat, but the wind can rise quickly on such a big water so always take care.

Rossmore Jetty

At Rossmore jetty you can have great sport for rudd over 2 lb, and after heavy baiting from the rocky margin to the left I took bream.

Caravan Park

Lough Derg Caravan Park offers an ideal situation, with fishing from stands into good water for bream. The owner, Mike Mannion, fishes and feeds the swims regularly, so the good shoals do not wander far from here.

This is a lovely place to fish, looking over at the Arra Mountains, which slide into the opposite side of the lake. I have legered here into 12–14 feet of water and taken great catches, including bream to 7 lb. For information on these swims, contact the owner: Mike Mannion, Lough Derg Caravan Park, Killaloe, Co. Clare.

Scarriff

The Scarriff River enters Lough Ree below Scarriff and the slow-moving water down from the quay at Tuamgraney holds some bream and perch. Up river from Scarriff, and closer to Lough O'Grady, there are better swims for bream to 3 lb, rudd and perch. The lower section of this river near the lake yields good pike in the autumn.

O'BRIEN'S BRIDGE

With Mount Pellier on the left bank, the village of O'Brien's Bridge in Co. Clare is the last of the rural coarse-angling centres on the Shannon. Fishing here is in the big, wide river and also in the many East Clare lakes just a short distance away towards Broadford and Tulla.

Population 451
OS ½-inch Map No. 15
Limerick 9 miles, Broadford 6 miles, Tulla 12 miles, Dublin 112 miles

---

RIVER SHANNON, O'BRIEN'S BRIDGE   (R66 67)

Below the Parteen Dam there is a match stretch which can accommodate 60-plus anglers. During matches, access to the top pegs is easy from a path which leads to waterside parking. For normal fishing, there is easy foot access up river to the well developed stretch, where swims are cleared and pegs numbered.

The river is wide and a short distance above the first stile there is a small island of rushes. Above here, in 12–18 feet of water, there are some good swims where prebaiting will reward you with 50–80 lb of good bream. The river here produces rudd, and with roach now appearing in this stretch it is reasonable to assume that an explosion of this species will occur here soon.

Five hundred yards below the bridge there is easy access right to the waterside for handicapped anglers at The Arches. This point is below the overhead cables and there is a concrete strip along the bank. Here there are good bream shoals, with rudd, perch, some roach and pike.

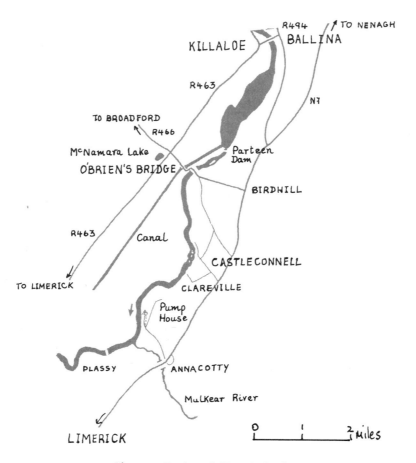

Shannon Region, O'Brien's Bridge

Across the bridge and up the hill to the left there is access by the cemetery to some good swims behind Inishlosky Island. Here the depth is 12–20 feet and there are bream and some very good shoals of rudd to 2 lb.

PADDY McNAMARA LAKE
(R66 66)

This 10-acre lake lies close to O'Brien's Bridge at the junction of the R463

Limerick–Killaloe road and the R466 O'Brien's Bridge–Broadford road. This quiet water is named after my late colleague and friend, Paddy Mac. Patrick – to his Clare friends – had worked in fisheries in his home county for thirty years organizing, surveying and developing the waters there. It is fitting that the locals should have named a lake after this fine gentleman of the water.

A shallow lake, it has some good swims near the easy access from the road. Fishing is into 8–11 feet of water, with a

HELP THE PIKE SURVIVE
PUT IT BACK ALIVE
DEN HECHT NICHT
        GEFAHRDEN
IMMER ZURUCKWERFEN
POUR QUE VIVE LE BROCHET
FAUT LE REJETER

WILDLIFE SANCTUARY

Local clubs are keen to conserve stocks of pike. This sign is erected on the River Shannon at O'Brien's Bridge

weedy bottom. The lake had held some small rudd and perch and over the years Paddy stocked it with tench and carp. Now those fish – tench to 4 lb and carp to 6 lb – are coming to the net. As those fish thrive and anglers enjoy good sport in this corner of Co. Clare, my memory of a dear friend will never diminish.

RIVER SHANNON

The River Shannon from the Parteen Dam to Limerick holds salmon and you are reminded that the water is controlled by the Electricity Supply Board. The river also holds good stocks of coarse fish, as at O'Brien's Bridge, but the coarse angler must exercise care not to fish the private and restricted salmon waters. If in doubt, always seek information at a local level or from the ESB.

Castleconnell (R66 63)

Turn west at Castleconnell, the N7 Nenagh–Limerick road, and follow the road up river to the car park at the World's End. A quarter-mile by the diving board there are good swims for bream. I have taken fish to 4 lb in 15–20 feet of water close in. Seldom fished, this stretch also has some roach, which will soon change the fishing pattern here.

Nearly ¾ mile south of Castleconnell a road to the west off the N7 leads to the

Joseph Maloney Jr, at O'Brien's Bridge. This is a wide stretch of the River Shannon where the depth is 15 to 20 feet and holds bream and roach

well-known salmon-fishing Clareville stretch. Five hundred yards downstream the sluggish river produces great catches of roach in the cold months of the year. Bream, too, appear in the summer, and catches up to 80 lb are taken.

Annacotty   (R60 64)

This stretch down river from Castleconnell and Clareville is approached off the main N7 road at the village and under the bridge by the Mulkear River. Turn left after 1,100 yards and after another ¼ mile left again through the big gates to the pumphouse.

Parking is beside the water and access is easy. Fishing along this low bank to the left and right can be rewarding, with good catches of bream, rudd, roach, hybrids and perch. I have explored the river between here and Clareville by boat. Fishing is great for rudd × bream hybrids over 5 lb and rudd galore to 2 lb. Bream abound here, with lovely fish to 6 lb, but these swims can only be reached by boat.

Limerick City   (R61 59)

The river just up from the heart of the city and above the canal at Plassy holds great stocks of bream, which average 3½ lb. The best swims are just below the old navigation posts where the depth is 7–10 feet. Great catches to 200 lb of bream to 5 lb are taken here.

This wonderful section of the river was once popular with anglers but is now seldom fished. Sadly, this area is now frequented by undesirables and you must keep a vigilant eye on your parked car and tackle. The best access is from the new housing development, College Court, and then down to the pegs. Check locally about access and parking before fishing in this, the last section of the long River Shannon.

COROFIN, CO. CLARE

Corofin is a lovely village beside the game-fishing water of Inchiquin lake. The village is also the gateway to the Burren, a country with distinctive scenery.

Population 314
OS ½-inch Map No. 14
Ennis 8 miles, Gort 15 miles, Limerick 32 miles, Shannon 24 miles

ATEDAUN LAKE   (R29 88)

Just to the right of the R460 Gort road ¼ mile from Corofin, parking is at the waterside. The River Fergus flows from Inchiquin Lake through this rich water. The margins are shallow and during the summer there is a prolific growth of weed in its clear waters. This is a special lake, one of my favourites, and it keeps drawing me back. Just pull up some of the weed and turn over some waterside stones and you will see the mass of invertebrates which provide food for the quality fish here. It is a little wonder that Atedaun Lake holds big stocks of lovely rudd, well over the Irish record weight of 3 lb 1 oz. This lake is exposed and has no bankside vegetation but there are massive boulders along part of the shore and in the water. Rudd fishing is best on calm days, when you can see the cruising shoals. Loose-feed in a clear area from a boat and the Irish record could be yours. This rich water yields great tench of over 6 lb in May and June. Good pike and perch are also to be found here and legered rudd in the winter will reward you with some cracking pike. Boats may be hired at Burke's shop in Corofin.

BALLYCULLINAN LAKE
(R29 86)

This reed-fringed lake is one mile from Corofin along the R476 Ennis road. Fishable only from a boat, its clear water holds rudd to 2 lb, with some bream only and a fair stock of those fighting rudd × bream hybrids which are over the specimen weight of 3 lb. The lake also holds a stock of pike around 8–10 lb. For boat hire, contact Burke's shop in the village.

There are several lakes north of Corofin which have the same characteristics, reeded with rocky margins. These lakes provide fair sport for pike, perch and some rudd.

EAST CLARE LAKES

The area between the villages of Tulla, Feakle and Broadford has a great number

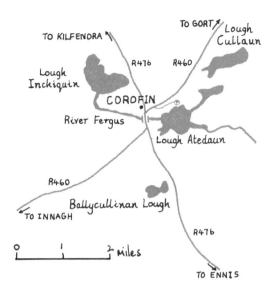

Shannon Region, Corofin

of lakes which offer a variety of species in this lovely coastal county.

ROSSLARA LAKE   (R53 82)

This rich 45-acre lake is 4 miles north-east of Tulla and has easy access from a car park. It is reeded in most places but there are good swims to the right and over the stile. Fishing is into 6–12 feet of water, with the near swims beside the island being shallow. There is weed here and tench to 6 lb can be found in early-morning sessions. The water also yields good bream to 5 lb and an abundance of small rudd and perch. This rich water is always worth exploring and some day you will find me fishing the nooks along the southern margins from a boat.

MARYFORT LAKES
CASTLE LAKE   (M52 81)

These two small waters are just a short distance from Rosslara Lake.

Castle Lake is about 2 acres and has soft margins, but here there are tench to 4 lb. Nearby is the 10-acre Maryfort Lake, which can be reached over a field. It is fringed with reeds but there is one short clean stretch where you can fish into 8–12 feet of water. I have enjoyed great evenings here with rudd galore to 1 lb and small tench to 3 lb. The lake also holds a small stock of small bream and some hybrids.

DROMORE LAKE   (R55 83)

Take the R352 Bodyke road and after 5 miles turn left onto the R468 Feakle road. Turn left again at Biddy Early's Lake and after ½ mile you will find Dromore Lake on your left. This water has a thick belt of reeds and soft margins. I put my boat on this lake and without pre-baiting got right into lovely bream, which averaged 4 lb. I float-fished at 5 feet close to the reeds and lilies, taking rudd to 1½ lb, but soon my fishing ceased as pike scattered the shoals. I was prompted to return for a winter session of pike and took fish to 16 lb.

SILVERGROVE LAKE
(Lough Bridget)   (R56 80)

Alongside the R352 Bodyke road 5 miles from Tulla, this is a long lake with an untidy shape. It can be fished at several places.

Shannon Region, Tulla

There is parking at the main road and a path leads to the first swims on the 'Island'. This area is liable to flood, as the banks are low. There are some top-rate swims to the left here and then to the right, at the corner. This is a great fishery which yields tench over 6 lb and also bream to 6 lb.

The small road to the right off the main road leads to car parks which give access to another section of the lake. Here at Kelly's Shore there are good perch to 1 lb and rudd to 1¾ lb. The lake can also be fished along the western side, but access is over private land at Derrymore.

COOLBAWN LAKE   (R55 80)

Turn right off the Bodyke road 4 miles from Tulla and left at the crossroads. Coolbawn Lake is small and settled between hills. Access is easy over one field and there are good swims here for tench to 4 lb. This is another of those small Clare lakes where you can have comfortable fishing for rudd and bream. Fishing is over a weedy and often dirty bottom, where you could lose lead. I have found good results here on the waggler set at 8–10 feet.

KILGORY LAKE   (R54 78)

Four miles from Tulla turn left off the Broadford road and then right at the signpost. There is parking near this 65-acre lake, which has a thick belt of reeds round its margins. This is a rich water with a good stock of bream to 5 lb and tench to 6 lb. Rudd and small perch dominate and on many a summer session

I found a host of good pike feeding on those fish along the margins.

There are good swims to the left of the entry to the stile and farther along at stands near the end. To the right of the car park entry and over the footbridge the last few swims are also productive. Fishing is into 10–14 feet of water and there is some weed. Prebaiting on this good water and regular feeding during fishing will hold the bream. This lake responded instantly to a heavy raking one morning for tench, which came to my sweetcorn-baited size 10 hook, fished close in on a float.

DOON LAKE   (R55 74)

One mile west of Broadford, Doon comprises two lakes joined by a narrow channel. A big water, it can be fished from many sides.

Doorus Shore

The car park is signposted off the O'Callaghan's Mills–Tulla road 2½ miles from Tulla. Foot access is down a long, steep hill. The bank is good and fishing is into 7–12 feet of water with some bottom weed. This is a most productive stretch, with bream galore around 1½–2 lb. There is an abundance of rudd and perch along this area. Roach, recently introduced, are now giving good sport here.

Creamery Shore

Access is easy from the roadside picnic area. The bank here is low and liable to flood. The bream swims are to the left into the forest. This area fishes best, when there is a fresh wind blowing from the left.

O'Donnell's Shore

This section of the lake faces north and is easily accessible from the roadside car park on the Broadford–Kilkishen road. The bank is low and fishing is into shallow water. Long casting is essential to pick up the abundant bream of 1–2 lb. This area has rudd and perch and now roach are adding another dimension to the water. There is also a good stock of small pike in this lake which no doubt will thrive on the recently introduced roach.

SHANDANGAN LAKE
(R47 72)

This lake lies to the left of the R462 Killishen–Limerick road 1 mile from Tulla.

A weedy and reed-fringed water, it has soft margins and on viewing it you will nearly feel the tench. Parking is along the narrow road, with fishing from some nearby stands. I took 50 lb of lovely rudd here in a short session and watched the display of tench spawning in late June. Those tench to 5 lb were only 10 feet from my swim but their thrashing about did not frighten the usually shy rudd.

The small spur off this lake called Hogan's Lake has very soft margins, where there are one or two swims. This area is the home of some great tench and it is worth exploring. Access is over private land and you should seek permission from the landowner.

THE CULLAUN CHAIN
(Rathluby, Stone's, Callaghan's, Cullaun and Gortnacorragh Lakes)
(R47 73)

This is a string of gems. Near the well-signposted tourist attraction at Crag-gaunowen, these five lakes lie below steep hills which command panoramic views.

This is the lovely Callaun Chain of lakes in Co. Clare which produces rich stocks of quality bream, tench, rudd and pike

The top lake, Rathluby, is heavily fringed with rushes and reeds but there are some clear swims. Hardy anglers will carry a boat over the fields to this water. Permission must be got to cross land here and anglers must keep the bank free of litter. Rathluby Lake is seldom fished and the tench over 6 lb, bream over 7 lb and good rudd enjoy complete freedom. The lower lakes are approached to the right (nearly opposite the Craggaunowen en-

try) by Mr O'Brien's house through a gate and to parking overlooking Callaghan's Lake.

The second water of the Chain, Stone's Lake, is a reeded water with stands and is reached by a stile. The margins have beds of lilies and fishing is often from the big stones opposite. Here there is a good stock of tench of over 6 lb and bream to 8 lb. A lovely water!

The next lake is heavily reeded with

Tim Queally, local Tulla angler, landed the lovely two-toned bream of 9 lb 6 oz on Stone's Lake

some fishing space, and again there are tench, some bream and rudd.

Callaghan's Lake, near the car park, is also reeded and has some swims for tench, rudd and some bream.

Cullaun Lake is big and has no good fishing swims from the bank, but from a boat you can have some good sport close to the top near the entry of the stream from Gortnacorragh Lake.

Gortnacorragh Lake is inaccessible and unfished and it is fantastic for big fish. It lies in a forested area and is shaded. On many occasions I have gone up the stream to this great water for those rudd × bream hybrids which tip the scales at well over 5 lb.

The Cullaun Chain is a great place to explore. Don't forget the pike rod – they grow big here.

GARRURA LAKE   (R49 79)

This small lake is signposted to the left of the road about 1 mile east of Tulla. Access is easy. With reeds, it has a soft margin but yields, from the few swims, some fine tench to 5 lb. There are also some small rudd and perch in this water, which fishes best in May and June.

CLONDANAGH LAKE
(R50 83)

North of Tulla town, turn right at the junction with the R462 Gort road. Cross the crossroads after 2 miles and then right at the next crossroads. The reeded lake has waterside parking. Bank space is limited and fishing is into 10–12 feet of water, with some weed. The water holds only some bream but I landed good hybrids to 2½ lb with rudd also to 2 lb.

Listed above are most of the waters in this area which are fishable from the bank. Most of them hold bream. However, there are many other lakes here which have wide belts of reeds and rushes and hold stocks of perch, rudd and pike. Some of these waters should be explored for good pike. With roach now in some waters in this part of Ireland, it is only a matter of time before that species enters the big pike and perch waters and provides additional food for the pike.

Fin Lake, Rosroe Lake and Castle Lake south of Kilkishen are well worth a try for pike fishing from a boat. And Lough Graney, in lovely countryside north of Feakle, has given me great sport from a boat for pike and also good bream to 6 lb.

South-Western Region

South-Western Fisheries Region

This region comprises the waters in Counties Cork and Kerry. The main river system is the River Lee, which flows east from its source in the mountains between the two counties to Cork City. This mixed fishery and the beautiful Lee Valley dominates the region and is of great interest to the coarse fisherman.

MACROOM, CO. CORK

Macroom is a busy market town which is dominated by the lovely River Lee, whose waters broaden at the big manmade lakes which feed the nearby hydroelectric power station.

Population 2,480
OS ½-inch Map No. 21
Cork 24 miles, Mallow 25 miles, Dublin 184 miles.
Club: Cork and District Pike Anglers Club

LOUGH ALLUA (Inchigeela Lakes) (W29 68)

Rising west of Macroom, the River Lee flows through beautiful country to Lough Allua. This long lake, through which the river flows, lies between Ballingeary and Inchigeela and is sometimes called Inchigeela Lakes. It holds a big stock of perch and some rudd, which provide the fodder for the good head of pike. This water can be fished from the bank along the north road (R584) near Inchigeela and farther along where the road runs close to the water. Along the southern shore, there are several places which provide good bank fishing and these too are near the road. Many anglers troll for pike here and boats may be hired from Creedon's Hotel in Inchigeela.

MIDDLE RIVER LEE (W36 72)

Along the left bank of the Lee from Toons Village to above Dromcarra bridge there are some deep pools which hold pike and perch.

THE GEARAGH (W32 71)

The Gearagh is a strange area of alluvial forest, sometimes under water, with many old tree stumps. There is good

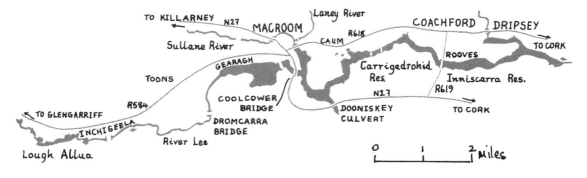

South-Western Region, Macroom

fishing for pike and perch from the old Gearagh road (north side) and at Quarry Pond.

MacLONIAGH BRIDGE

Fish the sandpit backwater area above the bridge for pike, perch and some rudd.

COOLCOWER BRIDGE

This stretch is best fished from the south bank to the point. Then you can move south towards MacLoniagh Bridge but in this area beware of the submerged snags. This area produces a lot of perch in the summer months.

The big reservoir can be fished from a boat by permission, but do remember that those submerged tree stumps will cause problems.

DOONISKEY CULVERT, BALLYTRASNA

This small spur off the big lake is approached off the N22 Cork road. Good sport for rudd is provided in a small pond below the minor road.

CARRIGADROHID RESERVOIR   (W39 72)

This area lies along the northern road to Cork (R618) near Caum Church. The bay approached by the old road to the right holds a good head of perch and rudd. Two small ponds near here, McCull's and Buckley's, hold perch, rudd and (McCull's) tench.

Farther down the system there are several places worth a try. The small bay at Rooves bridge holds small perch and rudd.

NOTE
The waters of the Lee system are controlled by the ESB and all regulations must be adhered to. The waters also hold brown trout and you are advised to note all club rules. Pike-angling clubs in this area have a ruling that all pike caught in these lakes be returned alive to the water.

Anglers wishing to put boats on either reservoir must obtain prior permission from the ESB.

Anglers who catch tagged pike are requested to give details of location, weight and size of fish to the South-Western Regional Fisheries Board.

THE LOUGH, CORK CITY
(W66 71)

This 10-acre lake can be approached off the Western Road in Cork City. When I first visited it, I was surprised to find that it was schoolboys who had learned to tackle this unique water. This is the lake which holds the record Irish carp, weighing 25 lb.

The lake is surrounded by a green area and a concrete path runs along the margin. There is an island near one side and the whole water is a wildfowl sanctuary, with hundreds of birds. The scene on a summer's day is one of mothers with children enjoying themselves and being entertained by the foraging birds.

I found setting up in the late evening and fishing through the night to be the most rewarding and peaceful approach. With 20-lb carp present, you cannot fish light; above all, you must not leave line or tackle around in this bird sanctuary. Carp respond to most baits here, and sweetcorn still produces fish over 20 lb.

The shallow water also holds small tench to 3 lb and there is also a big head of small rudd and perch. There are also some eels and a specimen of 7 lb 13 oz was recorded here some years ago.

Southern Region

Southern Fisheries Region

This region includes waters in Counties Offaly, Laois, Kildare, Carlow, Kilkenny, Waterford and Cork. The two main river systems are the Blackwater (sometimes called the Munster Blackwater), which flows eastwards through Co. Cork to enter the sea at Youghal; and the Barrow, which flows south from Co. Offaly to the sea near Waterford. These two systems provide the bulk of the coarse fishing in the region but there is one gem of a lake which demands inclusion.

RIVER BLACKWATER

(R56 98)

Rising in the borders of Co. Cork and Co. Kerry, this lovely river is fed by many smaller waters before flowing on through Mallow, Fermoy, Lismore and Cappoquin. A mixed fishery, it holds salmon, trout, roach, dace, perch, some pike and eels. Over long stretches the fishing is controlled by clubs or is in private ownership. Anglers must have permission to fish in these places and permits are obtainable locally at the main centres.

MALLOW, CO. CORK

This town on the River Blackwater lies in rich, wooded and pleasant agricultural country at the top of the Blackwater Valley.

Population 6,916
OS ½-inch Map No. 21
Cork 22 miles, Fermoy 19 miles, Macroom 26 miles, Dublin 148 miles

RIVER BLACKWATER

Coarse fishing in the vicinity of Mallow is good, but it is seasonal. There is easy access to a pool at Polagurum, on the south bank above the swimming pool and viaduct. The slow-moving water here produces good roach and dace. Just below the viaduct, on the north (left) bank over the footbridge, you will find some good swims. At the viaduct the depth is 10 feet and further along it drops to 2 feet.

At the Creamery stretch, where the depth is 2–3 feet, swims along the left bank fish well when there is colour in the water from late summer through the winter. Below Mallow bridge the Castle stretch is shallow, and then at Lover' Leap Rock there are good swims along the left bank with a depth of 7–8 feet.

Further down river in the Paddock Field stretch you will find a depth of 2–5

feet. You will find a long and even stretch at the Coursing Field, 1½ miles from Mallow along the right bank. You must respect landowners' property and seek permission to cross land here, where there are horses.

FERMOY, CO. CORK

Fermoy is dominated by the River Blackwater, which flows both over fast shallows and then through some deep, slow-moving stretches.

Population 3,310
OS ½-inch Map No. 22
Cork 22 miles, Mallow 19 miles, Lismore 16 miles, Dublin 137 miles
Club: Fermoy Coarse Angling Club

RIVER BLACKWATER
(W82 99)

This lovely river has a moderate flow and some wonderful fishing in accessible stretches. However, the river is liable to sudden floods, which can change fishing conditions. The normal routine is to loose-feed lightly, but in heavy water conditions much more bait is needed. The river is easily fished with a waggler or a stick float in the faster water. However, I recall trying out a new leger rod here and picking up some great roach on caster hookbait.

Barnane Walk

Access is up from the Grand Hotel and by the Boat Club. The top of this stretch is two fields away and here the water is shallow. At this end there are dace and a lot of brown trout. Along the path at The Walk there is a depth of about 10 feet, with good stocks of roach and dace. Fishing is good here down to the bridge,

in front of the hotel. You should not drive your car up along The Walk.

Jones's Field

This is a short stretch down river along the left bank from the bridge. It is approached just off the Lismore–Dungarvan road 200 yards from the corner. The bank here is good but swims are limited to about five. Fishing is into 4–5 feet of fast water. This area fishes well in the early months of the year.

Hospital Stretch

The entry to this good stretch is 1 mile along the Tallow road, with parking along the road margin. Access is over one short field to the right bank of the river. Here the bank is high and the near swims produce good catches of roach and dace.

There are some swims in the wood, but they are hard to reach if you are carrying full gear. Beyond the high viaduct there is an open field and the river then has shallows at the island, with swims yielding small roach in the early months.

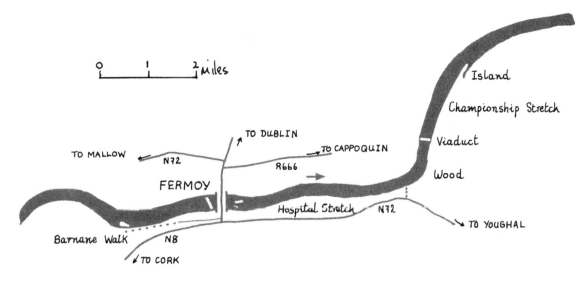

Southern Region, Fermoy

Championship Stretch

This fishery is reached from the Hospital stretch by an arduous trek through the wood and under the viaduct. I wonder how many will still have the energy to fish.

The depth here is 12–15 feet and fishing is from an open clean bank. Here again you will encounter roach and dace, together with countless small brown trout. The Championship Stretch is so called because it was here that we held the 1968 CIPS Championship. On that day the heavens opened to put the great River Blackwater into flood.

The river in the Fermoy area sometimes yields good perch, while the dace run to 1 lb and roach to 2 lb.

CAPPOQUIN, CO. WATERFORD

At the small town of Cappoquin the lovely River Blackwater changes direction to flow south and enter the sea at Youghal.

Population 902
OS ½-inch Map No. 22
Dungarvan 10 miles, Lismore 4 miles, Fermoy 21 miles, Dublin 130 miles

---

RIVER BLACKWATER
(S10 99)

I was fortunate to be around when the river at Cappoquin was the Mecca of all roach anglers. In the town there was a waterside bacon factory which was to influence the River Blackwater and create one of Europe's finest roach stretches. Here the river is backed up by the tide nearly to Lismore, several miles up river in this beautiful valley.

Let me tell you about the fishing at the once famous bacon factory, which was 200 yards down from the bridge. When pigs were slaughtered, the air was filled with loud screeches and this was the signal for anglers to be at the ready, with rods set up with float tackle. The swims were directly behind the gable wall of the factory and from there several spouts projected out, level with your chest or nose! In a short time, the spouts began to emit a trickle of blood, and from the moment it hit the water it appeared that every roach in the river was in the stretch. With the now great gush of blood, and the water becoming red, there was a surge from the massive roach population, which fed noisily on the congealed blood.

Now for the gruesome bit! The hook-bait was congealed blood which you pulled from the outflow near your nose. Roach after roach of over 2 lb were taken in those crazy conditions. Lawrie Robinson cracked the Irish record with a blood-lured fish which tipped the scales at 2 lb 13½ oz. Later, in 1972, Ronald Frost, with worm as bait, caught a fish to equal that record weight. Disaster struck this stretch when the bacon factory closed down and the food supply was cut off.

Good roach still remain in some parts of the river here, but more particularly there is a big population of quality dace in this stretch of the river.

The River Blackwater is a controlled salmon water and you are advised to check locally on where the coarse-fishing stretches are.

DURROW AND BALLINAKILL, CO. LAOIS

These are two small and picturesque villages near Abbeyleix in eastern Co. Laois. The small rivers Erkina and Owenbeg drain the few lakes in this area and flow into the River Nore.

GRANTSTOWN LAKE
(S34 80)

Throughout this book you will detect that I have some favourite waters in this country. I cannot subdue my enthusiasm for this one, which is situated in a forest in Co. Laois. Grantstown Lake is a lovely water surrounded by trees and ringed with a thick belt of reeds. You can walk over bank which is just soft and then, separating the reeds, reveal this still and quiet gem. As you savour the view, you can smell fish. There are at present some openings where you can fish, but together with the Forest Service, the local club intends to provide other facilities to cater for a limited number of anglers.

On my first visit to this lake, I found that it was easy to float fish. I set up for the expected tench as the water was shrouded in the early mist, and was soon into a rod-bender. But this was of another species which this water produces – a cracking perch which weighed 2 lb. Rudd to 2 lb cruise around the margins, and the occasional hungry pike often makes the quiet water erupt, as those lovely rudd scatter to escape. The tench fish best in the early and late hours, and I have had catches to 80 lb with fish to 5 lb. There is a thick layer of stonewort on the bottom and the nearby wall of the shelf has a carpet of that weed. When you hook a tench, be prepared for a fight as it burrows into the strong weed. A fabulous water!

For information and permission to fish this lake, contact the Secretary of the Durrow and District Angling Association in Durrow.

MASK LOUGH (Mass Lough) (S47 81)

This is a 4-acre lake close to Ballinakill village. There is a road along one side and a forest on the opposite bank, where there is an access path to some swims. Depths here are about 5–8 feet and there are dense beds of lilies. The small water yields some good tench to 4 lb and has a good stock of small rudd, perch and some small pike.

GILLS POND

Also beside Ballinakill, this is a 2-acre lake which was created artificially. The crystal-clear water has dense beds of white lilies and the bottom is covered with stonewort. At first glance you will think twice before fishing, but with strong tackle in the few clear swims you could land tench to 4 lb.

Both Mask Lake and Gills Pond are within the property of the Salesian Brothers' farm and you are asked to respect the owners' property.

RIVER BARROW

Rising in the Slieve Bloom Mountains, this rich water flows east by Portarlington to Monasterevan, where it is first of interest to coarse fishers. Strengthened by tributaries, the river, now 3–5 feet deep, turns south and flows on by Vicarstown to Athy. The river is now navigable but traffic is light on the Barrow and it does not trouble the angler. Further south there are some active boating and canoeing clubs and when competitive events are on it is best to move to one of the river's many quiet fishable stretches.

The river flows on through Carlow, Borris and Graiguenamanagh to St Mullins, where it becomes tidal and coarse fishing ceases. Here in April–May coarse anglers take out their light spinning rods with small spinners and cover the river at high water for twaite shad.

The River Barrow is a mixed fishery, holding salmon, brown trout and coarse fish. You must always be aware of the interests of clubs along this watercourse and should call into the local tackle shops in the towns on the river to acquaint yourself with club regulations.

Without question this is one of Ireland's finest coarse-fishing waters and yields fish of exceptional quality. The normal flow of water is steady to fast, but with rain the River Barrow can flood quickly and have a hard pull. There is a heavy growth of weed throughout, with belts of rushes in the upper shallow regions. While quality fish are found in the top section, it is from the middle to the lower section of the river that top-class specimens appear in greater numbers.

It is important to use appropriate tackle for this fast-moving and rich, weedy water, where quality fish are common. Here I use my stiff-action leger rod, with Drennan Specimen Plus 4-lb BS line and size 10 or 12 hooks for bream fishing. I will increase the strength of my terminal tackle if I find exceptionally big fish.

The Barrow is ideal for piking in the winter months. With no weed to contend with and miles of towpath, it is easy to cover long stretches of clean, open water. In those cold months of the year the fodder fish are near the canals, and it is there that you will find pike to 30 lb.

At the time of writing, there is no confirmation that roach are in the Barrow, but it is only a matter of time before those prolific fish enter this rich water and so compete with other species for food.

Rudd of over 2 lb are common in some sections and I believe that fish to 3 lb have been taken. There are some shoals of really big perch here and I recall meeting an old-timer near Monasterevan who told me about the 6-lb-plus perch which he caught in the stretch above the town bridge. Big perch do occur at many places right down to the famous Clash stretch near Graiguenamanagh.

Bream are common throughout, but once again this species increases in quantity as one progresses down river. The quality of these much sought after fish in the Barrow system is superb. I recall getting into the bream below Borris on one occasion and as I took 5-, 6- and 7-lb bream one after another I just wondered where the small fish were. Stories abound along the water of salmon anglers with hooks baited with big lobworms catching bream well over 10 lb. I can well believe it!

For fighting fish, it is hard to beat rudd × bream hybrids of 4, 5 or 6 lb. Here the hybrids are a lovely golden colour and are often confused with rudd. Fish well over the Irish record weight of 5 lb 13½ oz are taken – mostly in the Graiguenamanagh area, though specimen-sized hybrids do occur right up the river to Monasterevan.

Tench were stocked into this fast-moving river in the 1960s and now appear all over the system. Quite naturally, these fish, which like quiet water, are to be found in or near the canal stretches, but, surprisingly, many are taken in the weedy water where there is a considerable flow. Again, the quality of tench in these canal stretches is good, with fish to 7 lb being caught. I should add that the big tench here do not come easily to the hook. Perhaps again it is a case of weaning them from their rich natural food. The eel angler will find fish galore in the Barrow but I must honestly say that eels have caused me considerable annoyance when bream or tench fishing in the late hours. Eels of about 6–8 oz are common, but some fish over 4 lb are taken at times.

The rich and beautiful Barrow is fished a lot by coarse anglers but perhaps it is the absence of roach which has kept the majority away from it. My advice is to tackle up properly and have a go at one of our great rivers.

MONASTEREVAN, CO. KILDARE

Monasterevan is a small and tidy town at the junction of the River Barrow and the Barrow branch of the Grand Canal.

Population 2,143
OS ½-inch Map No. 16
Kildare 7 miles, Dublin 31 miles, Athy 12 miles

RIVER BARROW   (N63 11)

Above the town the Black River joins the Barrow and at this point quality perch to 3 lb appear in the early season. Spinning with a small silver bait, I have taken fish to 2 lb in the shallow but then weedless stretch just above the bridge. Later, I fished with big lobs while searching for bream and my best fish was a perch to 2¼ lb.

Below the historic Moore Abbey, local trout clubs control some stretches and you should check locally what club regulations are in force.

Belan

This stretch reached by turning east off the N7 Monasterevan–Portlaoise road left of Jamestown Cross. After 1 mile turn left again – the small road over the canal leads to the river. Along this long stretch to Athy the Barrow is shallow in most places, with islands of rushes. To the left of the parking, the access – over private land – leads to an area where there are some clear patches of water. The depth is 4 feet and weed growth heavy in summer. Fishing this area on many occasions I have taken rudd to 2¼ lb, some bream and a lot of good rudd × bream hybrids of over 3 lb. Here I sometimes used a stick float but, as the clear passage for the float was limited, I went on to using a stiffer leger rod with a feeder and got good results.

In normal conditions the Barrow has a steady flow but after rain it can fill up quickly, intensifying the flow. After many days of rain the river rushing through is no joy to fish!

Down river above Dunrally Bridge near Vicarstown some fine perch over 3 lb are taken. At Bert Bridge, the islands of rushes continue and, if you can find a clear place, try for those big rudd.

ATHY

The River Barrow and the Grand Canal dominate this industrious town in Co. Kildare. Prominant at the river bridge is White's castle, built by the Earl of Kildare in the sixteenth century. This historic area has seen many a battle but now the only struggles are those between anglers and big bream just below the bridge.

Population 5,076
OS ½-inch Map No. 16
Monasterevan 12 miles, Kildare 16 miles, Carlow 12 miles, Dublin 43 miles
Club: Athy Anglers' Club

RIVER BARROW   (S69 94)

Within the town the river is easily accessible. The stretch down from the bridge along the left bank is where the concentration of bream is intense in the early season. In May–June, shoals of bream, some over 8 lb, move in here to provide fantastic sport. The shoals move up from the stretch down below the canal junction and careful monitoring is vital if you are to hit the fish. The swims along the left bank are opposite the presbytery. The river is fishable along the right bank near the modern Dominican church, but in the shallow margins there my only success was in taking rudd to 2 lb.

Above the town there is a long stretch where the depth is only 3 feet during the summer, but again in the early season some good catches of bream averaging 3½ lb are taken.

The canal junction with the river is below the town, and from now on the regular features of open towpath, navigation channel and short canals are of intense interest to the angler. The river now seems to gain stature, with stocks of quality fish increasing. Fish shoals are localized, so do not expect 8-lb bream or 3-lb rudd to appear quickly in your swim. Heavy baiting and patience are vital to catching fish, especially in this rich water.

Below Levitstown Cut, there are some good swims with easy access from the R417 Athy–Carlow road. I once saw rudd below Maganey bridge and quickly set up my rod to discover that my maggot-baited hook took rudd × bream hybrids of over 3 lb. Lovely fishing!

You are reminded again that local angling club regulations apply in this stretch, where there is brown-trout fishing.

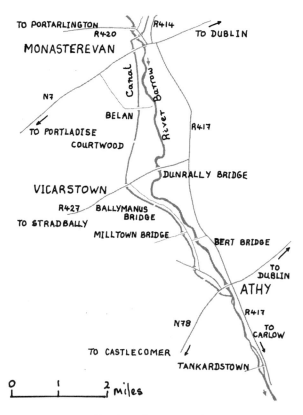

Southern Region, Athy

CARLOW

This is a pleasant town which was a Norman settlement on the east bank of the River Barrow. The town on the west bank of the river is called Graiguecullen.

Population 12,079
OS ½-inch Map No. 19
Athy 12 miles, Waterford 50 miles, Leighlinbridge 8 miles, Dublin 20 miles
Club: Carlow Angling Club

RIVER BARROW   (S72 78)

Up river of the town on the left bank is a sugar factory and here there are some shoals of good bream. Access to this stretch is off the Athy road to Brennan's bacon factory and then by foot along the waterside path. I found good fishing in the weedy section directly beside the cemetery. The river has a moderate flow and is wide at this point, and extensive baiting is necessary to hold the bream. This stretch is used by members of the active Carlow Rowing Club and so becomes crowded on days of competitive events.

Down river along the right bank in Graiguecullen and by the Carlow lock there is a good match stretch. The first pegs here, just below the canal, are uncertain because of the rush of water and silting. Farther along the high bank, or 'track', the pegs yield great fishing, with bream catches to 80–100 lb taken in matches.

Below this stretch there is a productive canal called Lanigan's, where the bank is high. Access to this point is gained from the Graigue–Oldleighlin road. Here I experienced some fine sport for bream, rudd or hybrids one evening as I looked down from the high bank at the fish taking my worm-baited hook. Keeping a low profile

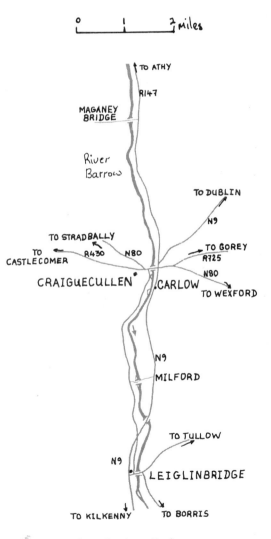

Southern Region, Carlow

I also saw tench, but it took sweetcorn to entice them. A great stretch, but do not cast shadows over the water. When the lid of my bait box fell down the steep bank and hit the water all the fish in my swim disappeared!

This wonderful fishery progresses at the usual steady pace to Milford, where the river gains momentum. This is a lovely scenic area of trees, islands, weir, canal and the old ruins of a mill. There is a controlled game-fishing stretch here, so be sure to check locally on the regulations in force. There are some good swims below the bridge along the right bank just above the point where the canal enters the river. Two swims can be approached over the lock from the lifting bridge on the canal. The other swims are in the private property of Mrs M. Quinn, at the Locks Guesthouse, and are to the up-river side of the canal. Here the river is weedy with the usual steady pull. Bream will respond to heavy baiting, and the rudd to careful, accurate loose feeding.

RIVER BARROW

Leighlinbridge, Bagenalstown, Goresbridge, Borris   (S69 65)

From Leighlinbridge the towpath follows the left bank of the river down to St Mullins.

I found rudd of over 2 lb just above the bridge 200 yards along the tidy bank at Leighlinbridge. The canal stretch down river is close to the R705 Bagenalstown road and here at Rathellan shoals of good bream to 5–6 lb appear in may–June. It was below Bagenalstown (Muine Bheag) that the Irish record pike weighing 42 lb was taken and it is no surprise that pike over the specimen weight of 20 lb are taken here every year.

Local game-fishing clubs control many stretches of the river and you are advised to make yourself aware of their regulations.

GRAIGUENAMANAGH, CO. KILKENNY

Graig is a prosperous market town and was once a centre of great ecclesiastical importance. The great Cistercian abbey set in this picturesque land of river and mountains is now fully restored. The area along the left bank of the river in Co. Carlow is called Tinnahinch.

Population 1,410
OS ½-inch Map No. 19
New Ross 12 miles, Borris 7 miles, Dublin 74 miles
Club: Barrow Valley Tourist Association

RIVER BARROW   (S71 44)

The character of this great river changes dramatically near Borris, as it pours into what is called the Barrow Valley. From here down to the tidal stretch there is wonderful fishing in breathtaking scenery.

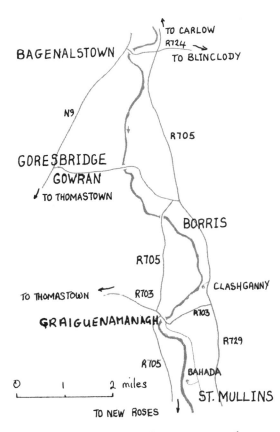

Southern Region, Graiguenamanagh

Clashganny

The Borris–Graig road gives easy access to Clashganny, where there is a weir and the usual short canal with a lock. Parking is at the car park beside the lock-keeper's house. Up river from the lock there is a fine long stretch where there are great stocks of coarse fish. How I dream of setting out with a pike rod on a crisp winter's day to sink and draw a dead bait through this accessible and lovely pike water!

Below the weir and on the island, which is approached over the lock, there are some swims in slack water which

often hold bream. Try it if you enjoy the sound of rushing water and the possibility of fighting 4-lb bream in a lovely swim. This stretch is controlled by local game-angling clubs and you will notice salmon anglers along the right bank. Below from the canal lock and parking area is a stretch which must be regarded as one of Ireland's best for quality fish. The fast water from the weir pours behind the islands and along the far right bank. At the bend to the left 500 yards downstream, backed by a cliff with tall trees, the water along the towpath is slow while the fast water continues to rush along the salmon stretch opposite. The good pegs are along the bend of the river and in this lovely setting you can settle in for some fantastic fishing. The slack water near the left side is about 6–8 feet deep and it is here that you could encounter bream to 11 lb, rudd over 2½ lb, rudd × bream hybrids to 5 lb, perch over 3 lb, pike over 20 lb and eels over 5 lb. Good tench to 6 lb appear in Ballykeenan canal stretch just a few casts down river. Few waters in Ireland can produce such quality fish.

Look at the catch of an Essex angler, Tom Coster, who in 1984 at Clashganny caught the following specimen fish: bream 10½ lb, perch 4 lb, pike 22 lb and tench 6¾ lb. That was the most remarkable recorded catch of quality coarse fish in any Irish water.

Graiguenamanagh Bridge

The bridge at Graig gives easy access to a stretch upstream which yields good rudd and perch but only some bream. Below the town bridge at Tinnahinch small rudd abound, but I found bigger fish below the lock.

The rich waters of the River Barrow between Borris and Graiguenamanagh at Clashganny

Bahana

The river becomes more stately as it cuts deep into the hills and it is at Bahana that good coarse fishing can next be found. This stretch is approached east through a forest off the Graig–St Mullins road. There is parking near the water. The best swims are at the entry to the forest going down the hill and beside an old well, which still provides lovely clean, cool spring water. The setting is beautiful with a view across the river to Brandon Hill, and 4-lb bream which come to hook baited with worm and caster are a bonus in these most pleasant of surroundings. While river traffic is generally quiet, you may be surprised by boats appearing round the corner and sailing quite close to the far bank. In May and June you will often find the bream along the right bank; later they move over to the deep water.

Below the Bahana stretch, weir and canal, the river is tidal. Salmon angling interests are strong in this area and this is the lower limit of coarse fishing in the River Barrow, though the fast water below the weir produces big bream.

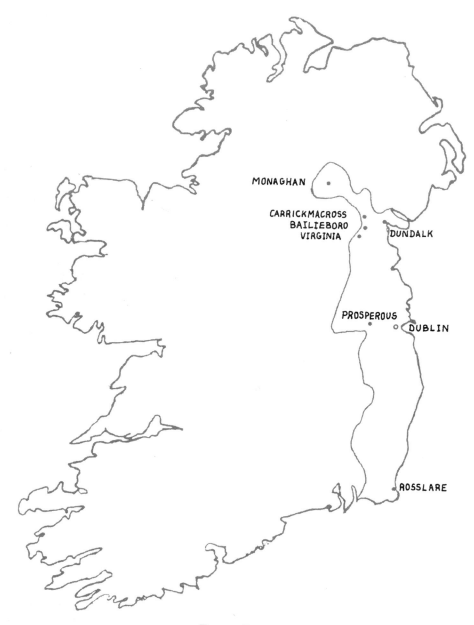

MONAGHAN

CARRICKMACROSS
BAILIEBORO
VIRGINIA

DUNDALK

PROSPEROUS

DUBLIN

ROSSLARE

Eastern Region

Eastern Fisheries Region

The Eastern Fisheries Region extends along the eastern seaboard and includes lakes and rivers in Counties Cavan, Monaghan, Louth, Meath, Kildare, Wicklow and Wexford. The coarse-fishing waters of interest to us are in the hilly districts of Counties Cavan, Meath and Monaghan, where there are lakes with top-quality fish. From Dublin City inland to the flat lands of Co. Kildare and Co. Meath, the Grand Canal and the Royal Canal provide great sport for the big population of anglers. Several small lakes in the southern part of this region hold good tench and perch, but they are not included here because I have not fished them thoroughly.

The River Liffey flowing through Dublin provides some interesting roach fishing but most of this river is controlled by game-angling clubs or is in private ownership. The Blessington Lakes, which hold some good pike, are controlled by the Electricity Supply Board.

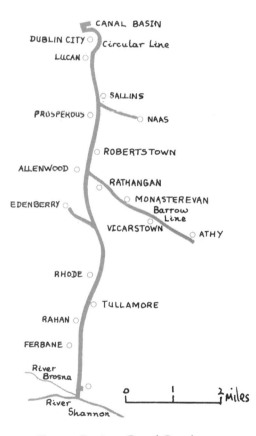

Eastern Region, Grand Canal

GRAND CANAL AND ROYAL CANAL

Nearly two hundred years ago work began on the Grand Canal in Dublin and in 1804 the first boat passed through at Shannon Harbour on the River Shannon.

The canal was used extensively for commercial traffic, with busy centres along the main route and various branches soon being added. The Royal Canal, which was completed later, linked the River

Liffey in north Dublin with the River Shannon at Clondra, Co. Longford, 85 miles away.

The Grand Canal is now used only by pleasure boats, mostly from a point outside the Dublin area. The Royal Canal is closed to navigation and many stretches have been dewatered.

Fortunately, there has been active and enthusiastic interest on the part of local amenity groups and others to develop and open sections of the Royal Canal. Both canals hold great stocks of fish over their length from the Dublin bases to the Shannon. These great and valuable natural amenities within Dublin City and through the midlands must be protected to provide recreation for the big population of young anglers who get pleasure from wetting a line.

Over the years I have surveyed the canals along every mile from Dublin inland, and have researched to provide up to date information for this publication. I was carried away with the enthusiasm of the tiny anglers fishing a junior competition in weedy conditions on the Royal Canal near Lucan, and especially with that of the young lad who landed a small tench and carp. But I was shocked when I returned to this lovely water just a short time ago to find a dredger operating along the same stretch providing a clean, weedless and fishless canal with a good flat bank!

The information on these canals is up to date at the time of writing, but such things do happen, you should check before setting out for a serious fishing session.

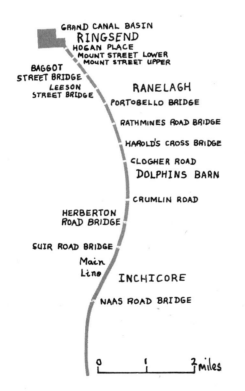

Eastern Region, Grand Canal and Circular Line

GRAND CANAL, DUBLIN CITY

The circular line from the Ringsend Basin to Suir Road Bridge is an exceptionally good fishery within the city limits. The basin, beside the River Liffey, holds a good population of roach, rudd, some bream, lots of small perch and some good quality rudd × bream hybrids. In this deep and weedy water the shoals are localized and local information will help you get results.

From Lock 1 to Lock 4 at Baggot Street there is a fair stock of small roach and perch. The next stretch to Leeson Street Bridge is again fair for roach. The next stretch, from Ranelagh Road to Rathmines (Lock 5 to Lock 6), is weedy, but here there are better-quality roach and also good rudd. Some years ago, just above Lock 6, there were lovely roach in great numbers and catches of over 80 lb were common, but that is no longer the case. Now you could take 25–30 lb of fish here in a session.

The next long stretch by Dolphin's Barn to Suir Road Bridge and Lock 1 on the main line holds a big population of roach, some rudd, some bream, and also a good stock of hybrids. This fine stretch will yield roach to 1 lb and roach × rudd hybrids of over 1 lb. This section of canal has clean water and a big growth of milfoil and hornwort weed.

From Lock 3 on the main line at Inchicore to Lock 5 near New Bridge there is still clean water with pondweed, and you will find small perch and roach. In the evenings you will see tench to 3 lb cruising through the weed. The next section, from Lock 5 to Lock 7 at Ballyfermot, yields some bream and small perch galore. Here, too, you will encounter pike to 12 lb.

Tench to 4 lb appear in the next stretch, from Lock 7 to Lock 8, but fishing here is difficult in the clear water. There is easy access to the canal section from Lock 8 by the Guinness filter beds to Clondalkin at Lock 9. Tench are present in good numbers here and come on the feed mostly in the very late evening or early morning, with sweetcorn as bait.

From here and at Aylmer's Bridge roach stocks decline, but tench, some bream and rudd appear at intervals all the way to the next active section of the canal.

PROSPEROUS, CO. KILDARE

This is a small village on the L2 Celbridge–Edenderry road. There is an active coarse-fishing interest here, and an angling festival is held annually.

Population 765
OS ½-inch Map No. 16
Dublin 22 miles, Edenderry 15 miles, Naas 7 miles, Mullingar 40 miles, Athy 29 miles
Club: Prosperous AC

GRAND CANAL

Sallins to Edenderry (N83 27)

From Sallins the curving canal crosses the River Liffey and this stretch has long been popular. I rate highly the section from Lock 16 at Digby Bridge to Lock 17 at Landenstown Bridge, with parking on the green patch of grass at the bend in the road. Here it is a delight to see big tench over 6 lb nosing their way quietly through the weed in the early morning. This area offers excellent fishing from mid-April to early June, and some fish are taken right into September. I recall fishing for rudd above this stretch and to my surprise began taking brown trout to 12 oz.

The Landenstown stretch between Locks 17 and 18 along the wooded lands

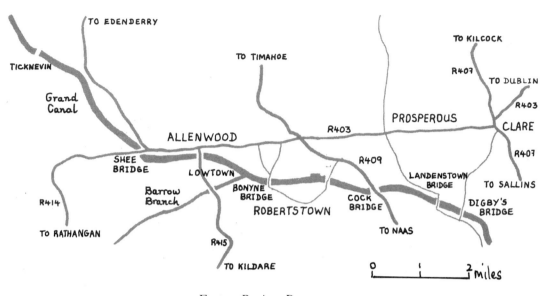

Eastern Region, Prosperous

of Landenstown House also holds tench and some small carp. From here the road turns away towards Prosperous, the main coarse-fishing centre in this area.

The stretch from Cock Bridge to Bonynge or Healy's Bridge is seldom fished, perhaps because there is no water-side road, but there are some great shoals of bream here. Just above Healy's Bridge the canal widens and I have had great bream fishing there in the evenings. All along this section of the canal by Roberts-town to Lowton there are good bream to 4 lb.

The main line after Shee Bridge and above the Bord na Mona Bridge is a match water. The results of catches taken during competitions here do not reflect a true picture of the canal, which offers great sport for bream in quiet evening sessions. Further along at Lullymore near the Bord na Mona briquette factory, bream, some rudd and perch are to be found, but my objection to this area is the fine peat dust which blows over at times and brings on a thirst.

From Hartly Bridge to Lock 20 at Tick-nevin the canal is high and exposed for the first time. I have found this section patchy, with the best fishing for bream and rudd in the evenings. The high canal now passes over the bogs to the 'Tunnel'.

The Grand Canal at Prosperous holds good stocks of bream at 3 lb

The canal in this area was recently breached, and over a large stretch we cannot expect any fishing for some time. Access to this section is from Edenderry and there is waterside parking along the exposed stretch.

GRAND CANAL

Edenderry to Shannon Harbour

The Edenderry branch holds an abundance of small perch, rudd and some small bream. There is access on the main R402 road at Colgan bridge to a short stretch where there are better-quality bream and some good rudd × bream hybrids.

Between Rhode bridge and Toberdaly bridge, bream shoals with fish to 2 lb appear, together with rudd and the common perch. I always wanted to fish the Red Girls stretch in the hope that I might come across some relations of the lovely ladies who lived in the nearby house between Rhode and Daingean. I was blessed only with lovely red-finned rudd near Killeen bridge.

The canal for a long distance now has some isolated shoals of bream, which you can spot if you take a stroll along the bank on a quiet evening.

Below Tullamore, you will find good stocks of bream, rudd, perch and some small hybrids. There are some good shoals of bream to 3 lb at Pollagh, down from Plunkett bridge and along the path on the left side. The bank is more accessible at Derry bridge, and about ¼ mile above this point I have enjoyed many a session for great rudd to 1½ lb. Pike stocks here are good and often when a feeding fish strikes for its food you will see the canal erupt with small fish.

The Grand Canal continues to show good fishing above Armstrong bridge near Ferbane and bream appear in numbers in the weedy and shaded stretch below Lock 33 on the right bank by the old mill.

Above L'Estrange bridge near Clonony Castle on the R357 there is a path along the right bank and here good catches of rudd and small bream are taken. Many anglers blown off the River Shannon in stormy weather will find this quiet area rewarding.

Below Shannon Harbour the River Brosna joins the Shannon and near this point the canal reaches the end of its 85-mile journey from Dublin. Below the last lock the bank is high and clear; then it drops to a level from which you can fish. The River Brosna flows in directly across from here and in high water the strong current hits the high bank. When the water is high, fish down close in water which may be 10–14 feet deep. In normal conditions the shoals will remain farther out and often feed on the edge of the gentle flow. The area produces good bream to 6 lb, with rudd over 1 lb and also quality rudd × bream hybrids. In the early season hungry pike will hunt this area in search of food after spawning.

Remember that at Easter, the many private boats which were wintered up at Shannon Harbour will rev up their engines and head down into the river and through your swim!

GRAND CANAL BARROW BRANCH
Lowtown to Athy

Just below Lock 21, where there is foot access only, I took some of my best ever canal rudd. Here in the weedy stretch there are lovely dark golden rudd over 2 lb. Above Rathangan bridge there is a very big stock of small rudd and some small bream. The stretch below Spenser bridge (Lock 23) looks good but stocks are poor, so forget it. However, close to Umeras Bridge the angling picture is much brighter, with good stocks of small bream. Here you can set your target at 20 lb. Above Monasterevan the canal fails to produce good catches, but along the right bank below the main N7 road some tench to 3 lb can be taken.

The canal now runs parallel to the River Barrow which flows directly south. A short distance from Vicarstown, the stretch from the Camal aqueduct to Ballymanus bridge has a good population of tench, many of which show the rare black colour. This section is reeded and has much weed, which gives good cover for the good stocks of rudd, tench, perch and pike. Take care when parking along the narow road and keep your tackle clear of the road.

Tench are also found at various swims up to ½ mile from Miltown bridge. Along the high stretch beyond this bridge, with good natural surroundings, I have had tench to 5 lb. Close to Athy, between Cardington bridge (Lock 26) and Lock 27, the quality of fishing greatly improves, with a good head of good bream and a big stock of small rudd. This section of the canal is well worth a try and will yield catches to 20–30 lb. The canal joins the River Barrow below the Dominican church in Athy and the many short canal stretches downstream are considered in Chapter 7.

TAGGED FISH IN IRISH CANALS

The Central Fisheries Board in conjunction with the Office of Public Works has been involved in fishery investigations into the movements of fish in the canal. It is hoped that the information gathered will provide the foundation for fishery management decisions on the siting of angling competitions, restocking programmes, predator control operations and other fishery matters. As part of this programme, large numbers of fish in the canals have been marked with numbered floy tags near the dorsal fin. Each floy tag carries a lettered code. Some tags may have a thin algal coating. Gentle scraping will remove this and reveal the number.

Anglers who catch tagged fish are requested to give details of the number, species, location and weight of fish to the Central Fisheries Board, Dublin.

ROYAL CANAL

Dublin City

The canal joins the River Liffey and stretches from Spencer Lock through north Dublin. The canal rises steeply through double locks, where there is good-quality water. The early stretches hold few good fish and it is only at Lock 6 and Lock 7 (Liffey Junction) that a fair stock of roach and some pike around 5 lb appear.

The roach population improves above

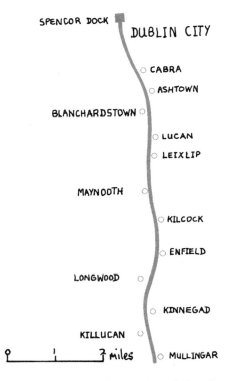

Eastern Region, Royal Canal

Lock 7 by Broome Bridge to Reilly's Bridge and Lock 8. Here you will find quite a good population of pike (5–10 lb) and eels galore. Above Reilly's Bridge and Campbell's Garage, the canal along the right bank takes on a different character. Here you can enjoy good sport for roach to 10 oz and perch. Your target here is a catch of 20–25 lb.

Stocks of nice pike are found near Longford Bridge at Ashtown. The long stretch from Lock 12 at Granard bridge near Blanchardstown to Lock 13 near Carton House is a superb fishery.

Clonsilla

Near Clonsilla the canal has a high bank, and for many miles on it produces lovely fishing in weedy conditions. Roach of well over 1 lb, good tench and carp have been recorded here. At the time of writing, however, a dreaded dredger has been operating in this area and I fear the worst for the fine fishing stretch in the short term.

This section of the canal is accessible to tourist anglers who want to wet a line on the way home from Cavan, Leitrim or Monaghan. From the N3 Cavan–Dublin road turn right just over the bridge at Clonee and then follow the Lucan sign. From the N4 Mullingar and Athlone road turn left at the lights at the bottom of the hill in Lucan, then right over the River Liffey and left up the hill. Take the first left after the bridge and after ½ mile you will find parking at the boathouse.

I do hope that this stretch will recover and that soon we can all enjoy the great sport which was experienced until recently.

At Deey bridge near the Carton House estate a surprise awaits the keen angler – some good carp to 6 lb roam the weedy section. On the Dublin side (east) of Cloncurry bridge the towpath from Lock 17 is overgrown but there is access over the old bog road. In this stretch there is a big stock of good roach to 1½ lb, some rudd, bream and an amazing mixture of hybrids. This good canal stretch also yields tench to 5 lb and is well worth a session.

Enfield to Mullingar

Just below Enfield, on the N4 Mullingar road, a small road to the left leads to some fishing in deep pools in the canal. Tench appear at many places along the shallow and weedy section from here.

Five miles west of Enfield, turn right (north) after the shop and then right at the Y junction and on to the bridge. Just 100 yards beyond the bridge take the dirt road to the left and left again when you arrive at the quarry. Access to the famous Blackshade match stretch is by the kind permission of the landowner. From Mullingar take the first left by the church ½ mile from Clonard village, and then left again on to the canal bridge.

The canal is to the left and near the quarry. Here the Royal Canal is at its best. The towpath has some bushes and the opposite bank has emergent vegetation with scrub. A lovely setting and wonderful fishing in this quiet rural stretch. The canal has the usual weed but is easily fishable at all times, yielding good bream around 3 lb with some fish to 5 lb. I have fished here many times and during the summer months paticularly I have seldom failed to land tench of about 3–4 lb. There are tench over the specimen weight of 6 lb, with rudd and perch over 2 lb in this match length.

The water is consistent and Brian O'Donoghue, an enthusiastic local angler, tells stories of breaking the ice during the winter months to catch all species, including tench. Farther along some sections of the canal, still shallow and weedy, hold rudd and tench. Near Mullingar the Downs Stretch on the south bank has deeper swims with tench.

West of Mullingar the canal is dewatered, but there is a growing interest in restoring the waterway. In years to come this great amenity will, I am sure, be the home of great stocks of fish, if all the organizations concerned work together in the interests of the sport.

Brian O'Donoghue plays a bream of 5 lb in the lovely Blackshade Bridge stretch of the Royal Canal

RIVER LIFFEY

The River Liffey rises high in the Wicklow Mountains overlooking Dublin and near Blessington its waters are trapped to form a reservoir. The Electricity Supply Board controls the fishing in this area. Flowing quickly to the lowlands of Co. Kildare, on its way to Dublin the river is a good game fishery and is controlled by local clubs. Before setting out to fish for coarse species you are advised to check on local regulations and get permission to fish from the following clubs: Electricity Supply Board, Clane Anglers, Sallins Anglers, North Kildare Trout Anglers, Dublin and District Salmon Anglers' Association. All the tackle shops in Dublin will advise you.

LEIXLIP RESERVOIR

The Leixlip Reservoir, a big water controlled by the Electricity Supply Board, has some fine fishing for roach, some rudd and bream, but it is for the hard-fighting specimen hybrids that anglers flock to the few swims there. Access to the end of this water and the well beaten pegs is by foot from the Salmon Leap pub. Anglers must have permission to fish on the property controlled by the ESB.

RIVER LIFFEY

Lucan Bridge to Dublin

A short strech of the Liffey ½ mile below Lucan bridge and opposite the CPI factory holds good stocks of roach in 6–9 feet of water. The Strawberry Beds stretch, up river from the Angler's Rest pub, has easy access but this is an area of heavy road traffic. Space is limited and depths vary from 6 to 10 feet in water which produces good roach and hybrids. Note that the Dublin and District Salmon Anglers' Association controls the waters here.

Access to the last coarse-fishing stretch of the Liffey is off the South Circular Road at Islandbridge to the Memorial Park. This stretch opposite the rowing club has had its ups and downs but is now producing good fishing, especially for those competing in matches. Depths vary from 3 to 13 feet and there is a fair to good stock of small roach, perch and some hybrids.

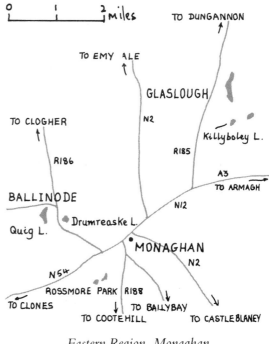

Eastern Region, Monaghan

MONAGHAN

A busy market county town, Monaghan is situated in hilly country. Once known as the ancient territory of Oriel, it was ruled by the powerful MacMahon clan.

Population 6,250
OS ½-inch Map No. 8
Castleblaney 14 miles, Carrickmacross 25 miles, Ballybay 11 miles, Dublin 74 miles

---

PETER'S LAKE

This is a small pond in the town of Monaghan. It is accessible and has a small fringe of reeds and lilies. Within an urban area, it provides young anglers with good sport for small roach, small bream, hybrids and perch.

QUIG LOUGH

This 25-acre lake is near Ballinode, down a small road to the left. Parking at the end of the road must be done with care. Foot access is easy. The lake has a thick fringe of reeds and fishing is along one bank which has some stands. This is a good water with depth of 14–16 feet and a thick carpet of stonewort in most places. In May and June the lake produces good tench and my best fish here weighed 5 lb 14 oz. It took bread. Also here are roach, rudd, hybrids, perch and pike, which make this an attractive fishery.

DRUMREASKE LAKE

The lake lies just off the R186 Monaghan–Tydavnet road and parking along this busy road must be done with care. The water has a heavy margin of reeds and fishing is from stands. It was on 17 May 1983 that I got a phone call from a Dublin angler, Colm Quinn, who reported that he had caught some big roach × bream hybrids. I rushed to the lake to weigh his fish, one of which went 3 lb 15½ oz, a new Irish record.

Those hybrids don't come easy, but you will be entertained by the big stock of roach, small bream and perch.

ROSSMORE PARK LAKES

These are several small lakes in the Forest Park near Monaghan town. The margins of some make them unfishable, while others have a few open swims which allow you to cast a line. Small rudd, small roach, perch and some small tench are all that these waters provide.

KILLYBOLEY LAKE

Near Glaslough village, this is a 20-acre lake with easy access. The margins are soft and there is a belt of reeds round the water, which is fishable from stands. The depth is 4–6 feet with a muddy and sometimes weedy bottom. The water provides good sport for small rudd, tench, perch and pike.

GLASLOUGH LAKE

This lake is within the estate of Mr D. Leslie and permission to fish must be obtained from him. It has a history of big pike and I went there in April 1972 and took my first 30-pounder. A lovely lake overlooked by Glaslough House and surrounded by rich woodlands, the margins are mostly reeded. It also holds a big stock of quality roach, which no doubt provide good food for the big pike. Access is limited to those who have permission to fish on this private water.

CASTLEBLANEY, CO. MONAGHAN

Castleblaney is a busy market town beside Lough Muckno. It is named after Sir Edward Blaney, to whom a grant of land was made by James I.

Population 2,490
OS ½-inch Map No. 8
Carrickmacross 10 miles, Monaghan 14 miles, Dundalk 16 miles, Dublin 61 miles

Club: Castleblaney Angling Club

LOUGH MUCKNO

This large and picturesque lake received scant attention from coarse anglers in the past, but with the introduction of roach the angling scene has undergone a complete change. This natural amenity is just a short stroll from the town and it can be fished from the bank in several areas.

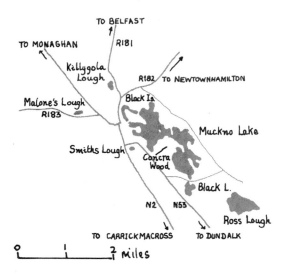

Eastern Region, Castleblaney

Black Island

Past the old gateway to the Hope Castle demesne the slip road to the left leads to a waterside car park. Foot access is then over the bridge and through the forest to the right. There is a match stretch here with the first pegs facing the south-west and the second section facing the south-east. In windy conditions fishing can vary considerably. The bank is good and fishing is mostly into 8–10 feet of water. The stretch yields good catches of roach and small perch.

During the winter months pike are never far away from this shore, and fish to 30 lb have been taken. To the left of the bridge Gas Lake holds bream, but access to this water is difficult at the moment. In the early season, some great catches to 50–70 lb can be taken here.

White Island

To the right of the car park and slipway is White Island, which offers some good bank fishing. However, access to this point is possible only during dry summer conditions. I have fished here a lot and found good bream to 4 lb with a lot of small roach. I suggest that you approach this area as I do, by boat only.

Concra Wood

The approach to this state forest is off the N53 Castleblaney–Dundalk road and access is by the permission of the Forest Service. The forest road to the left runs close to the heavily timbered waterside and the parking near the end gives access to some swims. At this point the lake narrows to a neck and then opens out to another large section. In this second section, facing south, there are just a few swims which in summer, after heavy baiting, will yield good catches of nice bream to 5 lb. This area, known as the Belfast Steps, is ideal for winter piking, as there is a sharp drop-off to 25–30 feet and fish over 30 lb are taken by legering. Please handle all pike with great care and return them alive to the water.

South Lodge

This section of the lake is also reached from the Dundalk road. There is an open parking area and slip after ½ mile. Used a lot by boating enthusiasts in the summer, this area with limited bank space does produce nice roach fishing in the early months of the year.

Toome Stretch

Half a mile beyond South Lodge turn left and then off this narrow road over private ground to parking. The bank at this section of the lake is firm and clean. The swims to the left are shallow, with the depth and fishing improving as you progress down the bank to the gate. At this point the depth is 20 feet over a gravel bottom but further along it shallows to 10 feet. Here there are roach but fishing varies more than at other sections, as the fish do not seem to take up permanent residence. Here too, winter piking is rewarding and records show some great fish taken here. Some anglers fish sections of the lake just off the road which runs along the northern shore. You should note that access over land is only through the good will of landowners and permission must always be sought.

SMITH'S LAKE

This 2-acre lake lies beside the N53 Castleblaney–Dundalk road. It has soft muddy margins, with a growth of lilies and some reeds. While stocked with tench in the past, it has never really produced great fishing. It does retain some tench to 4–5 lb, which come on the feed in May and June. The small water also yields some small roach, bream and perch.

KILLYGOLA LAKE

This 6-acre lake lies beside the R181 Castleblaney–Keady road. Take care parking at the dangerous bend. Seldom fished, this water with limited swims is well worth a try as it has a good stock of bream to 7 lb. In May and June tench are also taken, which makes this small border water a surprise package.

CARRICKMACROSS, CO. MONAGHAN

Carrickmacross is a busy market town which gained a reputation all over the world for its delicate lace. The area now has a reputation in the angling world for its quality coarse fish.

Population 2,005
OS ½-inch Map No. 8
Castleblaney 10 miles, Cootehill 20 miles, Dundalk 15 miles, Dublin 55 miles

Club: Carrickmacross Coarse Angling Club

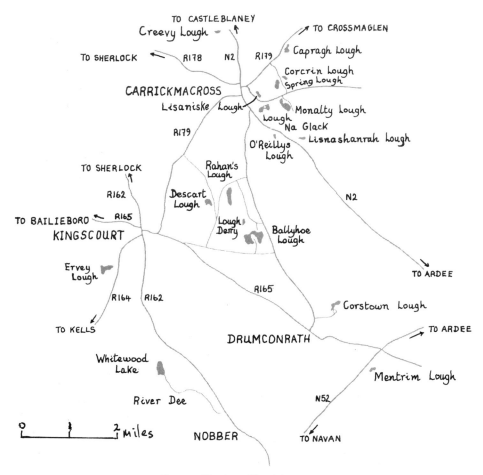

Eastern Region, Carrickmacross

LISANISKE LAKE

This 13-acre lake lies to the north of the R178 Dundalk road close to Carrickmacross. Tucked under the main road, it is exposed, and fishing is from stands. A shallow water with depths of 3–7 feet and a good bottom, it produces good catches of small bream, roach, hybrids and perch.

LOUGH NA GLACK

This 85-acre lake is one of Ireland's richest waters and is also one of the most popular with those seeking big coarse fish. Just ½ mile from Lisaniske Lake and to the south off the Dundalk road, there are a few access points to the lake. The first access from Carrick is to the right at a dangerous bend and down a narrow road through a wood to a car park where there is a slip. At a glance you will take in the nature of the lake, which has a thick belt of reeds and soft margins in most places. To the right the Proules River flows quietly into a section of the lake which is shallower than the rest. In rainy conditions, the river here can carry a lot of water and so affect what fishing there is in this area. There are some stands along here but this is not the most productive area.

The next approach to the lake is from the private property of the Nuremore Hotel and over the golf course to the wooded shore. I must stress that anglers should respect the property of all concerned and appreciate that the owners have the right to restrict access. Directly down from the hotel the Hotel Bay has some swims to the right and left. The depth is 8–10 feet in this area and the margins are soft. To the left of here is the Island, where the lake narrows before opening out to another section which also has excellent swims. This area is directly across the water from the slip and Proules River inflow.

This exceptionally good lake has a thick growth of all kinds of weed and you need only to pick up a handful to see the great numbers of invertebrates which provide food for the fish. During the summer months the vast growth of the common starwort in the bays will often interfere with your line.

This lake, like so many rich waters, is moody and fishing patterns vary a lot. However, it can be said that early-morning fishing during the summer produces the fish. Fishing for bream continues right through from March to November, but with a slow period in midsummer. That the shoals move all over the lake is a certainty and the sure way of locating them and then baiting up is to monitor their movements if the weather is calm and if you have the time to sit and observe. When your swim comes alive and you land your first 9- or 10-lb bream, do not expect the good sport to continue on the following day – the shoal may have moved on.

In the early days I took rudd galore over 2 lb but now those fish are few. Bream to 11 lb are here and we await that one big fish that will crack the Irish record weight of 11 lb 12 oz. Rudd × bream hybrids over the specimen weight of 3 lb are there and it is no surprise to find tench to 6 lb in this rich water.

DICK'S LAKES

Just beside the golf course and approached easily from the N2 Dublin road, the first lake to the left is remarkably deep. The best swims are on the opposite side from the road. Here you will find some small bream, small tench, roach, rudd and perch. In this pond, too, the occasional eel to 3 lb is taken. When the golf traffic is heavy keep your head down, because some miscalculated shots could land in your swim.

MONALTY LAKE

In the early days the Inland Fisheries Trust carried out technical surveys of coarse-fishing waters all over Ireland. My duties took me to Monalty Lake and it was with expectancy that I cast my first line there in 1970. I was bowled over with the results and later, with little trouble, I enticed Norfolk angler Ray Webb to the lake. Early reports had shown that the water held great stocks of big rudd × bream hybrids and, sure enough, when we fished it they came to our nets in great

John Mills with a specimen rudd x bream hybrid taken on Monalty Lake, Carrickmacross

numbers. This great water has changed little since then.

Near Lough na Glack, it is approached to the right off the Dundalk road, with parking at a lay-by in front of a house. A shallow lake, there is one spot on the near bank where a cast out from the tall tree will reach a depth of 12–14 feet. The hybrids and bream were originally to be found mostly at this point, but in later years they could be caught all over. Bream to 10 lb and hybrids of over 6 lb are taken in this marvellous lake. The fish can be found in the shallows and their movements are often dictated by the weed growth, which comes and goes. On the colder days, however, that small deep area is where you will find the fish.

Because of the heavy forest of weed which appears in this lake, I have always brought my boat along and, on finding a clear patch, baited up heavily and waited. The top half of the lake towards Carrickmacross is sometimes only 3–4 feet deep and I recall on a brilliant sunny day taking 84 lb of big rudd in a short session in that very shallow area.

The shallow and muddy water at the main road side holds some cracking tench of over 6 lb and it is remarkable that few of them move into the main and deeper part of the lake. With a light flat-bottomed boat you will, with difficulty, get into that area and have great sport, particularly in May and June. Just like its neighbouring water Lough na Glack, this lake of quality fish does not respond on a regular basis. On a calm morning, a sharp eye will at least reveal where the fish are.

CORCRIN LAKE

This good water is approached off the Dundalk road 2½ miles from Carrick. The lake is beside the road and has easy access. The margins, sometimes soft, have some growth of reeds, but there are good swims with fishing into 15–18 feet of water. It yields bream to 4 lb and tench to 6 lb, with perch, some rudd, roach and hybrids.

CAPRAGH LAKE

The Carrickmacross area is blessed with many lakes holding quality bream and this water lying beside the R179 Carrickmacross–Culloville road is one of them. The near margins are weeded and the shoreline is varied, with peaty areas of soft ground and then some solid pegs to fish from. The wooded area near the road produces good fishing, but try walking round the far bank, where there are good productive swims.

Fishing is into 8–15 feet of water, dropping to 30 feet in the centre. This is a rich water where fishing is slow at times. It produces its best results in the early mornings. With patience and a careful approach, you will find bream to 9 lb, rudd, roach and hybrids. The lake has a small stock of tench to 6½ lb but I can well believe that Capragh will turn up fish over 7 lb some day. As for pike, there are some big ones over 20 lb here. A great fishery!

RAHAN'S LAKE

This 100-acre lake is part of the River Glyde system and lies beside the road between Carrickmacross, Kingscourt and Drumconrath. The only access is along the right side of the lake over a stile and then over one field. The margins are peaty and fishing is into 6–8 feet where the bottom is soft with some weed at times.

Prebaiting followed by constant loose feeding will bring the good bream to 4 lb, roach and hybrids on the feed. I've had tench to 5 lb at the top end of the lake where it shallows to 3–4 feet. This shallow lake is a good fishery which yields great catches taken easily on the float.

LOUGH DERRY

Near Ballyhoe Two Lake (described below under Drumconrath) and also close to

Rahan's Lake, this is another rich water which yields quality fish. Please note that there is no fishing on one side of this lake, where access is private. Access to the fishable part is over three fields. The banks are good with some marginal reeds. There is some weed and fishing is into 6–12 feet of water.

This is a moody water so do not expect to land into fish at a cast. Give this rich water special attention and you will find bream to 9 lb and tench of over 6 lb in

your swim. There are also some rudd, roach and good hybrids.

CREEVY LAKE

Two miles from Carrick off the Castleblaney road, this 48-acre lake is a mixed fishery controlled by the Eastern Regional Fisheries Board. It holds brown trout and a good stock of small rudd and perch. The staff of the Fisheries Board nearby will be glad to give you information.

DRUMCONRATH

Drumconrath is a small, tidy village in north Co. Meath and is situated in an area of lakes which extends across the boundaries into Cavan and Monaghan.

Population 1,313
OS ½-inch Map No. 13
Carrickmacross 11 miles, Kingscourt 9 miles, Dublin 40 miles

Club: Drumconrath Angling Development Association

BALLYHOE ONE LAKE

The approaches to this lake are from Cross Guns crossroads between Carrickmacross and Drumconrath, and first left from Kingscourt off the Kingscourt–Drumconrath road. The access road is to the football pitch, with the lake to the left. Parking is beside the water. The bank is open and clean, with some reeds and soft ground to the right, where there is fishing from stands.

Ballyhoe One is a great favourite – and no wonder! It yields some great catches of bream and tench. Bream to 4 lb are common and, with rudd and roach present, the lake holds a rare mixture of hybrids. The lake responds consistently to early and late fishing for tench to between

6 and 7 lb in May and June and produces good fishing again after the spawning season. Fishing is into 8–12 feet of water over a mostly clean bottom.

BALLYHOE TWO LAKE

This section of the big water is to the right further along the football pitch approach road. The margins are shallow and often covered with a thick growth of weed, making fishing impossible, but it was here that I took lovely rudd over 2 lb in the pre-roach days. My advice is to fish this rich water from the far bank.

Access is left off the road to Lough Derry. Here there is car parking and access to the shore is easy. Clear bank space is limited. You will find tench in this weedy water and for a serious summer session for tench the best bet is to fish from a boat. In the winter, when the weed has gone, you will find some cracking roach to near 1 lb.

CORSTOWN LAKE

Turn right 1 mile from Drumconrath on the Carrick road. Parking is at the waterside of this 37-acre lake, which is tucked under a big hill. Corstown has a long history of producing good catches when rudd were the dominant species. Now, with roach present, good bream to 4 lb are still taken and your target here is 40–50 lb, but that figure is conservative.

The margins are peaty, with a thin fringe of reeds. There is a depth of 5–15 feet and the bottom is fairly clean. From the car park, walk along the left or right banks to the swims near the high pylons, where the best results are obtained.

MENTRIM LAKE

An access road south off the N52 Ardee–Kells road leads to waterside parking at this 5-acre lake. The water is reeded and a good margin of lilies betrays the fact that this is a rich water. The lake has its moods and while bream to 6 lb are present they are often slow to respond to your bait. Tench to 6½ lb have been taken on this lake, where fishing is from stands. There is some weed and the depth is to 20 feet.

WHITEWOOD LAKE

A short distance from Nobber, this 100-acre lake used to receive scant attention from anglers but now there is a good stock of roach present and the angling scene has changed. Access is easy and parking is at the waterside. Much of the shore is reeded but there are some clear swims where it is possible to cast into 8–15 feet of water. In the winter months you will find good quality (over 10 oz) roach, with a good head of pike feeding freely. There are some bream present but much baiting is required to get them on the feed.

DESCART LAKE

This good water is approached from the Carrick–Drumconrath road at Cross Guns crossroads or from the Kingscourt–Drumconrath road. Parking is at the roadside car park, with foot access over two fields to the left. The bank has some clear swims but the ground can be soft in rainy conditions. There are some lilies along the margin and fishing is into 8–13 feet of water. This water yields some great catches of bream to 4½ lb and also holds a good stock of roach, some rudd and hybrids. Small perch abound and there are pike too, mostly about 5–8 lb.

BAILIEBOROUGH

Bailieborough is situated in high, hilly country in east Co. Cavan. It is from here that waters of the tributaries of the River Boyne flow towards Virginia. Just a short distance to the north of the town, the waters of the Erne system flow through the Annalee River near Shercock.

Population 2,203
OS ½-inch Map No. 13
Cavan 20 miles, Virginia 8 miles, Shercock 8 miles, Cootehill 15 miles, Dublin 52 miles

Club: Bailieborough Tourism and Angling Association

TOWN LAKE

This lake in Bailieborough is only a fair water, producing small roach, small bream, perch and pike.

PARKERS LAKE

This is a rich water which holds good stocks of bream to 5 lb. There is a heavy belt of reeds round the lake, which also has soft margins. The only way to fish this water in comfort is from a boat and then you could have catches of well over 80 lb of lovely bream. Access is over private ground near the town. If the water ever becomes more fishable, you must give it a cast.

CASTLE LAKE

Turn off the Bailieborough–Shercock road at the milk factory and after ½ mile turn left into the forest. Parking is at the end of the lake, whence the many good swims must be reached by foot.

For 50 yards beyond the barrier to the left there are good swims facing southwest. Here you will find bream in the early season particularly. The best pegs to the right of the parking area are 130 yards along the road past the other barrier. There are stands to the left and fishing is from an open clean bank. The river enters the lake opposite and the swims here are the favourite haunts of bream to 4 lb. Catches of over 100 lb are common.

The bottom is mostly clean with some weed. Depths vary, but most of the fishing is into 5–14 feet of water. Roach, perch, some rudd and small pike are also to be found in this good fishery.

Anglers should note that this lake is situated in the lands of the Forest Service and you are requested to respect all regulations by not lighting fires and leaving no litter. Parking is only at the access near the main road entry, and the barriers, if open, are not an invitation to proceed farther with your car. Barriers in any forest are open only to allow forestry workers access and may be closed at any time.

DRUMKEARY LAKE

This 40-acre lake lies on the left 1 mile farther along the Castle Lake access road. There is parking near the lake along a narrow road. This is a fine fishery. The banks are good and fishing is into 8–12 feet of water, with some weed in the summer. Facing the prevailing wind, the shore here at the roadside fishes best in windy conditions. I like fishing this water and have had comfortable and easy sessions, taking catches to 60–70 lb of bream to 4 lb. In recent years perch have increased in number. Fishing with bread to overcome the problem, I took some rudd, which I thought had all gone. There are hybrids and good roach here with some quality pike.

GALBOLIE LAKE

Galbolie Lake is a 25-acre water just beside the Bailieborough–Cavan road. An attractive water, it holds some good roach but has a poor stock of bream. Fishing in general is not very good and I advise you to try some of the more productive waters in this area.

VIRGINIA, CO. CAVAN

Virginia, situated on the shores of Lough Ramor in Co. Cavan, is a small and attractive town, which twice won the national award as Ireland's tidiest town.

Population 612
OS ½-inch Map No. 13
Cavan 18 miles, Bailieborough 8 miles, Ballyjamesduff 6 miles, Kells 12 miles, Dublin 51 miles

LISGREY LAKE

One mile north of Virginia beside the N3 Virginia–Cavan road, this water is fishable from stands. Reeded in most places, the margins are soft and the fishable area is to the right along a path. Just a fair water, it holds small roach, small perch and some small bream. Not really worth serious attention.

RAMPART RIVER

The Rampart River flowing from the high ground of Bailieborough in Virginia has some good swims which are approached by the Ball Alley. With depths to 8 feet, in the mid-season they give good sport for bream to 5 lb. In the early months, I have had great roach catches here, with good

fish to 12 oz. The river then rushes down through shallows to the big Lough Ramor.

LOUGH RAMOR

Tourist anglers travelling north from Dublin on the N3 have their first sight of water at this big lake to the left of the roadside. In the past this water held fair stocks of bream, some rudd, perch and pike. When roach entered the lake, and anglers concentrated on some sections of this big water, they located the bream as well. The lake is now a great fishery and gives superb sport for bream to 3 lb, roach, hybrids, perch and some good pike.

The southern section of the lake which

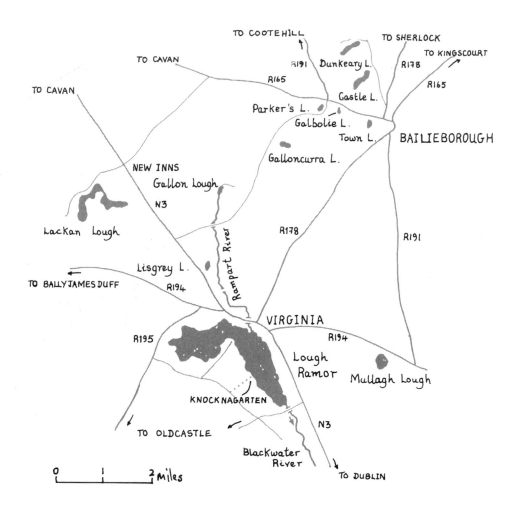

TO COOTEHILL

TO SHERLOCK

TO CAVAN

TO KINGSCOURT

R191 Dunkeary L.

R178

R165

R165

Castle L.

TO CAVAN

Parker's L.

Galbolie L.

Town L. BAILIEBOROUGH

Galloncurra L.

NEW INNS

Gallon Lough

N3

Rampart River

R178

R191

Lackan Lough

Lisgrey L.

TO BALLY JAMES DUFF

R194

VIRGINIA

R195

R194

Lough
Ramor

Mullagh Lough

KNOCK NAGARTEN

TO OLDCASTLE

Blackwater
River

N3

TO DUBLIN

0   1   2 Miles

Eastern Region, Virginia

is visible from the main road is quite shallow and has a maximum depth of 10–12 feet. The western part of Lough Ramor to the right of the quay in Virginia has depths to 35 feet near Crane Island. In general, this big water has shallow margins and many of these areas are unfishable because of rocks. In low water during the summer many rocky hazards can be seen all over the lake.

Fishing for roach – and, indeed, for bream too – is varied. In the early months the roach in the southern sections provide great sport, and here too one can take great catches of bream in late April, May and June.

*Barrie Nicholson, Ireland's bait farm owner, with his mixed catch of bream, roach and roach x
bream hybrids on the western shore of Lough Ramor near Virginia*

The west-facing amenity area beside the quay in Virginia comes into its own when fresh winds blow onshore. To the right of here, below the golf course, access is easy to a few swims only. The uneven and shallow bank to the milk factory also produces bream in the early summer. It should always be remembered that access over land is only through the good will of the landowners and permission must be obtained to cross fields.

On the western side of the lake at the narrow waist of water directly opposite the quay at Virginia there are six good swims in the wood at Coronagh.

The main fishing stretch is approached from the east off the N3 Virginia–Dublin road at Maghera Cross. Cross the Nine-Eyed Bridge and the River Blackwater and turn right at the crossroads. After ¾ miles, beside the vacant low stone house, turn right by the private houses through a gate to the waterside. Respect the landowners' property and do not camp or leave litter here. Here at Knocknagartan the bank is low and fishing is into a shallow section of the lake, with depth of no more than 10 feet. I introduced my friend, Barrie Nicholson to this section of the lake one April. He is a bait-farm owner and he proceeded to give it a liberal supply of all the tasty baits that he produces. The water was fresh and unfished for perhaps six months, and we had great sport taking bream and roach galore. After heavy fishing over the following months, however, this shallow area can go off easily. In form, this stretch can yield catches up to 200 lb but it does pay to study the amount of bait you should apply. In colder weather the bream will move off to deeper water.

The spot where the water leaves the lake at the Nine-Eyed Bridge can offer good roach fishing in the early season. Anglers are advised not to enter the area at the caravan park, where there is private property.

During the winter the lower section of this big lake is worth trying for pike of over 20 lb. Near Crane Island there are some great sharp shelves where pike lurk in the cold months of the year.

NADREEGEEL LOUGH
(Lackan Lough)

Turn west off the N3 Virginia–Cavan road at New Inns onto the R196 Bally-jamesduff road. There are two lakes here, connected by a thick belt of reeds, and the roadside lake is easily accessible. Fishing is from stands into 8–12 feet of water. There is a big stock of great roach, some rudd and good hybrids. I often put a boat on this water and fish it from the far bank, where there is clear ground. A great lake to float-fish for roach and hybrids of over 1 lb. The lake also holds good pike and perch.

A Fishing Cruise on the Shannon System

When the fish go off the feed we try new tactics and ponder the reasons for our lack of success. After another long period of inactivity we are prone to a bit of dreaming about the possibilities of fishing on the other side of the water. Then we think of the long haul of carrying tackle round the shore . . . and isn't it getting a bit late. Suddenly the fish are back on, but now it's time to go home for a bite to eat. How often have you thought that you should go back fishing after the evening meal? Have you ever thought of rising at the crack of dawn to get those feeding fish which on some waters go off as soon as the early sun hits the water? But what a bother it all is!

The answer to all those dreams can be answered by a cruise on the River Shannon or the Erne and living, eating and sleeping with the fish. There are marvellous opportunities, with hire-cruiser operators based at many places on both systems. It is a wonderful experience to take your boat out to some isolated water and go fishing in a place which may have never seen a rod before.

Plan your expedition with care and above all remember two golden rules. First, take care and always be alert to possible dangers when on the water. Second, do not be tempted to move a lot when on the water. Select your swims, bait them and do not ramble on. Give your baited swim a chance – it will come alive and you will have the fishing of a lifetime. In a boat you can rise early to see the morning mist on the water. You can reach for the rod with one hand and put the kettle on with the other. You can explore, go behind islands, have your evening meal, and then watch the evening sun drop in the sky as the big rudd move in to take your bread-baited hook. That is the life!

THE BOYLE RIVER AND LOUGH KEY

Drum Bridge on the Boyle River is the upper navigable limit in the west of the Shannon system. There is an island along the left bank where the slow-moving river enters Lough Key. To the right by the red marker and inside Bingham Island, Kerin's Bay holds great stocks of bream in May and June. Moor the boat at the end of the river and take the dinghy into the shallow and weedy bay. Fish the inner part of the bay to the right.

Lough Key holds good stocks of bream, roach and pike. The section of the lake between Ash Island and the big Bullock Island is particularly good for pike. Note that there is a shallow rocky section in the middle of the inner bay.

J. Richards with a good catch of bream to 4 lb on the Boyle River at Knockvicar

Bream fishing has always been productive in the narrow part of this big lake where the river leaves it. Anchor along the reeded right bank downstream of the lake and fish the margin for bream.

Below Knockvicar, the Boyle River enters Oakport Lake. This rich water has bank facilities along the southern side, but the wooded top side has yielded great catches of bream, rudd, roach and hybrids for me. Anchor close to the reeds to the right of the red marker, where it can often be shaded and calm. You can also explore this water and fish near the island, where a friend of mine once took a 20-lb pike on a wobbled rudd. This good water will produce great bream catches if you concentrate on it.

Below Cootehall the river enters the interesting Drumharlow Lake. This lake in the past held massive stocks of big rudd over 2 lb, but now, with roach present, those rudd are fewer and the water holds a good head of hybrids. Anchor in the bay to the west (right bank) above the red and black markers at Inishatirra Island. Here you will have great sport for good roach and hybrids. To the east of Drumharlow Lake and north of Inishatirra Island, the inner bay has some good shoals of bream along the right bank where the fringe of reeds is thin. Farther into this bay there are some dangerous shallows.

From here the Boyle River joins the River Shannon a short distance above Carrick-on-Shannon.

THE UPPER SHANNON AT LEITRIM

The main river flowing from Lough Allen is fast and narrow, but it is worth a visit near the upper limit of navigation, particularly in May and June. The fast river below Battlebridge holds big stocks of roach and anglers fish the left bank below the start of the canal. Tie up at the jetty and use your dinghy to fish the right bank, downstream of where the land-based anglers fish. Here you must monitor the movement of roach but if you are there at the right time you will have great sport. The river is fast and you will get best results on the pole or with a stick float.

FROM CARRICK TO LOUGH BODERG

At the Carrick Marina in the main flow from the finger piers you will find bream and roach which are not bothered by the boat traffic. On the east or left side of the second section of Lough Corry there is a big but shallow bay with some rocky

hazards. Anchor near the black marker just above the island and enter the bay in a dinghy. This is a great place for bream in May and June, with an abundance of fish around 3 lb. Here, too, you will find pike in the winter months.

At the entry to the Jamestown Canal you will always have good bream fishing. Moor at the quay at the canal beside the bridge and explore the section of the main river along the left bank, just below the reeds and the small inlet, ¼ mile above the main bridge. This is a great area for bream, roach and good-quality hybrids. I have spent many happy days here and have never failed to catch. A great part of the Shannon!

Below the Albert Lock at the point of the main river again, fish near the red marker for tench in May and June. The river up towards Drumsna holds good stocks of roach, bream and hybrids. Try the reeded margin on the left bank 200 yards down from the black marker and across from the small island. This section, with the busy main road visible down to the left, holds good bream.

Down river and under the railway bridge, the river enters the heavily reeded Lough Tap. Try the bay along the eastern side. This is good pike country but beware, as it shallows close in.

LOUGH BODERG, KILGLASS AND TERMONBARRY

The character of the river is changing now and soon we will reach the home of good rudd. As you go down river south through Lough Boderg, Derrycarne Forest lies to the left and the big, shallow bay holds very big stocks of bream in

May and June. Anchor in a safe place and explore this bay from a dinghy. I have often launched my small boat at Derrycarne and moved up to fish near the point of the forest and into the bay, which is protected from the south-westerlies. This area will give you fantastic bream catches.

West of here, to the right going down river, you will enter a new world – an area which is heavily reeded with clear water and an abundance of lovely rudd over 2 lb. The quay at Carranadoe bridge is a good base for exploring for rudd and tench. The small and nearly inaccessible pond, 300 yards out on the finger jutting into Lough Boderg, holds tench to 5 lb. You will also find some tench and rudd in the bay to the right of the black marker.

From the moment you enter Carnadoe Lake you can be on the look-out for big rudd nearly anywhere. The waters here are all heavily reeded, with margins of lilies in many places, and the depth is 4–5 feet. The jungle of high reeds provides fantastic small and shaded bays where you can moor safely and fish to your heart's content. With the nose of your boat tucked into the reeds, you are beautifully concealed in my favourite waters of the Shannon.

Beyond Carnadoe (Carranadoe) Lake you come to Carrigeen Cut to the left and a sharp right bend round an island through the reeded channel to Grange Lake. The Grange River, sometimes shallow, enters the top of Grange Lake at the quay. When this river is high with good flow the fishing here for bream and rudd × bream hybrid is in a class by itself. I have fished by mooring directly out from the flow in the protection of the reeded margin. By long casting you will find great shoals of fish which move along the edge of the flowing water. Try fishing the bay to the top of the island about 300 yards from the red marker. This is an excellent area for hybrids over 4 lb.

Before entering Carrigeen Cut I have often taken great catches of rudd over 2 lb just to the left near the red marker and between the black and red markers to the right. Boat traffic is heavy at times at this junction, but in the evening the sport is vintage stuff. You can moor in the cut, but watch out for other boats.

Kilglass Lake has a slightly different character, with shallow margins and light belts of rushes. Near the island I have fished on the calm side for great rudd × bream hybrids of well over specimen size, but the pattern of fishing in this lake is to stalk the rudd and hybrids from a small boat. There is a jetty at the bottom of the lake and there is also good mooring at the mouth of the Mountain River, where the bank is clean and firm. This river – which is sometimes weedy and, upstream behind Church View Guest House quite shallow – has provided me with many small roach. Explore the lake from here, and look out for the rudd cruising in the rushy margins on summer days. For comfortable fishing in lovely isolation and the chance to take the Irish record rudd over 3 lb 1 oz this section of the Shannon is excellent.

Back in the main navigation, Lough Scannell has a great stock of bream in the far eastern section, which is not far from the main road.

A forest skirts the eastern side of the narrow channel leading into Roosky. At the top of Pigeon Island you will find bream. Moor or anchor just off the current on the western side.

ROOSKEY, TERMONBARRY AND LANESBOROUGH

Below Roosky Lock the river is reeded but there are some isolated clear spaces which have good bank fishing, especially below the pylons at Cloneen on the right bank. Lough Forbes is a big, open water, with wooded lands around Castle Forbes on the eastern side. This is a good water for pike and the bay south of Yellow Island should be explored from a small boat. The next two bays along the eastern side, especially the southern one with the small island, deserve attention from the pike angler.

The Camlin River mouth has a good bank near the bend. This is an ideal stretch to bait up and fish for good-quality bream, roach, hybrids, tench, perch and pike. There is little flow here and in the early season catches of well over 150 lb can be taken in a short session. It is in situations like this that I question the use of keepnets. Here you could fill one, two, or even three. Why? On my last piking trip at this spot a cruiser, skippered by an angler, raced at top speed through our swim, taking one of my floated dead baits with him! The lesson is to slow down when you see anglers with rods out. Always remember that the wash from a fast-moving boat will cause stress to fish held in keepnets.

Below the weir at Termonbarry the river widens, and here in the early months fishing is top-class. From the quay below the lock you can set out to explore the fast-moving water below the weir, where there are good roach. An interesting area, but you must search and find those fish in the currents and eddies.

There is excellent fishing in the canal mouth beside the Camlin River. You can easily tie up to the bank, but remember that the area can at times be busy with traffic. At the right time you will find roach and some good bream to 5 lb at the side of your boat.

In the main navigation the reeded margin below the black marker is well worth a serious session for bream. Bait up heavily and you will find bream of over 6 lb and some cracking roach. This area is good for pike in September, when fish of over 20 lb are taken. Remember to put pike back alive. Big trout over 10 lb come into this section of the river in the late season.

Below here the river narrows in the Cut and ¼ mile downstream the River Feorish enters the Shannon from the west. In the narrow channel there is fabulous roach fishing in the early months (March–May). Here I have had fish over 1 lb and catches of well over 100 lb are possible. The shallow, weedy mouth of the sluggish Feorish River fills up in May and June with fantastic bream to 8 lb and rudd × bream hybrids to 5 lb. Roach also come in here, with fish to over 1 lb. It all adds up to one great area to concentrate on for a few days.

From this point downstream the river has many shallow and weedy areas, where there are hidden banks of peat silt. Some quiet backwaters are attractive to the eye of the angler, but beware of that peat silt, even if you approach it in a small boat.

As described in Chapter 5, Lanesborough offers splendid bank fishing near the bridge and the hot-water outflow. But it also presents the boat fisher with wonderful opportunities. In July and August, look out for the shoals of bream to the

P. Dighton with the record Irish rudd x bream hybrid which tipped my scales at 5 lb 13½ oz. The fish was taken below the bridge along the left bank of the River Shannon at Lanesborough

right of the river. Anchor just 50 yards out to the right of the flow, and when you see those bream and hybrids you will have great sport.

LOUGH REE, FROM LANESBOROUGH TO ATHLONE

Out from Lanesborough you can anchor near the black buoy or nose your boat into the reeds just round from the Cut. The area here with a few islands has shallow, weedy places, and from this weedy section you can again enter the main navigation near the markers. This Ballyclare area, overlooked by the bungalow, is a great haunt for all species from April to July. Here you will find very big bream to 10 lb, rudd × bream hybrids to 5 lb, rudd, some roach, and tench to 6 lb. At the bottom of the Cut and to the west of the markers there is an abundance of perch.

The shallow, weedy bay on the right holds good pike in the early months of the year.

The main channel of the Cut can at times yield great bream catches, but I have found that the shoals are not resident in this stretch, but move from one section of the lake to another.

Lough Ree is a massive reservoir of specimen fish, but there are two problems for boating anglers. Safe moorings for large boats or cruisers are limited; and, because of its size, this big lake can be dangerous for those using small boats. The great shoals of fish all over the lake never see a hook, and as we explore and discover more safe sections I predict that this great treasure will be opened to more anglers.

I have found bream and rudd galore out from Portrunny in Cruit Bay and up towards the shallow (sometimes only 3 feet) inlet below Rinany, where the Hind River enters the lake. The area is exposed, but with a waggler fished from my small boat at anchor I picked up some great fish in calm conditions. In Black-brink Bay you will find safe anchorage in 25–30 feet. The inner part of this bay round from the point of St John's Wood is a good place for tench. You will find these fish close in and also up to the Lecarrow Canal near the red markers. This area fishes well in May and June. You will also find tench in the canal, but the best chance here is to fish it at first light when they are feeding and before the boat traffic starts. There are great rudd to over 2 lb here and in the northern part of this bay just below the outer black marker, and in the shallow margin you will find bream. Close to the shore to the north-east of Rindoon you will find a good open, sheltered area

where in the late season legered dead bait will yield good pike in 15–30 feet of water.

In the bay along the eastern side of Quaker Island, opposite Priest's Island and Cashel on the mainland, you will find bream and rudd in 8–12 feet of water. This sheltered area is well worth a try. Why not stretch your legs on the interesting island here, which is steeped in history?

To the east, off the main navigation for cruisers, are Saints Island and Inny Bay. This section of the lake – from Pollagh across by the many Black Islands to Inchturk and Muckanagh Point – is only for the person who is fully acquainted with the water. There is quite deep water south of King's Island and also south of Inch Bofin, but then there are some shallow rocky areas which make navigation dangerous. There is very deep water close to Bethlehem Point, while Inny Bay has a flat bottom with an average depth of 8 feet.

At the mouth of the River Inny there is a cluster of reeds, and to enter it in a small boat you must follow an S course. The depth of the river is 10–13 feet and at this point you will find great rudd × bream hybrids and bream in April and May. Entry to the clean southern bank of this big bay is through a channel hidden in the tall reeds ¼ mile up from the bottom in front of the bungalow. Once in the channel you can take your small boat along the high embankment to within 200 yards of the end of this cul-de-sac to fish for bream to 8 lb, rudd × bream hybrids to 5 lb and tench to 5½ lb. This area only fishes well in May and June. My echo sounder is put to good use in this part of the lough – as indeed it is in every water I fish from a boat. I stress that only experienced sailors should enter the Inny Bay area, and at no time should hire cruisers move off the recommended navigation channel.

The Inner Lakes to the south of here can be reached via Coosan Point. The first lake, Killinure, is heavily reeded with shallow margins, and ½ mile in at Stranmore I found rudd in great numbers. On a calm evening you will find those lovely fish cruising close to the surface in most of this area. An excellent spot is the sheltered area west of Temple Island, reached by a sheltered reeded channel, or from Portaneena jetty. It is full of rudd in the summer months.

Ballykeeran Lough is reached by a narrow channel near SGS Marina, where there are all facilities. This sheltered water holds a big stock of rudd × bream hybrids to over 3 lb. From this spot I have pushed my small boat through the reeds near the white mooring buoy, got out and fished one of the small ponds on Friar's Island. This is just one of the countless surprises to be found on this magnificent waterway. The ponds, though slightly reeded, yield some cracking tench to 6 lb as well as hybrids.

Coosan Lough is reached by a narrow channel off the southern shore of Killinure Lough. It is another shaded water, tucked away, which offers serious fishing. You may find some boat traffic here, but only during the high season and when boats shelter from the big lake in stormy weather. Coosan Lake is heavily reeded with much marginal weed, but it is a rich water, holding good stocks of rudd, bream, hybrids and tench, all of good quality and many over specimen size. There are several old mooring posts to which you can tie up your small boat for a

serious session. Remember that in a rich water which is seldom seriously fished you will need to groundbait heavily and wait for some time to get the fish into your swim. Have patience and you will be rewarded with great sport. These rules apply to most places, but particularly to the rich unfished waters of Lough Ree.

Halfway between Robin Island and Hodson's Pillar along the western side of Lough Ree at the wooded peninsula from Yew Point, there is a great but short section along the reeded margin where the depth is 12–25 feet close in. Here, from August to October, after heavy baiting, you will pin down great shoals of big bream to 10 lb and hybrids.

The sheltered eastern side of Beam Island and Big Yellow Island are two more along the countless spots on this great lake that will yield superb catches of big fish.

FROM ATHLONE TO BANAGHER

Below Athlone the Shannon flows through flat country which floods easily in the winter months. Indeed, during the spring and summer the flood remains in some areas. The boat user will have to exercise care in navigation in these conditions, and the normal fishing haunts become obliterated by water.

Great shoals of bream, rudd and tench are to be found behind Long Island. Anchor along the eastern side at the bottom of this island opposite Old Town, and fish up behind the island. I have had wonderful sport with rudd over 1 lb, tench to 4 lb and bream to 4 lb. The twisting river holds those fish right down to Shannonbridge, and there is safe mooring at some places on to the western (right) bank.

Just above Devinish Island you will find great bream fishing below the red marker. I have explored behind this island from a small boat, taking specimen-size rudd × bream hybrids to over 3 lb and lovely rudd to over 2 lb. The same area is well worth a try for big pike.

Below Shannonbridge, on the right (western) side below the red buoy, there is a bay opposite the island on the left bank. Here in 15–25 feet of water I found great shoals of big rudd × bream hybrids to 5 lb. Above and near the bridge there are big rudd, and round the corner in the River Suck you will find the bream. You will find some good bream shoals up the River Suck and I have approached this area in my small boat and fished from the right bank of the river.

From the safe mooring in the channel, behind the island below Shannonbridge, explore the hot-water stretch below the power station. Fish the right bank above and below the Bord na Mona bridge. Here on many occasions I have taken specimen rudd and hybrids. This right bank, which is easily accessible by a boat, will produce fabulous catches if you concentrate on the one swim and groundbait heavily.

Down river from this point, after the second black marker, there is an island alongside the western bank. Anchor below the island and with a small boat you can enter another backwater which will reveal good fishing. A weedy channel from the backwater leads to the Clonfert Ponds, which are shallow and weedy. Come here in May and June and you will be startled, as I was on one occasion, by the massive stock of fish. I moved into this area in total silence, smelling fish. Just the occasional moorhen crossed my path and, as I stood up to look around and push my boat silently forward, the whole area erupted into a massive surge as shoals of fish became aware of my intrusion. I was shocked, but recovered quickly to cast my float tackle into the teeming mass of bream which I could see round my boat. It was after catching several fish that I found what they were feeding on, as all those bream threw up small fry. A most unusual diet for bream! But my maggot-baited hook then brought me a catch that I will always remember. Below the measured half mile and a short distance above Lehinish Island you can moor along the left bank. Behind the bank you will find a lovely small backwater pond with a narrow access channel from the river. Here there is top-class fishing for rudd to 1 lb, tench to 5 lb, hybrids, bream and perch.

Behind Lehinish Island and the island below that, rudd, hybrids and bream are in abundance. The area here can be explored from a safe mooring on the left bank below the canal and River Brosna. Near the old lock along the western bank I have taken rudd and tench.

Down river there is a fantastic backwater which is described under Banagher in Chapter 5. A small channel which leads into this great water. From April to June I have often thought that all the fish in the River Shannon were here. Many times I would start catching bream after bream on maggot and worm bait, followed by rudd × bream hybrids, then rudd, then tench. For variety and great catches I rate this spot one of the best on the Shannon. The water is quiet, with a depth of 3–8 feet, and sometimes weedy. A sheltered area at all times, it is a perfect place for float fishing. Tench to 6 lb are taken in May and June and early-morning sessions with maggot or sweetcorn as bait will produce outstanding results.

FROM BANAGHER TO PORTUMNA

Below Banagher, the well-known Pea Factory swim described in Chapter 5 still produces good fishing. I always found that fishing from the Inishee Island side – approached only by boat – gave the best results. From here to below Victoria Lock at Meelick there are many islands, but do not be deceived by the quiet backwaters, as the tops of those islands are often silted up.

From the quay above Meelick weir you can fish several places up river along the western (right) bank, particularly opposite the black marker, where I once took some great bream and hybrids in 12–15 feet of water. However, it is dangerous to enter the area along the right side in a small boat because there is a strong current, therefore keep to the left.

Just round the corner behind the lock you will find bank mooring near the point of the Old Canal. Here I had superb results trotting down the fast water for rudd. This fast water then combines with the outflow from the Little Brosna River and the junction is fantastic for floating for rudd to well over 2 lb and hybrids of over 3 lb. The fast water which flows

Hugh Gough fishing in luxury from the stern of a cruiser. This bream came to the net above Meelick on the River Shannon

down from the weir enters on the western side above the red marker. With a small boat I have explored this area of rocky, weedy shallows and am always fascinated by it. Rudd and hybrids abound. The key is to anchor and watch carefully for signs of fish. With a stick or Avon float, cover all the river to find the fish – the shoals lie in veins of currents. Here too, in September and October, you will find big pike hunting for food in the shallow water.

The backwater and drainage channel can also be approached from here and fished from the bank. Below Friars Island and Big Island you will find tench. These waters are also the home of the ubiquitous big rudd and perch.

The wide Shannon below Meelick is reeded in most places, but there are some open sections in the reeds where you can moor and fish. At the top of Bally-macegan Island you can find safe mooring at the right bank opposite the red marker. The bank here is good and lightly reeded. Here you will find the answer to all your dreams. There is fantastic bream fishing along this stretch and you can sit on them in this convenient setting. In the main navigation you will find that the short few swims of the Milne Stretch yield good bream and lovely big rudd. Just below Portland Island and above the smaller island you will find bream, but above here the backwater is used by water skiers during the summer months.

LOUGH DERG, FROM PORTUMNA TO KILLALOE

At Portumna the river, now wide and reeded, enters the last of the Shannon's great lakes. Lough Derg is a beautiful lake, 25 miles long and bulging to a width of 9 miles in one place. It has great depths, to 100 feet in places, and like other Shannon waters can be dangerous in stormy weather. Always keep an ear to the weather forecast before venturing out on a big lake.

Fish stocks are good, with an abundance of good bream, in some cases to 8–10 lb, a very big stock of lovely rudd to 2½ lb, with many fish to 3 lb. Rudd × bream hybrids to 5 lb are found in places, but may not be as common here as in Lough Ree. Great shoals of tench are to be found along some of the western bays which are rarely if ever fished. The ubiquitous perch are all over the lake and good pike to 30 lb are also taken here. Local anglers tend to restrict themselves to the pursuit of the trout by dry fly, dapping and trolling, or to trolling for pike, and seldom use other methods. At the time of writing it has come to my notice that a few roach have been caught in Lough Derg, so it is only a matter of time before this last section of the Shannon is invaded by those prolific breeders.

Like other big Shannon lakes, Derg has many shallow and rocky margins. The lake must be treated with respect and great care must be taken when using a small boat, by which I mean one of 18 feet, which would be safe on this water in a mild wind.

The lake has scores of small islands, which offer great shelter for fishing. Remember that the prevailing wind is south-westerly. Take your boat out on a calm evening and explore the reedy and rushy margins where those rudd can be seen. Always keep a sharp eye out for bream rolling, and then set about baiting up for a serious session.

Close to the eastern bank below Slevoir Point out from Terryglass Bay you will find bream along the shore in 10–15 feet of water. The headland north of Gortmore Point also holds good bream in good water very close to the bank. In the colder months try legering dead bait from the bank at this point for good pike. Along the western side of the lake just below Cregg Point and above Goose Island where there are reeds, bream are also to be found close to the bank in 8–12 feet of water.

Just south of Bellevue Point, and above the small bay, there is sheltered water for bream fishing quite close in with a depth of 10–15 feet with some weed. Further along the eastern shore there are many small islands and rocks north of the big Illanmore Island. Along the mainland at and down from Curraghmoore Point there is good bream water close in.

Directly west of the Split Rock is Rossmore Pier, where you can have great sport. One evening I set out in my small boat around the rushes and, on seeing rudd, I baited up by pushing small squares of bread down some rushes. The bay was calm and I looked forward to an early-morning session. During the night the wind rose and I was awakened by the constant banging of a loose plank under the pier. The lake was now being treated to a force 4 wind, but in the bay beside the boat it was quite protected and calm. I moved out and took rudd galore of over 2 lb and then came back for breakfast. My leger rod was set up on the boat and before the kettle was singing I was into bream around 4–5 lb.

This is a great area for bream and rudd and you will also take tench close inside the reeds. The Woodford River which enters here is narrow and shaded, with some reed. I found it to be full of small perch.

South of Benjamin Rocks and the second red buoy are Nutgrove Bay and Dog Island. Just above Dog Island you will find tench in the calm mornings or evenings in late May and June. Tench are now more abundant along the bays here. Between the red markers at Bunlany Island and the big Hare Island tench come into the margins of the bay, and the reeded Church Bay also holds big stocks during the spawning season in June and July.

Across the lake on the eastern side there is great bream water at Urra Point inside the black and red markers of the navigation channel. This area can be explored from the safe mooring at Dromineer. Youghal Bay is big and deep with some great stocks of pike. From Garrykennedy harbour, set out to the right and after 1 mile, quite close in, in 15–25 feet of water, you will find pike in the colder months of the year. The inner part of the bay is shallow but does yield bream in May and June. West out of Garrykennedy, the deep shore is worth fishing for pike by deep trolling.

Back along the western side of Lough Derg, the many islands and bays are all homes of good bream and rudd. Of particular interest, however, is the channel between Cribby Island and Inishparran, where you will find not only pike but good bream to 8 lb.

I have fished around most of the islands in the Mount Shannon Bay and Scarriff Bay and have never failed to locate bream and rudd. At all times you will find perch, which are the dominant species in Lough Derg. With such fodder food in abund-

Lough Derg at the bottom of the Shannon system is a big and beautiful water

ance, pike in the 8–12-lb range are common throughout the big lake. North of Scarriff Bay, just above the mouth of the Scarriff River towards Rabbit Island, bream appear in massive shoals in April, May and June.

The lake now narrows, but is still remarkably deep, with depths of over 100 feet in places. The western side has lots of small islands, rocky margins and belts of rushes. I describe in Chapter 5 the good bream fishery at the Lough Derg Caravan Park in Tinarina Bay and it is from here that I have set out to explore the small inlets for bream and rudd. The scope is enormous, with massive shoals of quality fish behind every small island. The eastern side of the lake, with depths to 50 feet at a cast from the shore, offers great opportunities for winter piking with legered bait.

The lower section of Lough Derg is most scenic and from Ballyvalley Point the lake tapers into a narrow channel to Killaloe and Ballina. Here there is much boating activity, but the perch are to be found right down to the bridge and are also in the Old Canal. I have found rudd to 2 lb near the canal entry and just above that small bream appear in numbers.

We have come to the end of the great Lough Derg and our boating fishing trip on the Shannon. There is fantastic potential in this final section of the wonderful waterway, many years of exploring and experimenting still to be done, not only on Lough Derg but also in Lough Ree and the other big lakes.

Using my echo sounder along the shore under the high Arra Mountain I found a steep shelf dropping off to 40–60 feet extending for about 3 miles down from Parker Point. I located single fish close to that shelf at 25–30 feet. Were they big pike or trout? I would like to try deep trolling there, but that is in the future.

In several bays along the western side I have seen the water turn to a greyish white as massive shoals of tench churned up the marl bottom during spawning. Then my echo sounder has shown a super-abundance of bream shoals roaming throughout the rich water. I have sat in quiet sheltered bays, doing my usual thing of observing, only to find great areas erupt as great shoals of rudd were agitated by hungry pike on the prowl.

The Shannon waters are there for all of us to discover.

BOATING AND FISHING HINTS

Experienced boat users will understand my regular reference to safety on the water and particularly to safe mooring. The experienced boat owner, being familiar with the water, may take liberties. He will also be able to quickly take up my hints on finding the fish on the Shannon.

Hire cruiser tourists, on the other hand, must stay within the navigation channels as instructed by the cruiser hire operators. Moor at the known safe places shown on Shannon charts.

Anglers who have a lot of gear should be careful to store everything so as not to cause obstructions on board. If tackle is kept on deck, have plenty of rope to secure rods, nets and other items. Sheets of plastic can be used to cover tackle at night and in rainy weather. Always keep maggots safe and dry by covering them at all times.

The waters of the River Shannon are controlled, so remember that if you nose your boat onto the bank and the water drops an inch or two you will have difficulty getting off!

You may need extra anchors, so bring some strong plastic bags, which when filled with stones and secured by ropes will do the job. Always take care of engines on small boats. Secure the engine and, when in a lock, beware of colliding with other boats.

Boat users should always slow down when passing anglers. Remember that the wake from a boat will toss a keepnet about and that fish will be damaged. A speeding boat will sometimes kill fish in these conditions. Land-based anglers are tempted to change swims often, but when you are living on the water the temptation is even greater. When you have selected your swim, bait it heavily and wait. Do not ramble but stay with your swim for days.

You can arrange with Irish Angling Services to have bait for you at centres along the Shannon. Details are given in the Appendix.

Pike anglers on boats must abide by all regulations and laws, and you are advised to return all pike to the water alive.

Appendix

ACCESS TO FISHERIES

Access to the waters described in this book may be across private property. Inclusion in the book does not imply that there is a right of way. Fishermen must always take care to get the owner's permission to cross private land.

While walking the banks of lakes and rivers in Ireland I am always conscious of the fact that we have our fishing only through the goodwill of those landowners. That is why I have dedicated this book to them. Show your consideration by keeping to the Country Code.

Always respect landowners' property.

Do not enter or cross fields without permission.

Never drive a car into a field.

Never cross meadows; always walk along boundary fences or by the waterside.

Litter such as plastic bags, fishing line, and other items should never be left at the waterside. Remember that discarded tackle kills. Take your litter home in your bait bag.

Close all gates.

Never light fires.

Use a bit of common sense out there and be a good sport!

LICENCES AND PERMITS

Northern Ireland

All anglers of 18 years of age who fish for coarse fish must hold a Fisheries Conservancy Board Coarse Fishing Rod Licence for each fishing rod used.

A permit is a separate document issued by the owner of a fishery which confers the right to fish in the owner's fishery. An owner may be a private individual, a company, an angling club or a government department.

There is no close season in Northern Ireland for coarse fishing. Licences and permits are issued for a season or for 15 days and are available from hotels, tackle shops, travel agents and the Northern Ireland Tourist Board.

The Department of Agriculture has developed a number of so-called 'free' fisheries throughout Northern Ireland. On these coarse fisheries no department permit is required. However, anglers using these waters must hold the appropriate rod licence. These fisheries are privately owned waters where the fishery owners have agreed to permit the public to fish and the landowners have allowed access over their land. It is important to remember that the owners of free fisheries reserve the right to close down access at any time. In addition, an owner who suffers damage to his land or livestock either through vandalism or because of the carelessness or thoughtlessness of anglers is justified in prohibiting access.

Republic of Ireland

All anglers between the ages of 18 and 66 require a State Rod Licence to fish for coarse fish. At the time of writing an annual licence costs £10 and a 21-day licence £5. There is no close season for coarse fish.

COARSE-ANGLING LAWS

1   It is illegal to use live fish as bait.
2   The only legal method to catch fresh-water fish is by rod and line.
3   It is illegal to transfer live roach from one water to any other water.
4   A person may not fish with more than two rods at any time.
5   It is prohibited to take and kill more than three pike on any one day.
6   It is prohibited for any person to have in his possession more than ten dead pike.

Notes

Anglers who catch roach to use as bait should kill them immediately and not carry live fish around with them.

Anglers should never take fish such as roach, carp or tench and transfer them to other waters.

Fish may only be taken by rod and line.

It is therefore illegal to use nets, otter boards and long-lines (unless by licence).

Anglers should respect local club regulations and, in the interest of conservation, never kill pike. Guest-houses, hotels and shops such as butcher's should never retain pike in freezers.

BAIT

Irish Angling Services offer all the bait that is required for coarse fishing.

Red maggots are now the most popular hookbait, followed by casters and white maggots. Worms are also available from this producer. White and brown bread-crumb baits, with a variety of additives, can also be supplied.

Bait may be ordered in advance and, by arrangement, be left at a centre where you fish. A list of those who stock such baits follows.

I am often asked how much bait is required. Most Irish coarse-fish waters do not see a hook from October to April, and it is natural that when starting off considerable baiting is necessary. For roach, in most waters, 3–4 pints of maggots and casters will be needed in a day. For bream, such as in the Shannon, worms and casters are vital to success. At least 10 lb of cereal groundbait should be used in a day and I have often returned to my car for more bait on those big waters.

Cereal bait mixed with casters and worms, with worm and caster hook bait, will get you those bream. During the summer some waters will not take much baiting, but they are in the minority.

Do not forget that bread still remains a good bait, not only for rudd but also bream and tench.

BAIT STOCKISTS

Northern Ireland

Home, Field and Stream, Church Street, Enniskillen. Tel: (0365) 22114

Erne Tackle, Main Street, Lisnaskea, Co. Fermanagh. Tel: (03657) 21969

Dave Ensor, Aghnacarra House, Carrybridge, Co. Fermanagh. Tel: (0365) 87077

Tyrone Angling Supplies, Omagh, Co. Tyrone. Tel: (0662) 44827

Field & Stream, Killyman Street, Moy, Co. Tyrone. Tel: (08687) 84556

Rankins Sports, Royal Avenue, Belfast. Tel: (4) 322657

Lisburn Sports, 9 Smithfield Square, Lisburn. Tel: (492) 77975

D. McKeown, 155 Moira Road, Lisburn. Tel: (492) 81275

Sidney Beckett, 56 High Street, Lurgan. Tel: (07622) 23352

Tedford Sports, 28 West Street, Portadown. Tel: (0762) 338555

Bannview Squash Club, Portmore Street, Portadown. Tel: (0762) 336666

Republic of Ireland

Mr Nicholson, Ardlougher House, Ballyconnell. Tel: (049) 26258

McMahons Gun Shop, Main Street. Tel: (049) 34438

McMahons Hardware, Bridge Street. Tel: (049) 22400

Mrs Dunne, Hilltop Farm, Kilduff. Tel: (049) 22114

Mrs Carol Braiden, Kilduff House, Kilduff. Tel: (049) 22452

Mrs Mundy, Deredis, Butlersbridge. Tel: (049) 31427

Magnet Sports, Town Hall Street. Tel: (049) 31812

Mrs Brady, Lakevilla, Killykeen Area. Tel: (049) 31513

Mrs Iris Neill, Lisnamandra Farm House, Crossdoney. Tel: (049) 37196

Mrs Smith, Drumbran. Tel: (049) 38185

Mr C. Fay, Cabragh House, Cavan Road. Tel: (049) 52153

Mr Brian Hanley, Dromore View, Carrick Road. Tel: (042) 41466

Mr Jim McMahon, Carrick Sports Shop. Tel: (042) 61714

Del Wilson, Hill View, Bree. Tel: (042) 46217

McElwaines, Main Street. Tel: (042) 65341

Jack O'Neill and Son, Main Street. Tel: (049) 39738

Eamonn Grey, Breffni Arms. Tel: (049) 35127

Mrs F. Kinkade, Lakeside. Tel: (043) 83242

John Maloney, Glebe House. Tel: (078) 31086

Mr Phil Elderton, Main Street. Tel: (078) 44080

The Creel, Main Street. Tel: (078) 20166

Aisleigh House, Dublin Road, Carrick-on-Shannon. Tel: (078) 20313

Michael Healey, Lakeside Store, Main Street, Lanesborough. Tel: (043) 21491

Mr B. Burton, Woodlands, Dublin Road. Tel: (0905) 43123

Mr Dermot Killean, Main Street, Shannonbridge. Tel: (0905) 74112

Mr Sean Egan, Shannon Side House, West Lodge Road. Tel: (0902) 94773

Mr J. Phelan, Silver Spring House. Tel: (045) 68481

Mr J. Presscott, 73 Woodlands. Tel: (045) 79341

Mr Rory Harkin, 17a Temple Bar. Tel: (01) 772351

O'Malleys Fishing Tackle Shop, 33 Dominick Street. Tel: (044) 48300

The Tackle Shop, Rahan. Tel: (0506) 55979

Griffin Hawe Ltd., 22 Duke Street. Tel: (0507) 31575

Mr J. Crean, Vicarstown Inn. Tel: (0502) 25189

John Boyd, Motor & Sport, Castle Hill Centre. Tel: (0503) 42677

Michael McCabe, Brandon View House, Ballyogan. Tel: (0503) 24191

Mr Owen O'Carroll, Oak Park Lodge. Tel: (0509) 47143

Mr Joe Maloney, Riverside, O'Brien's Bridge, Nr. Limerick. Tel: (061) 377303

Mr Jack O'Sullivan, 4 Patrick Street. Tel: (025) 31110

Mrs Flynn, River View House, Cook Street. Tel: (058) 54073

USEFUL ADDRESSES

Central Fisheries Board, Mobhi Boreen, Glasnevin, Dublin 9

Electricity Supply Board, Fisheries Division, Lower Fitzwilliam Street, Dublin 2

Bord Failte (Irish Tourist Board), Baggot Street Bridge, Dublin 2

Irish Tourist Board, 150 New Bond Street, London W1V 0AQ

National Coarse Fishing Federation, Blaithin, Dublin Road, Cavan

Fermanagh Tourism, Lakeland Visitor Centre, Enniskillen, Co. Fermanagh

Northern Ireland Tourist Board, 38 High Street, Sutton Coldfield, West Midlands, B72 1UP

Northern Ireland Tourist Board, River House, 48 High Street, Belfast BT1 2DS

Northern Ireland Department of Agriculture Fisheries Division, Hut 5, Castle Grounds, Stormont, Belfast BT4 3TA. Tel: Belfast 31221

Northern Regional Fisheries Board, Station Road, Ballyshannon, Co. Donegal. Tel: (072) 51435

Northern Regional Fisheries Board, Corlesmore, Ballinagh, Co. Cavan. Tel: (049) 37174

North-Western Regional Fisheries Board, Abbey Street, Ballina, Co. Mayo. Tel: (096) 22623

Western Regional Fisheries Board, Weir Lodge, Earl's Island, Galway. Tel: (091) 65548

Shannon Regional Fisheries Board, Thomond Weir, Limerick. Tel: (061) 55171

South-Western Regional Fisheries Board, 1 Nevilles Terrace, Massey Town, Macroom, Co. Cork. Tel: (026) 41222

Southern Regional Fisheries Board, Anglesea Street, Clonmel, Co. Tipperary. Tel: (052) 23624

Eastern Regional Fisheries Board, Mobhi Boreen, Glasnevin, Dublin 9. Tel: (01) 379209

Index

Abbreviations: B = bridge; C = canal; I = island; L = loch/lake; R = river
Page numbers in italics refer to maps and illustrations

Also published by Unwin Hyman:

TROUT AND SALMON LOUGHS OF IRELAND

By Peter O'Reilly

The first comprehensive guide to the best stillwater gamefishing in Ireland by the Angling Officer of the Central Fisheries Board.

Number One bestseller in Ireland. Hardback at £14.95

TROUT LOCHS OF SCOTLAND

By Bruce Sandison

Fully revised, in its second edition and with 150 new lochs.

Now available in paperback at £9.95